Principles of Financial Control in the Public Sector

Plamena Georgieva Nedyalkova
University of Economics, Bulgaria

A volume in the Advances in Finance, Accounting, and Economics (AFAE) Book Series

IGI Global
PUBLISHER of TIMELY KNOWLEDGE

Published in the United States of America by
IGI Global
Information Science Reference (an imprint of IGI Global)
701 E. Chocolate Avenue
Hershey PA, USA 17033
Tel: 717-533-8845
Fax: 717-533-8661
E-mail: cust@igi-global.com
Web site: http://www.igi-global.com

Library of Congress Cataloging-in-Publication Data

Names: Nedyalkova, Plamena, author.
Title: Principles of financial control in the public sector / by Plamena Georgieva Nedyalkova.
Description: Hershey, PA : Information Science Reference, [2023] | Includes bibliographical references and index. | Summary: "The main thesis of the monographic work is that the principles of control determine the methodological foundations of financial control and are a means of improving the quality of control impact"-- Provided by publisher.
Identifiers: LCCN 2023008230 (print) | LCCN 2023008231 (ebook) | ISBN 9781668488836 (hardcover) | ISBN 9781668488874 (paperback) | ISBN 9781668488843 (ebook)
Subjects: LCSH: Finance, Public. | Finance, Public--Auditing. | Fiscal policy. | Economic history--1990-
Classification: LCC HJ141 .N43 2023 (print) | LCC HJ141 (ebook) | DDC 336--dc23/eng/20230310
LC record available at https://lccn.loc.gov/2023008230
LC ebook record available at https://lccn.loc.gov/2023008231

This book is published in the IGI Global book series Advances in Finance, Accounting, and Economics (AFAE) (ISSN: 2327-5677; eISSN: 2327-5685)

British Cataloguing in Publication Data
A Cataloguing in Publication record for this book is available from the British Library.

Advances in Finance, Accounting, and Economics (AFAE) Book Series

ISSN:2327-5677
EISSN:2327-5685

MISSION

In our changing economic and business environment, it is important to consider the financial changes occurring internationally as well as within individual organizations and business environments. Understanding these changes as well as the factors that influence them is crucial in preparing for our financial future and ensuring economic sustainability and growth.

The **Advances in Finance, Accounting, and Economics (AFAE)** book series aims to publish comprehensive and informative titles in all areas of economics and economic theory, finance, and accounting to assist in advancing the available knowledge and providing for further research development in these dynamic fields.

COVERAGE

- Banking
- Health Economics
- Fiscal Policy
- Internet Banking
- Managerial Accounting
- Bankruptcy
- Environmental and Social Accounting
- Auditing
- International Economics
- Economics of Migration and Spatial Mobility

IGI Global is currently accepting manuscripts for publication within this series. To submit a proposal for a volume in this series, please contact our Acquisition Editors at Acquisitions@igi-global.com or visit: http://www.igi-global.com/publish/.

The Advances in Finance, Accounting, and Economics (AFAE) Book Series (ISSN 2327-5677) is published by IGI Global, 701 E. Chocolate Avenue, Hershey, PA 17033-1240, USA, www.igi-global.com. This series is composed of titles available for purchase individually; each title is edited to be contextually exclusive from any other title within the series. For pricing and ordering information please visit http://www.igi-global.com/book-series/advances-finance-accounting-economics/73685. Postmaster: Send all address changes to above address.

Titles in this Series

For a list of additional titles in this series, please visit:
www.igi-global.com/book-series/advances-finance-accounting-economics/73685

Perspectives on Blockchain Technology and Responsible Investing
Sonal Trivedi (Chitkara Business School, Chitkara University, India) Rashmi Aggarwal (Chitkara Business School, Chitkara University, India) and Gurmeet Singh (The University of the South Pacific, Fiji)
Business Science Reference • © 2023 • 317pp • H/C (ISBN: 9781668483619) • US $250.00

Mainstreaming Cryptocurrency and the Future of Digital Finance
Hamed Taherdoost (University Canada West, Canada)
Business Science Reference • © 2023 • 330pp • H/C (ISBN: 9781668483688) • US $250.00

Handbook of Research on Designing Sustainable Supply Chains to Achieve a Circular Economy
Yanamandra Ramakrishna (Skyline University College, UAE) and Siti Norida Wahab (Universiti Teknologi MARA, Malaysia)
Business Science Reference • © 2023 • 697pp • H/C (ISBN: 9781668476642) • US $295.00

Emerging Insights on the Relationship Between Cryptocurrencies and Decentralized Economic Models
Dhanapal Kesavan (SRM Institute of Science and Technology, India) and N. Mari Anand (Department of Business Studies, University of Technology and Applied Sciences, Salalah, Oman)
Business Science Reference • © 2023 • 256pp • H/C (ISBN: 9781668456910) • US $250.00

Exploring Business Ecosystems and Innovation Capacity Building in Global Economics
Mihir Joshi (Banasthali Vidyapith University, India) Mohsen Brahmi (University of Sfax, Tunisia) Luigi Aldieri (University of Salerno, Italy) and Concetto Paolo Vinci (University of Salerno, Italy)
Business Science Reference • © 2023 • 393pp • H/C (ISBN: 9781668467664) • US $250.00

For an entire list of titles in this series, please visit:
www.igi-global.com/book-series/advances-finance-accounting-economics/73685

IGI Global
PUBLISHER of TIMELY KNOWLEDGE

701 East Chocolate Avenue, Hershey, PA 17033, USA
Tel: 717-533-8845 x100 • Fax: 717-533-8661
E-Mail: cust@igi-global.com • www.igi-global.com

Editorial Advisory Board

Table of Contents

Foreword

The book *Principles of Financial Control in the Public Sector* is relevant for its time. There is no such kind of research, which determines the importance and significance of this book. The research directed in this book aims to substantiate the principles of financial control, their classification and impact on the applied control procedures.

The used comparative analysis of the Bulgarian and foreign experience, as well as the reference to other research materials, achieve the overall chosen goal of the development. In-depth studies have been made of the applied and possible criteria for the classification of the principles of financial control, a scientific analysis of the hierarchical structure of the control system in Bulgaria has been carried out, the approaches to applying the principles of financial control, the factors influencing their application, are measurable. the sequence in the performed control procedures.

The book *Principles of Financial Control in the Public Sector* has the quality of an independent study with significant results for the theory and practice of financial control. Conceptual statements about the principles of financial control have the meaning of ideas that will receive their natural continuation for the future.

In this respect, the monographic work has the importance of an original contribution to the improvement of the control practice, it can be accepted as a foundation for other scientific studies on the subject. Its usefulness for the overall control system and in particular for the financial control system is indisputable.

In the study of the control environment, a good balance was achieved between the possible participation of different control bodies in applying the general principles of financial control.

Plamena Georgieva Nedyalkova
University of Economics, Bulgaria

Preface

The dynamic political and economic situation, both in the country and in the world, set some new and more complex goals and objectives for solving in front of control, which posed challenges in its scientific and practical field. And just as in dominoes, where after the fall of one tile, the others fall, so in control doctrine, under the influence and impact of these factors, not only the functions of control, the objects and subjects change, but also the principles of financial control change and improve. Many of the control bodies of the world's major companies and organizations have long come to the conclusion that in order to implement full, effective, and quality control, the following is necessary (Moffett, 2012):

1. The principles of control, which need to be observed during the control process itself, should be clearly and precisely defined and publicly stated.
2. The mechanisms for applying the principles of financial control should be properly defined. This process is very complicated, as it always depends on the pre-set control goals and tasks, on the control powers of the controller, as well as on the features and specifics of the controlled object.

Thus the principles of control, including the principles of financial control, go beyond the general theoretical framework and become a bridge that facilitates the detection of unregulated deviations of phenomena and processes occurring at both the macro-level (state level) and micro-level (specific enterprise, industry, department, etc.). This determines the degree of their importance and is one of the main motives determining the thematic choice for research, namely: principles of financial control. The urgency of the problem is determined by the fact that the principles of financial control are the main building element of the control technology, without which the control process cannot take place.

The stages for implementation of the principles of financial control and the methodology for research of their application in the control technology and in the control process are an object of research in the monograph.

The principles of financial control, applied by the control inspectors of The Public Financial Inspection Agency (PFIA), are a subject of research.

In order to study in-depth the implementation of the financial control principles by the agency, the information security on the implementation of the empirical part of this exhibition covers the following:

1. Two thousand four hundred and fifty reports on the results of the financial inspections carried out by PFIA for the period from 2007 to 2011.
2. The information disclosed in the annual reports on the activity of PFIA for the period from 2007 to 2011 and period 2019 to 2022.
3. The research results by various NGOs in the field of financial control, such as the Center for Study of Democracy and the Association for Combating Economic Fraud.
4. The results presented in the annual activity reports of the Public Financial Inspection Agency (PFIA) on the financial security of the country for the period from 2007 to 2011 and period 2019 to 2022.

Due to the large volume and number of information sources, only a part of them are presented in the development applications.

The main motives for choosing this specific object for research are:

1. According to a January 2011 report by SIGMA - Support for Improvement in Government and Management, the EU's main goal is to create a common market for public procurement. The European Community (EC) therefore supports the proposed legal requirement to remove all existing barriers and prevent the emergence of new ones related to the effective implementation of the public procurement within the EU. The report also emphasizes that this can only be achieved by applying the basic principles of financial control presented in the relevant regulations. (SIGMA, 2011).
2. The Public Financial Inspection Agency (PFIA), as one of the main control bodies of the state power, is authorized not only to check the procedures for assigning and implementing public procurement in Bulgaria but also to protect the public financial interests by applying the principles of financial control.

In connection with the presented subject and object, the purpose of the monograph work is based on the theoretical overview of the nature and classification of the principles of financial control to present both foreign experience in established legal procedures for the application of financial control principles and systematic stages of their study, and also to propose an adaptation of the established foreign practice and experience to the practice in the country. In order to achieve the outlined goal, it is necessary to solve the following main tasks:

1. To present theoretically the issues and problems related to the development and improvement of the principles of financial control. The aim is to lay a good foundation for empirical research by clarifying many of the theoretical postulates concerning the principles.
2. To study the factors that affect the applicability of control principles, taking into account the fact that the mechanisms for applying the principles of financial control are influenced by their interaction with the control environment and the processes of formulating the ultimate optimal control solution.
3. To apply the comparative approach in analyzing the established foreign practice with the practice in Bulgaria in relation to the implementation and impact of the principles of financial control.
4. To apply the evaluation approach to determine the impact of the principles of financial control in the control process.

The main thesis of the monographic work is that the principles of control determine the methodological foundations of financial control and are a means of improving the quality of control impact. Achieving a high quality of control impact is the cornerstone of any control process. It is, therefore, necessary, on the one hand, to improve the methodology of financial control so that the emphasis is on the quality implementation of the principles of financial control, and on the other hand, to establish a system of procedures for examining the impact of the principles.

Proving the presented thesis is connected with the following working hypotheses:

Hypothesis 1. In addition to the set goals and tasks to be completed by the PFIA inspectors, the control environment also influences the way of applying the principles of financial control.

Hypothesis 2. The methodology for determining the normative impact of the Public Financial Inspection Act and the Regulations for application of the

Public Financial Inspection Act on the controlled objects should be applied as a methodology for determining the impact of the principles of financial control regulated in these two normative acts.

The presented goal, as well as the tasks for its achievement, determine the structure of this work, the objects and the subject of study, as well as the methodological research approach of the work itself. The methods of synthesis, analysis, induction, deduction, observation, analogy and comparison are applied in order to achieve the thus defined goals and to complete the previously set tasks in the study work. A systematic approach was used to describe the sequence of processes. The visualization of various facts and data is carried out with the help of the graphic and schematic approach. The combined application of research methods and approaches is aimed at reaching final conclusions and presenting different recommendations. In studying the application of the principles of financial control in Chapter Three, the requirements of the European Commission to the country regarding the implementation of a methodology, when investigating complex economic and financial crimes in Bulgaria, are taken into account.

Regarding, on the one hand, the fact that the topic set in this way is comprehensive and a different research approach can be applied to its research, different from the one adopted for writing this work, and on the other hand, taking into account the previously set goals and tasks, the following limitations need to be presented:

1. Theoretically, issues such as the nature and tasks of financial control will not be explored. They are too comprehensive and still debatable among experts regarding whether control is a separate doctrine or a function of management; can control be considered a public attitude; as well as whether control is a function of accounting and law; is it possible to present financial control as a system built on a number of elements.

Due to the unresolved issues concerning the full disclosure of the nature of control, we assume that for the purposes of the study, control is presented as a function of management. It is the basis on which the structural systems of each self-established doctrine, such as management, are built. Taking into account the dialectical approach (Marx, 1988), it can be assumed that control cannot be considered in isolation from all other phenomena and processes occurring in the economy, and it should be assumed that it is not a constant but a variable.

In a broader sense, the term "financial control" should be understood as a process on the basis of which the maintenance of the order, legality and expediency of the sovereign activity of the state itself is carried out. On the other hand, in a narrower sense, this concept should be interpreted as a way to identify, present and summarize the identified financial gaps, weaknesses, deviations and violations of generally accepted domestic and government financial principles and norms in order to take measures and affecting the person causing the damage.

2. The ethical principles of financial control, such as democracy, transparency, immediacy, independent verification and a systematic approach, will not be studied in this work. The ethics of the control processes, as well as the ethical requirements to be observed, can be issues of self-study.
3. Individually and independently, each principle can be a subject of research in order to present its theoretical and practical aspects in more details. Given this circumstance, in this work we limit the study of the principles of financial control, focusing on the features of control principles, which are more significant and on the basis of which one control principle is distinguished from another.

The following problems were identified during the empirical research on the implementation of the principles of financial control by the PFIA inspectors, as well as during the study of their impact on the condition of the controlled object. The first main problem is the fact that the principles of financial control are a specific element not only of the implemented control technology, but are also an element of the control process. This element remains intangible and invisible in the control situation, as it has a qualitative but not a quantitative characteristic. It is this specificity of the researched object that creates difficulties in the application of research tools for its study. The second problem is that in the implementation of the principles of financial control, in the performing of the control process and especially in the final closing stages, the manner of their application is not disclosed in the control documentation. Based on the previous two problems, the third problem follows - lack of sufficient empirical information on the researched problem.

The book contains the following chapters:

Chapter 1: Evolution of the theory of the principles of financial control.

Chapter 2: Criteria for classification of the principles of financial control.

2.1 Classification of the principles of financial control according to the hierarchical structure of the control system of the country
2.2 Classification of principles according to the type and form of financial control.

Chapter 3: Normative regulation of the principles of financial control in Bulgaria.

Chapter 4: Influence and importance of the principles of financial control for preserving the financial security and stability of the country

Chapter 5: Factors influencing the implementation of the principles of financial control. Graphic design of the control environment

Chapter 6: Stages for implementation of the principles of financial control by the Public Financial Inspection Agency (PFIA)

Chapter 7: Methodology for studying the principles of financial control

Chapter 8: Impact of the principles of financial control on the quality of the inspection activity carried out by the Public Financial Inspection Agency (PFIA) in Bulgaria

Chapter 9: Evaluation of the results of the implementation of the financial control principles

Chapter 10: Comparative analysis of the results of the implementation of the principles of financial control in Bulgaria and in some countries with developed economies

In this study, the established methodology for determining the normative impact of a given normative act has been proven. It can also be applied as a methodology for researching the application of the principles regulated in the relevant normative act. Compliance with the regulatory requirements by the supervisors in the implementation of their control actions is carried out with the help of the control norms regulating certain provisions. Each norm of control has a certain structure, especially in regard to laws, decrees, regulations, acts, etc. The regulated rules are one of the constituent elements in this structure, and following them, the regulatory texts of the normative act will be achieved.

The proposed systematic stages for applying the principles of financial control, namely: the approval of a control policy, the approval of organizational technology for the implementation of a control process, and the development and implementation of an individual assessment system for evaluating the application of the principles of financial control, are a prerequisite for the establishment of a methodology for the study of these principles. The individual assessment can be formulated using the findings protocol, in which each inspector must individually and impartially assess the rules he follows in the control process. The assessment criteria are presented in the Expert Assessment Card on the application of the principles of financial control. The card should be prepared individually by the PFIA inspector, and the assessment data from it should be presented in the findings protocol. All information regarding compliance with the sequence of stages, and the indicators, on the basis of which the relevant assessment of the influence of the control principles is formulated, should also be revealed in the final reports of the inspection activity. The lack of this type of information, as is currently the case in PFIA's control practice, is a prerequisite for drawing a number of contradictory conclusions about the performed control process.

Correlation analysis as a statistical-mathematical method is applied as a method to prove the influence and impact of control environments on the controlled object. With the help of the graphic construction of the active, passive and corruption control environment, it was proved that theoretically the environments so specified can be distinguished from each other, but in practice, they are of a mixed type such as active-passive, active-corruptive and passive-corruptive. The complex nature and specificity of the control environment are a prerequisite for problems on the part of inspectors to qualitatively and effectively apply the principles of financial control. The more clearly defined the control environment, the easier the principles of financial control are applicable.

Considering all the presented research theses, evidence and information sources, on the basis of which the empirical study of the development was carried out, the following more important conclusions can be drawn:

1. The control principles are the main building block, on the basis of which not only the entire control process, but also the control technology, takes place. It can be assumed that they are the design or idea for its implementation and progress.
2. The control principles themselves are interconnected and form a single control system. Despite the existing variety of control principles, the characteristic is that no principle contradicts another. They complement each other and reveal the specifics of the controlled object.
3. There is no historical information and data on when exactly the principles of control appeared, but what is known is that they are the result of practical traditions existing since ancient times for the implementation of control in various forms and modes of manifestation.

4. The main problems that are a prerequisite for the incorrect and inaccurate application of the principles of financial control by financial inspectors are: a) the lack of an internally regulated methodology for a specific control institution for the application of the principles of financial control; b) the absence of a methodology approved for the control practice for researching the application of the principles of financial control; c) the violation of the sequence of control stages of the control process; d) the incorrect implementation of the control technology.
5. The development and implementation of a methodology for researching the application of the principles of financial control in Bulgaria should be within the competence of the Ministry of Finance. The obtained results should be provided and officially published by the National Statistical Institute, so that all interested persons have access to this information. In this way, we believe that control practice will be significantly improved because comparability of the obtained results will be realized for the same set control goals and tasks by the relevant control authorities. The development of such a methodology will contribute to the clarification and modern solution of a number of control problems, such as: the timely change of the control technology; the application of new rules of conduct in relation to the change in the country's political and economic situation; the introduction of stricter restrictive control measures, etc.
6. During the empirical study of the applicability of the principles of financial control, a number of practical problems were identified. This is due to the fact that the mechanisms for applying the principles of financial control are not sufficiently legally regulated, especially in regard to the specific (derivative) principles. This also proved our thesis that significant reform is needed in the control technology of PFIA regarding the principles of control since our country still does not have established traditions regarding the mechanisms and their application, as is the case in other countries belonging to the Anglo-Saxon control system.
7. The incorrect and inaccurate application of the principles of financial control by any control institution, including PFIA, is not due to inaccurate regulation of their nature in the normative acts but is a result of the lack of an internally approved methodology regarding the manner of their application. Therefore, the main recommendation we make to the control authorities is the development of such a methodology.

8. The proposed sample methodology regarding the application of the principles of financial control must be tailored to the specifics, goals and tasks of the control organization.

The limited volume of work and the problematic application of the principles of financial control are the main prerequisite for claiming that the research questions presented in this way are not exhausted. The completeness of the development refers only to the achievement of the previously set goals and objectives. An object of subsequent research could be the analysis of the dependence between the functions and principles of financial control. Similarities and differences can be explored between the principles on which control strategies are constructed and the principles that are implemented during the control process itself. The different points of view and opinions on the issues presented in each part of this study can also be the subject of independent research and analysis.

We believe that the topic set in this study is a major key, which helps much larger and more important issues for society to be investigated, such as, for example, the study of the mechanisms and applicability of the principles and norms of financial control applied by the European Commission as the main control body of the member states of the European Union. In addition, the principles and norms of control can be the object of study from the point of view of internal control for a particular company. Also, the subject of research can be the principles of financial control of other control institutions, not only the principles of PFIA. All presented alternative options for research once again prove the impossibility of covering and researching all current issues related to the principles of financial control in a single study.

The problems and questions presented in this work are a small part of the unexplained and unexplored problems in the field of control theory. It is likely that the proposed research approaches are not the only ones to investigate the questions presented. The methods proposed here to investigate problematic and practical issues, such as the method of applicability of principles to control theory, can be considered daring and too innovative. The presented study is a small attempt to outline the theoretical-applicable problems of the principles of financial control, as well as to present a research approach for their resolution.

Plamena Georgieva Nedyalkova
University of Economics, Bulgaria

REFERENCES

Marx, K. (1988). *Capital: A Critique of Political Economy*. Partizdat.

Moffett, J. (2011). *Control Principles and Role Hierarchies*. Moffett. http://www. moffett.me.uk

Acknowledgment

The author Plamena Nedyalkova would like to express her deepest gratitude to:

All contributors for being willing to share different research perspectives;

The manuscript reviewers for their suggestions and comments;

IGI Global for sending a timely invitation to prepare this manuscript and for continuing editing support;

I thank my family, who supported me in my scientific research work, I also thank those who "benevolently" put all kinds of obstacles in my way, because I was able to become stronger and for this work to find its international appeal.

Plamena Nedyalkova
University of Economics, Bulgaria

The dynamic political and economic situation, both in the country and in the world, set some new and more complex goals and objectives for solving in front of control, which posed challenges in its scientific and practical field. And just as in dominoes, where after the fall of one tile, the others fall, so in control doctrine, under the influence and impact of these factors, not only the functions of control, the objects and subjects change, but also the principles of financial control change and improve. Many of the control bodies of the world's major companies and organizations have long come to the conclusion that in order to implement full, effective and quality control, the following is necessary (Moffett, 2012):

1. The principles of control, which need to be observed during the control process itself, should be clearly and precisely defined and publicly stated.
2. The mechanisms for applying the principles of financial control should be properly defined. This process is very complicated, as it always depends on the pre-set control goals and tasks, on the control powers of the controller, as well as on the features and specifics of the controlled object.

Thus the principles of control, including the principles of financial control, go beyond the general theoretical framework and become a bridge that facilitates the detection of unregulated deviations of phenomena and processes occurring at both the macro-level (state level) and micro-level (specific enterprise, industry, department, etc.). This determines the degree of their importance and is one of the main motives determining the thematic choice for research, namely: principles of financial control. The urgency of the problem is determined by the fact that the principles of financial control are the main building element of the control technology, without which the control process cannot take place.

The stages for implementation of the principles of financial control and the methodology for research of their application in the control technology and in the control process are an object of research in the monograph.

The principles of financial control, applied by the control inspectors of The Public Financial Inspection Agency (PFIA), are a subject of research.

In order to study in-depth the implementation of the financial control principles by the agency, the information security on the implementation of the empirical part of this exhibition covers the following:

1. Two thousand four hundred and fifty reports on the results of the financial inspections carried out by PFIA for the period from 2007 to 2011.
2. The information disclosed in the annual reports on the activity of PFIA for the period from 2007 to 2011 and period 2019 to 2022.
3. The research results by various NGOs in the field of financial control, such as the Center for Study of Democracy and the Association for Combating Economic Fraud.
4. The results presented in the annual activity reports of the Public Financial Inspection Agency (PFIA) on the financial security of the country for the period from 2007 to 2011 and period 2019 to 2022.

Due to the large volume and number of information sources, only a part of them are presented in the development applications.

The main motives for choosing this specific object for research are:

1. According to a January 2011 report by SIGMA - Support for Improvement in Government and Management, the EU's main goal is to create a common market for public procurement. The European Community (EC) therefore supports the proposed legal requirement to remove all existing barriers and prevent the emergence of new ones related to the effective implementation of the public procurement within the EU. The report also emphasizes that this can only be achieved by applying the basic principles of financial control presented in the relevant regulations. (SIGMA, 2011).
2. The Public Financial Inspection Agency (PFIA), as one of the main control bodies of the state power, is authorized not only to check the procedures for assigning and implementing public procurement in Bulgaria but also to protect the public financial interests by applying the principles of financial control.

In connection with the presented subject and object, the purpose of the monograph work is based on the theoretical overview of the nature and classification of the principles of financial control to present both foreign experience in established legal procedures for the application of financial control principles and systematic stages of their study, and also to propose an adaptation of the established foreign practice and experience to the practice in the country. In order to achieve the outlined goal, it is necessary to solve the following main tasks:

1. To present theoretically the issues and problems related to the development and improvement of the principles of financial control. The aim is to lay a good foundation for empirical research by clarifying many of the theoretical postulates concerning the principles.
2. To study the factors that affect the applicability of control principles, taking into account the fact that the mechanisms for applying the principles of financial control are influenced by their interaction with the control environment and the processes of formulating the ultimate optimal control solution.
3. To apply the comparative approach in analyzing the established foreign practice with the practice in Bulgaria in relation to the implementation and impact of the principles of financial control.
4. To apply the evaluation approach to determine the impact of the principles of financial control in the control process.

The main thesis of the monographic work is that the principles of control determine the methodological foundations of financial control and are a means of improving the quality of control impact. Achieving a high quality of control impact is the cornerstone of any control process. It is, therefore, necessary, on the one hand, to improve the methodology of financial control so that the emphasis is on the quality implementation of the principles of financial control, and on the other hand, to establish a system of procedures for examining the impact of the principles.

Proving the presented thesis is connected with the following working hypotheses:

Hypothesis 1. In addition to the set goals and tasks to be completed by the PFIA inspectors, the control environment also influences the way of applying the principles of financial control.

Hypothesis 2. The methodology for determining the normative impact of the Public Financial Inspection Act and the Regulations for application of the

Public Financial Inspection Act on the controlled objects should be applied as a methodology for determining the impact of the principles of financial control regulated in these two normative acts.

The presented goal, as well as the tasks for its achievement, determine the structure of this work, the objects and the subject of study, as well as the methodological research approach of the work itself. The methods of synthesis, analysis, induction, deduction, observation, analogy and comparison are applied in order to achieve the thus defined goals and to complete the previously set tasks in the study work. A systematic approach was used to describe the sequence of processes. The visualization of various facts and data is carried out with the help of the graphic and schematic approach. The combined application of research methods and approaches is aimed at reaching final conclusions and presenting different recommendations. In studying the application of the principles of financial control in Chapter Three, the requirements of the European Commission to the country regarding the implementation of a methodology, when investigating complex economic and financial crimes in Bulgaria, are taken into account.

Regarding, on the one hand, the fact that the topic set in this way is comprehensive and a different research approach can be applied to its research, different from the one adopted for writing this work, and on the other hand, taking into account the previously set goals and tasks, the following limitations need to be presented:

1. Theoretically, issues such as the nature and tasks of financial control will not be explored. They are too comprehensive and still debatable among experts regarding whether control is a separate doctrine or a function of management; can control be considered a public attitude; as well as whether control is a function of accounting and law; is it possible to present financial control as a system built on a number of elements.

Due to the unresolved issues concerning the full disclosure of the nature of control, we assume that for the purposes of the study, control is presented as a function of management. It is the basis on which the structural systems of each self-established doctrine, such as management, are built. Taking into account the dialectical approach (Marx, 1988), it can be assumed that control cannot be considered in isolation from all other phenomena and processes occurring in the economy, and it should be assumed that it is not a constant but a variable.

In a broader sense, the term "financial control" should be understood as a process on the basis of which the maintenance of the order, legality and expediency of the sovereign activity of the state itself is carried out. On the other hand, in a narrower sense, this concept should be interpreted as a way to identify, present and summarize the identified financial gaps, weaknesses, deviations and violations of generally accepted domestic and government financial principles and norms in order to take measures and affecting the person causing the damage.

2. The ethical principles of financial control, such as democracy, transparency, immediacy, independent verification and a systematic approach, will not be studied in this work. The ethics of the control processes, as well as the ethical requirements to be observed, can be issues of self-study.
3. Individually and independently, each principle can be a subject of research in order to present its theoretical and practical aspects in more details. Given this circumstance, in this work we limit the study of the principles of financial control, focusing on the features of control principles, which are more significant and on the basis of which one control principle is distinguished from another.

The following problems were identified during the empirical research on the implementation of the principles of financial control by the PFIA inspectors, as well as during the study of their impact on the condition of the controlled object. The first main problem is the fact that the principles of financial control are a specific element not only of the implemented control technology, but are also an element of the control process. This element remains intangible and invisible in the control situation, as it has a qualitative but not a quantitative characteristic. It is this specificity of the researched object that creates difficulties in the application of research tools for its study. The second problem is that in the implementation of the principles of financial control, in the performing of the control process and especially in the final closing stages, the manner of their application is not disclosed in the control documentation. Based on the previous two problems, the third problem follows - lack of sufficient empirical information on the researched problem.

Plamena Georgieva Nedyalkova
University of Economics, Bulgaria

Chapter 1
Evolution of the Theory of the Principles of Financial Control

ABSTRACT

In the first chapter of the development, the questions regarding the theoretical concepts of the essence of the principles of control are considered, and a general definition is derived. The purpose of the principles for the control activity and their importance are presented.In this part of the development, different opinions of researchers and scientific specialists are presented in order to discover the different aspects of application of this concept in practice. The principles of control are the rules that determine the way in which the control process takes place.

Clarification of the nature and meaning of the principles of financial control, their form and manner of manifestation is required by the fact that they are "the scientific basis on which to build concepts and strategies for the development of control" (Donev, 1984). In addition, the principles of control are the fundamental basis on which the whole control process should take place.

Etymologically, the term "principle" comes from the Latin word "principium", which translates as "basis". Over the different historical periods, under the influence of a number of factors, the essence of this concept has changed many times, having different meanings and content. For example, from the remaining and preserved to this day fragments of Heraclitus, it is established that the ancient Greek word for principle "arcή" was originally used in the old times, and again, it means "foundation" (Yanev, 1928). At a

DOI: 10.4018/978-1-6684-8883-6.ch001

later stage, with the advent of Latin, the Latin word "principium" was used. It is interesting to note that even in the earliest handwritten books, the term "principium" was never presented with its own meaning, but was used in conjunction with words such as "AB LOVE" or "AB LOVE PRINCIPIUM"/ Start from the most important thing" (Ifandiev, 2009).

Today, the meaning of the term "principle" is very different from what it was in the Middle Ages and in antiquity. Principles are accepted as the basic starting point of a theory, science, or political system. They are also perceived as a guiding principle in life; ideas; views and beliefs (Bayrova, 1982).

Research in our country is still very scarce on the problematic issue of the theory of control, such as the question of the nature of the financial control principles. That is why, for its more complete and accurate study, we present the opinions of various world experts. In the process of researching various sources of literature in their nature and type, we came across the still debatable question of what the term "principle of control" means. It turns out that even specialists from the same control system interpret this concept differently. For example, if the statements of V. Burtsev and N. Kazakov are taken into account, despite the fact that both are representatives of the control system of mixed economies, it is established that they have different views on the interpretation of the essence of the principles of control. N. Kazakov defines the principles of control as guiding directions of the whole control process, on the basis of which the control itself acquires a leading and managing role. The application of a specific principle must be consistent with "the very nature and essence of control activities" (Kazakov, 2001).

According to N. Kazakov (Kazakov, 2001), the principles of control are the basic rules for carrying out the control activity itself. Effective state control will exist only when the principles and requirements for its performance are followed.

Taking into account all the historical data describing the political and economic events that took place in our country, it is established that the structure of the control system of Bulgaria belongs to the model of the countries with mixed economies. Therefore, this is the main reason why many of the views and statements of our researchers are close to those of other foreign experts belonging to the same control model of mixed economies. For example, according to Pl. Chipev (Chipev, 2002), the principles of control are "non-binding and do not aim to be detailed prescriptions for the national legislation. Their purpose is to serve as a starting point. ... These principles are evolutionary in nature and must be seen in light of the significant changes in conditions. "

According to other experts, the principles of control are uniform because they apply to the entire activity of the unified national control system, to all its subsystems (Velichkova, 1977), and according to K. Donev (Donev, 2002), the principles of control "are basic rules and requirements for its implementation".

If we compare the control model of the countries of mixed economies with the Anglo-Saxon control system, which includes countries such as the United States, Australia, America, Britain, etc., it is found that researchers from this control system present the nature of control principles in a specific way. Specialists from the Anglo-Saxon control system reveal the specifics of the principles of control, emphasizing the importance of the control process for the specific organization. For example, A. Schaad (Schaad, 2011) assumes that the principles of control are general restrictions imposed on a particular organization. These principles are regulated according to the goals of a higher body, and they are always consistent with the organizational hierarchy of the organization itself.

Another distinctive feature is that the Anglo-Saxon control system has adopted the idea that each organization uses a different set of control principles and has individual requirements for the implementation of the control process itself. The control principles are perceived as part of the corporate management framework of the corporation itself (Moffett, 2011).

Researchers belonging to the Anglo-Saxon control system have also long concluded that control activities must be carried out on the basis of clearly regulated control principles. Characteristic of this system is the strong influence of the large corporations on the processes of drafting the regulations themselves. All the legislation of these countries is subject to the possibility of regulatory action by specific public advocates (called lobbyists) performed on the financial bills. For example, US federal law officially regulates lobbying. For this reason, many of the generally accepted principles of control in the countries belonging to this control system are strongly influenced by the goals and views of the large corporations on the manner of implementation and conduct of control activities.

The control system of mixed economies, which includes not only Bulgaria but also all former socialist countries, differs in another way from the Anglo-Saxon control system. The financial control of these countries is influenced simultaneously by the state itself, which is a major regulatory body, as well as by the mechanisms of the market regulation itself. The development of the principles of control is strongly influenced by the specifics and goals of the state power itself. The strong influence of the socialist government and economy in these countries is a prerequisite for the difficult entry and implementation of newer, modern control methods and principles in the control activities of the controlling bodies.

So far, we have considered the opinions of the experts who believe the principles should be accepted as a rule of conduct. There are other views in the theory, which are determined by the different perceptions of the concept of "principle". For example, according to St. Marinova (Marinova, 2009), the principle is not a rule of conduct, but an idea that determines the creation and function of the norm itself. The content of the principle, in addition to being publicly approved, but also strictly legally regulated, logically precedes the creation and implementation of the norm. This opinion is also supported by specialists such as Apostolov (Apostolov, 1946), Tashev (Tashev, 2000), Kelsen (Kelsen, 1962), Hart (Hart, 1961), Dworkin (Dworkin, 1978) and others.

Taking into account all the above, we assume that:

1. From a historical point of view, the implementation of the principles of financial control precedes the period of their theoretical presentation.
2. The control principles are the main building block, on the basis of which not only the whole control process takes place, but also the control technology. It can be assumed that they are the idea for its realization and course.
3. The control principles themselves are interconnected and form a single control system. Despite the existing variety of control principles, the characteristic is that one principle does not contradict another. They complement each other and reveal the specifics of the controlled object.
4. There is no historical information and data on when exactly the principles of control originated, but what is known is that they are the result of practical traditions existing since ancient times for the implementation of control in various forms and ways of manifestation.
5. With the help of the principles of control it is possible to provide independent, accurate and objective information about the condition of the controlled object, as well as accurate assessment of the presence of quantitative and qualitative changes from the adopted generally accepted norms.

The question of the essence of the principles of control and especially of the principles of internal financial control was presented during the IX Congress of the International Organization of Supreme Audit Institutions (International Organisation of Supreme Audit Institutions – INTOSAI), held in Lim. During the congress in October 1977, the so-called "Lim Declaration on Guiding Principles of Control" was adopted (Lim Declaration, 1977). This declaration played a very important and fundamental role in the development of the supreme audit institutions. What is specific is that it does not exhaust the issue of the principles of control, but over time, it presented a regulated framework consisting of principles and prerequisites necessary for the proper organization, regulation and implementation of internal financial control (Donev, 2002).

A significant number of experts still agree that the two concepts, namely "principles of control" and "principles of financial control", overlap as meaning. But there are significant differences between them. The concept of "principles of control" is more general, as it refers to all control principles that are known in the overall control system of the country, namely: the principles of judicial control, the principles of legislative and the executive control. Also, the principles of control are pre-defined axioms, on the basis of which the overall framework for the state control process is built. In addition, they are a guarantor of the effectiveness of state control. Therefore, the principles of financial control should be accepted as basic rules for conducting only the financial control process. It is the principles of financial control that determine the nature of the financial control process itself - how democratic it is, how well the conditions for the lawful and successful course and completion of the control process are provided, and how the rights and legitimate interests of its participants will be protected.

On the other hand, applying the comparative analysis between the presented opinions, it can be assumed that in recent years there has been a theoretical and applied evolution of the principles of financial control. The evolutionary constructiveness is due to the fact that their purpose and role relate not only to the scope, conduct and establishment of the result of the control process but also to the organization and the subsequent assessment.

In conclusion, the following definition of **the principles of financial control** can be formulated: **they are rules of conduct that should be observed and especially applied by control bodies during the implementation of control technology and in the implementation of the control process from its beginning to its end**. Once established, a specific concept of the principle of financial control remains unchanged. The presented interpretations regarding the nature of the control principles and the principles of financial control will not be the only and the last ones revealing the essence of this researched issue.

REFERENCES

Apostolov, Iv. (1946). Evolyutsia na kontinentalnata talkuvatelna teoria. GSU YuF, N° 41

Bairova, M. (1982). *Dictionary of foreign words in the Bulgarian language*. BAS Publishing.

Chipev, P. (2002). In Search of Mechanisms for Better Corporate Control, Sofia: COALITION 2000

Donev, K. (2002). Darzhaven finansov kontrol – teoria i praktika. God. na IU Varna, 74.

Dworkin, R. (1978). *Taking Rights Seriously*. Duckworth.

Hart, H. L. A. (1961). *The Concept of Law*.

Ifandiev, G. (2013). It's time to take back the church. http://www.forumat-bg.com

Kazakov, N. (2013). Principles of regulation of internal financial control and forms of its implementation in the system of economic security of Russia. http://oad.rags.ru

Kelsen, H. (1962). *Theorie pure du droit*.

Lima Declaration. (1977). Lima Declaration of Control Guidelines. http://www.intosai4kni.org/wiki/ [seen on 14.07.2009]

Marinova, S. (2009). Towards the concept of legal principle. Economic alternatives, N° 5.

Moffett, J. (2011). Control Principles and Role Hierarchies. Available from: http://www. moffett.me.uk

Schaad, A. (2011). A Framework for Organisational Control Principles. Available from: http://www.alloy.mit.edu

Tashev, R. (2000). Contemporary legal positivism. Modern law, N° 5.

Velichkova, M. (1977). *Edinni printsipi, metodika i kriterii za kontrol*.

Chapter 2
Criteria for Classification of the Principles of Financial Control

ABSTRACT

In this part of the development, a classification of the principles of financial control according to various criteria and criteria is presented. It is therefore appropriate to assume that the principles that make up the overall control framework of executive control should also be classified according to the structure of the state apparatus as: 1. Principles of executive control of the Council of Ministers 2. Principles of administrative (departmental) control 3. Principles of specialized administrative control 4. Principles of executive control in local government

The question of classifying the principles of financial control according to different criteria has always been relevant not only from a theoretical but also from a practical point of view. We believe that the main prerequisite for this is that the classification is not just a grouping of principles by individual characteristics, but also a way to determine the interaction between the individual control principles in the implementation of the control process and technology. It can be assumed that there is still no uniform approach in the specialised books for the classification of the principles of control, including the principles of financial control. We assume that the existence

DOI: 10.4018/978-1-6684-8883-6.ch002

of different classification approaches is determined by the following more important prerequisites:

1. The control process is comprehensive and it is difficult to determine its boundaries.
2. The control technology applied by the different control bodies is different, which contributes to the diversity in the implementation of the financial control principles.
3. The historical development of control not only as a science but also as a practice, has influenced the change of the principles of control over the years and has led to the emergence of new principles that meet the modern theoretical and practical requirements of control.
4. The different economic and legal environment in which the whole control process takes place.
5. The different goals and tasks that are set before the control process, leading to different application of control principles.
6. Dynamically changing legislation, harmonizing with EU requirements, is a prerequisite for changing existing and introducing new control principles.

Despite the long historical roots of the emergence of control, there is still no consensus on the criteria on the basis of which control principles should be grouped. For example, the Anglo-Saxon control system pays more attention and priority to audit control principles. Comparing the research of this problem by specialists from the Anglo-Saxon control system with the one done by specialists from the control system of mixed economies, it is established that the problem has not been studied in depth. What the former socialist countries such as Bulgaria, Serbia, Poland, Hungary, Czechoslovakia and others adopted in order to quickly harmonize their control practice with EU requirements, is to implement and enforce all that the Anglo-Saxon control system has established for control principles. Countries belonging to the control system of mixed economies have made radical changes in the implementation of state control principles, adopting the regulated control principles of the EC through the amendment of its regulations. For this reason, and taking into account the above, we believe that for Bulgaria as an EU member state, it is necessary all control principles and especially the principles of financial control to be grouped and arranged on specific grounds. Otherwise, the impression will remain that these important rules exist, but it is not really regulated exactly what is the feature that unlocks their manifestation. With the help of Figure

1 we present the criteria according to which we group the control principles and classify the principles of financial control.

The presented criteria for the classification of the principles of financial control with the help of Figure 1 will help for a more detailed study of the features and specifics of the principles of control, including the principles of financial control. Each criterion is specific in itself and reveals in different ways not only the essence of the principle itself, but also helps to study important moments in the development of financial control as a science and practice. In this part of the study, an attempt is made to summarize a significant part of the existing opinions among scientists in Bulgaria on the criteria for classifying the principles of control, including the principles of financial control. The grouping of the principles according to certain criteria is, on the one hand,

Figure 1. Criteria for classification of control principles, including the principles of financial control

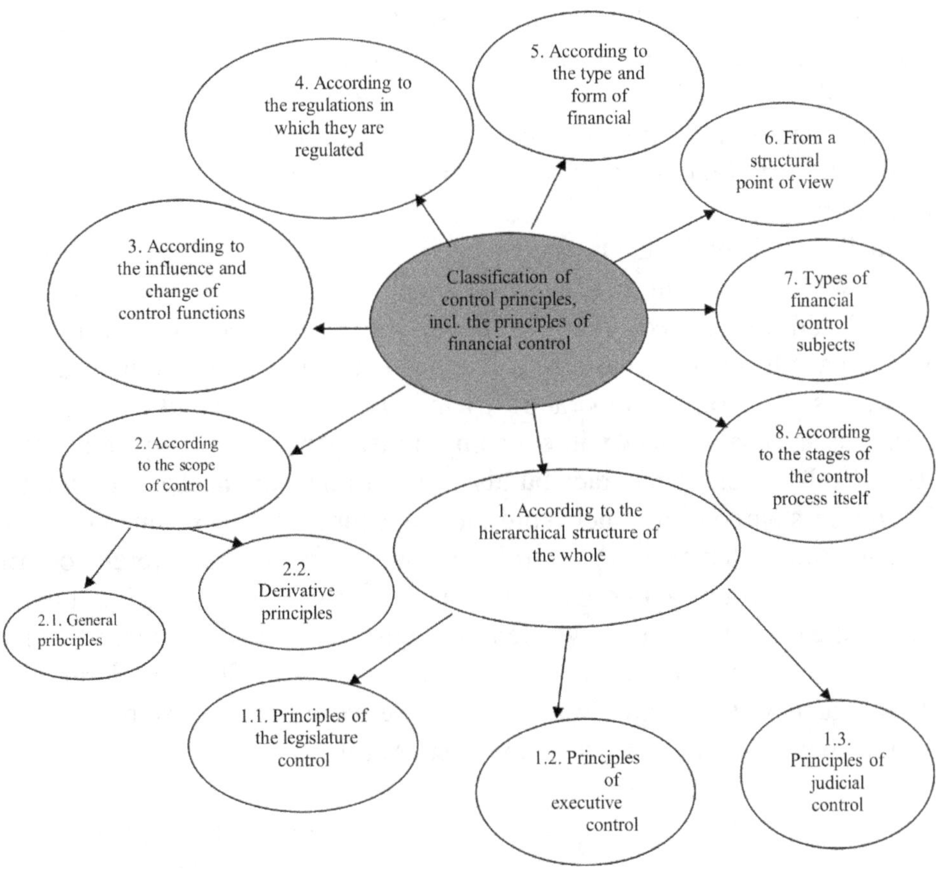

a creative process, depending on the directions set by the specialists for research, and on the other hand, it is a utopian process, chimerically grouping the principles according to specific criteria. The chimerical grouping of the control principles is established in the specific control situations, when it is most accurately proved that the theoretical affiliation of a given principle to a specific grouping criterion is not a prerequisite for its non-application in a specific control situation.

CLASSIFICATION OF THE PRINCIPLES OF FINANCIAL CONTROL ACCORDING TO THE HIERARCHICAL STRUCTURE OF THE CONTROL SYSTEM OF THE COUNTRY

The structure and organization of the country's control system are subject to the general theory of systems. They exist and function in order to achieve certain goals and objectives. They are built on the basis of the structure of state power and represent a set of separate elements (subsystems) that function as a whole. These subsystems are: legislative, executive and judicial control. The division of the main building blocks of the country's control system is subject to one of the basic principles of state power, namely, the separation of powers.

In his work entitled On the Spirit of the Laws, in 1748, Charles de Montesquieu (Hajoljan, 2012) was the first to declare that the functions of the state should be exercised by various bodies - legislative, executive and judicial, which have to interact, but also to control each other ". In Montesquieu's view, this is the only democratic way in which the rights and freedoms of citizens can be guaranteed without compromising the sovereignty of the state itself. Today, every democracy builds its government on this basic principle. Therefore, state control, which is presented as a function of government, unites all subsystems that exercise control, resulting in creating the overall control system of the country. In order to maintain the balance in each community, one of the most important unwritten rules has been adopted, namely, that no controlled system should exceed its scope of action, ie. not to be dominant. This is achieved through the relationship between the exercise of a power and the control that other bodies exercise over it.

Figure 2. Hierarchical structure of the control system of the Republic of Bulgaria

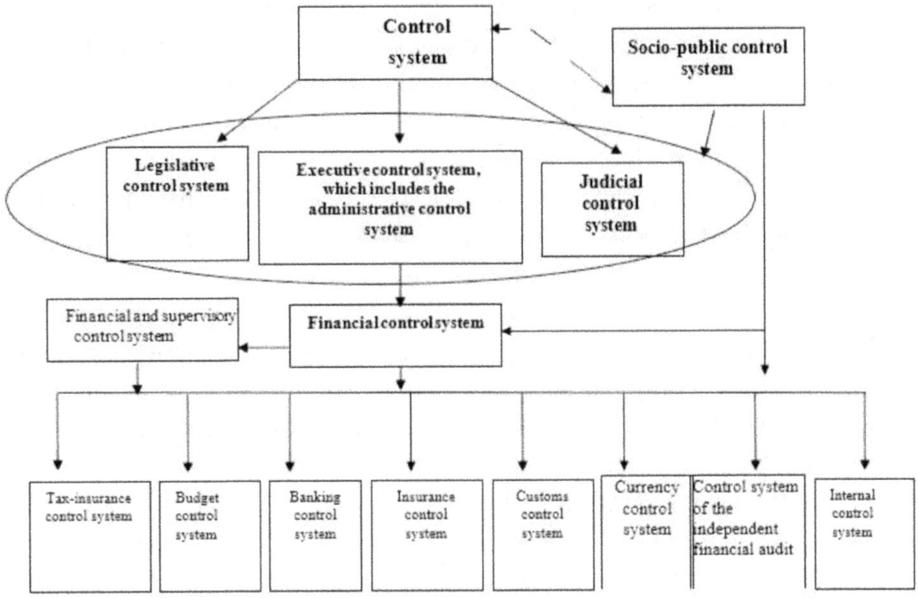

Each individual control subsystem is made up of separate elements (also called subsystems). With the help of Figure 2 the hierarchical structure of the control system of the country can be presented as follows:

1. The concept of "control system" is more general and comprehensive than the concepts of "legislative control system", "executive control system" and "judicial control system". This is determined by the fact that they (the legislative, executive and judicial control systems) are subsystems (elements) of the overall control system of the Republic of Bulgaria.
2. The control subsystems that make up the overall control system of the country are very diverse in appearance. This determines the complexity of development and the impossibility to cover all control subsystems and to study all control principles that build not only the systems themselves, but also their subsystems.
3. The control system helps to provide information to stakeholders by the state authorities. Information technologies, together with the control actions of the controllers, drive the mechanisms for the preservation of the state property and the society as a whole, without infringing on their autonomy and their statutory rights.

4. Control is an open system that can continuously include in its scope a variety of subsystems. The main objective of all subsystems is to ensure complete, effective and comprehensive control over the identified controlled objects. The purpose of the financial control system is: to understand the main financial processes; to establish key financial policies and objectives; to determine which processes are a prerequisite for maintaining the appropriate level of risk in the control environment; to apply best practices and continuously improve the philosophy for building effective control actions.

For the purposes of this study, special attention is paid to the control exercised by the executive branch to which the administrative control relates. Many of the issues of administrative control are a subject of research not only from a legal point of view but also from the financial control point of view. According to experts, administrative control is "control exercised by bodies included organizationally in the system of executive bodies" (Lazarov, 2009). Accepting the thesis of E. Zlatarev that financial control is a "specialized type of administrative control" (Zlatarev, 2007), we believe that among the known, existing in practice types of administrative control, for this work's purposes, it is necessary to emphasize the specialized administrative control, but only to the extent that it reveals the connection and dependence between the principles of administrative control and the principles of financial control.

Therefore, taking into account the above statement and refracting it through the prism of the goals and objectives of this study, it follows that to determine whether the emergence and development of the principles of financial control are influenced by the principles of administrative control, the following is necessary:

1. To determine whether administrative control and financial control have some similar goals and objectives
2. To determine whether the scope (perimeter) of the action of administrative control does not affect (does not enter) the scope (perimeter) of action of financial control.

The goals of the state financial control are numerous. One of them is the protection of public financial interests. It is regulated in Art. 2, para. 1 of the State Financial Inspection Act. According to the provisions of the same Act, the main tasks of the State Financial Inspection Agency are:

1. Carrying out subsequent financial inspections for the observance of the normative acts, which regulate the budgetary, financial-economic or reporting activity of the organizations and the persons under art. 4;
2. Establishment of violations of the normative acts regulating the budgetary, financial-economic or reporting activity, as well as of indicators for committed frauds;
3. Disclosure of damages caused to the property of the organizations and persons under Art. 4;
4. Bringing the perpetrators to administrative and criminal liability in the presence of the relevant legal grounds;
5. Detection of fraud and infringements affecting the financial interests of the European Community.

In Art. 4 of the Law on the State Financial Inspection, the legislator has presented in detail the organizations and persons who may fall under the scope of the financial inspectors performing financial control, namely:

1. Budget organizations;
2. State companies under Art. 62, para. 3 of the Commercial Law, as well as municipal companies;
3. Companies with a blocking quota of state or municipal participation in the capital;
4. Commercial companies, in the capital of which a person under point 2 or 3 participates with a blocking quota;
5. Legal entities that have obligations guaranteed by state or municipal property;
6. Legal entities under the Non-profit Legal Entities Act and impersonal companies under the Obligations and Contracts Act in which the state or the municipality participates directly or indirectly in their property;

Administrators of aid, recipients of state or minimal aid, persons financed with funds from the state or municipal budgets, under international agreements or programs of the European Union, as well as persons financed with funds from state companies under Art. 62, para. 3 of the Commercial Law - regarding the spending of these funds.

Regarding the administrative control, its main purpose is to protect the following:

1. National security and public order in the Republic of Bulgaria, as well as exclusive and sovereign rights of the state within the meaning of Art. 18, para. 1 - 4 of the Constitution of the Republic of Bulgaria
2. Personal and property rights of citizens and legal entities
3. Environment

On the other hand, the methods by which this basic objective of administrative control is achieved can be presented in the following sequence:

1. Carrying out inspections on documents and on the spot at the beginning and during the performance of economic activity, as well as during the performance of individual transactions and actions by persons who perform or intend to perform economic activity
2. Issuance of a license or registration for starting a business, as well as refusals to issue a license or to register
3. Issuance and refusal of permits and certificates for a separate transaction or action by persons who carry out or intend to carry out economic activity
4. Implementation of coercive administrative measures and initiation of proceedings for imposition of administrative penalties

The comparative approach to analysis shows that the goals and objectives of administrative control are more comprehensive than those of financial control applied by PFIA. The main purpose of financial control overlaps only one of the main objectives of administrative control, namely: protection of public and financial interests of the state. It is this overlap of one goal of administrative control with the main goal of financial control is a prerequisite for the applicability of the same principles in both financial and administrative control. For example, the principles of legality, professionalism, confidentiality, speed, procedural economy, etc., are inherent in both financial and administrative control.

The totality of all control principles builds the general conceptual framework of control. With the help of the control principles, we follow, on the one hand, the "deconstructed" change of the control framework itself over the years, and on the other hand, its "reconstructed" change.

A "deconstructed" change in the control framework is observed when it changes under the influence of natural factors. A "reconstructed" change to the control framework is observed in cases where its structure has been influenced by various political, economic and social factors. In order to obtain either a "deconstructed" or a "reconstructed" prismatic refraction of the control framework, it is necessary to comply with the condition that natural, social and politico-economic factors must influence, first, the change of the general control principles themselves and, based on this, to influence the transformation of the overall conceptual framework (Corcuff, 1973).

All set goals and tasks in public administration are arranged hierarchically from top to bottom according to their priority. For example, one of the most important and basic goals and tasks of any society is to preserve the political and economic stability of the community (Alexandrovich, 2008). Therefore, just as these goals and objectives are fundamental to a particular community, they are also common, as they apply to all participants in the community. The realization of these common goals and objectives is done only in compliance with certain common principles and norms that apply to all participants in the community.

According to the hierarchical structure of the state, the principles of control can be classified according to the characteristics of *the types of state control exercised by the state*, namely:

1. Principles of legislative control
2. Principles of executive control
3. Principles of judicial control

Each of these principles has the opportunity to study independently as an important building block of the overall control framework of our country. For the purposes of this work, we pay special attention to the principles of executive control, as the principles of judicial and legislative control are legal issues.

In turn, executive control is subdivided into separate subtypes according to the structure of the state apparatus. It is therefore appropriate to assume that the principles that make up the overall control framework of executive control should also be classified according *to the structure of the state apparatus* as:

1. Principles of executive control of the Council of Ministers
2. Principles of administrative (departmental) control
3. Principles of specialized administrative control
4. Principles of executive control in local government

The types of principles of administrative control presented in this way can be independently studied. E. Zlatarev (Zlatarev, 2007) accepts that financial control is a specialized type of administrative control. It is characteristic that the specialized administrative control affects only certain fragments of the control activity of the state. The principles on which the specialized administrative control process is based are determined by the scope of control. For example, when a fragment of the overall financial activity of the state comes to the attention of the control bodies, the principles on the basis of which the control process should take place will depend on the specifics of the controlled financial object. Therefore, the principles of financial control should be classified according to *the types of financial control subjects*:

1. Principles of tax and social security control
2. Principles of budgetary control
3. Principles of banking control
4. Principles of insurance control
5. Principles of currency control
6. Principles of customs control
7. Principles of independent financial audit
8. Principles of internal control

In the conditions of a dynamically changing market economy, the challenges faced by every political and economic community are the main factors that give rise to the need to set additional goals and objectives in order to achieve the previously set goals. All set goals and objectives should subsequently be considered secondary. Secondary goals and objectives are never at odds with pre-defined main goals and objectives. For the correct realization of the set secondary goals and tasks it is necessary to observe certain derived principles. The secondary principles themselves carry in themselves some of the peculiarities and specifics of the general principles. Another characteristic feature of the derived principles is that they are not intended to be observed by all participants in the community, but by specific persons who are entrusted with the implementation of secondary goals and objectives.

The hierarchical structure of the control system of the country, presented in Figure 2, is a prerequisite for the principles of control to be grouped into two main groups: the first are the so-called **general principles** of control, and the second are the so-called **specific (derived) control principles.** According to K. Donev (Donev, 2002), the general principles of control "reflect all possible requirements for the organization, conduct and completion of control, regardless of its forms, types, methods and subjects of control. The derivative principles of control are continuation, development and concretization of the general principles, in accordance with the organization, types, forms and the legal status of the subjects for state financial control".

Apart from the hierarchical structure of the control system, another criterion for the grouping of the principles of control, incl. the principles of financial control, to general and derivative principles, is the scope of control (Donev, 2002). The scope of financial control includes the financial relations between individuals and legal entities and the state regarding the formation, creation and distribution of the national product. While the scope of all state control includes not only financial but also non-financial relations arising between individuals, legal entities and the state. For this reason, the principles of control are divided into general and specific (derived) principles. Based on all the above, we assume that according to the scope of control exercised by PFIA, the principles applied by the Agency are specific (derived) principles of state control. On the other hand, in relation to the hierarchical place that the Agency occupies in the state structure of the country, presented in Figures 2 and 3, the principles of financial control of PFIA are a type of administrative principles of the executive power.

From Figure 3, revealing the classification of the principles of control, the following more important conclusions can be drawn: the principles of control are the basis of the structural construction not only of the overall control system, but also of the individual component systems. On the other hand, they are presented in a hierarchical structural relation and dependence. The existence of such a connection and dependence can be explained by the fact that there is a hierarchical connection and dependence between the goals and objectives in the overall control system of our country. Analyzing the presented Figure 3 from the bottom up we find that each type of control has its own specific principles, based on which, it differs from other types.

General (basic) principles of control are only those control principles which guarantee not only the protection of national wealth and state property but also the property of companies and citizens. General (basic) control principles apply to every share, industry, even a participant in society, in order to ensure and protect the vital interests of the population. Various examples of general (basic) principles can be presented from the control practice, but as the most significant and important we accept the opinion of K. Donev (Donev, 2012), that the composition of the general principles includes: *democratic centralism, the unity of political and economic leadership, the unity of sectoral and territorial governance, unity and collectivity, individual responsibility, collectivity and efficiency, objectivity and science*. The general (basic) principles are the cornerstones for the creation of control systems; they must be applied consistently both in cases of internal control and in cases of external control. It is important to note that these general (basic) principles are never independent of each other. The omission or incorrect application of one principle will always weaken the effectiveness of others. We believe that the principles can be added to these general principles: *people's sovereignty, constitutionalism, equality of citizens, political pluralism, the principle of separation of powers, equal rights of the parties, inviolability of the person, legality and independence.* The principles presented in this way are common not only to financial control, but also to legislative and judicial control due to the fact that they should be observed by all parties of the control process. The general principles of financial control "reflect all the essential requirements, rules and criteria relating to the elements of control, regardless of its types and forms, the bodies of implementation and the technology of implementation" (Donev, 2010). Many of the general principles of control presented in this way are regulated in the Constitution of the Republic of Bulgaria. The regulation of the general principles of control in this normative act is dictated by the fact that the Constitution is the supreme and fundamental law in the country. Any action of the control bodies should be in accordance with the constitutional principles, as otherwise their actions will be unconstitutional.

From the point of view of Western control practice, the general principles of control, on the one hand, overlap with the established principles in our practice, but also differ. The main prerequisite for this difference is the non-uniform organizational structure of state power. For example, in the United States, the basic principles are: Popular Sovereignt, Separation of Powers, Federalism, Judicial Review and Checks and Balances (The 6 Basic Principles, 2012). In Britain, the general principles of state control are: Parliamentary sovereignty, Principles of Democracy, Principle of Fairness, Principle of Legality, Principles of Judicial Review, Principle of Fairness and Procedural Due Process, and Principle of Freedom In Britain. On the other hand, control bodies in Italy should respect established constitutional principles such as: Equal Treatment, Principle of Equalisation, Principle of Fiscal Autonomy, Right to be Heard in Court, Defendant's Rights, and Responsibility of Public Officials (Italy – Constitution, 2012). According to the Italian Constitution, government officials and employees of other public bodies are directly responsible under criminal, civil and administrative law for acts committed in violation of rights. Civil liability, according to the Italian Constitution, extends to state and public bodies. On the other hand, the Italian Constitution does not include norms of economic relations, but of economic relations. There is a separate chapter three of the Italian Constitution, which pays

Figure 3. Classification of control principles

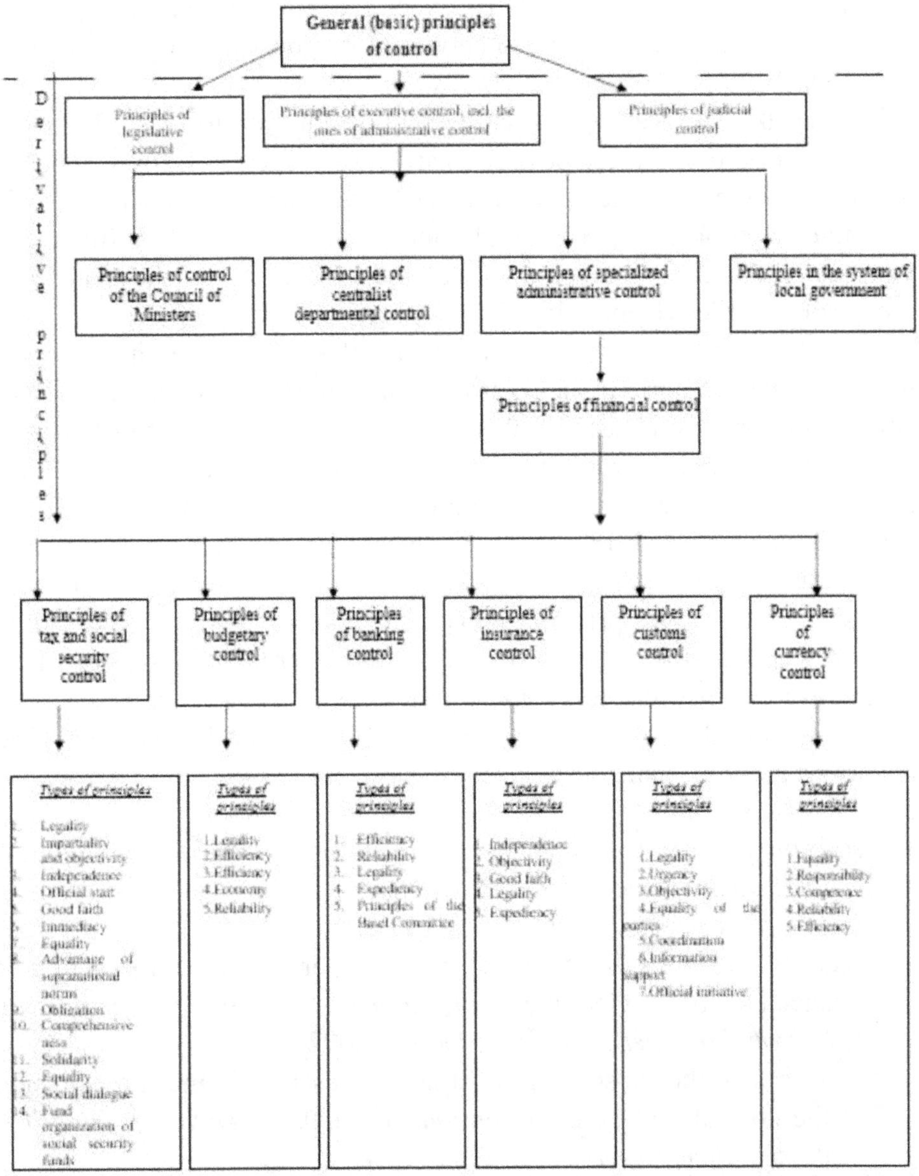

special attention to the "guiding principles of social and economic policy" (Italy – Constitution, 2012).

Therefore, the general (basic) principles of control should be defined as well-established ideas, if they are not integrated into the relevant regulations to be applied for both internal and external control purposes. In addition, the interpretation of these principles is a very meaningless action, especially when the principles are embodied between the input and output of control processes.

The specific (derivative) principles apply exclusively to a specific control body. We believe that these principles are always derived from the general principles, as they are effective rules, due to the impact of the first rules. In the reference books, they are found under the name "specific principles", which determine the organization of the subjective factor and the technology of control activities (Donev, 1984).

On the other hand, the specific principles determine the types of organizational structures in the control organizations (control bodies) (Hirsh, 1990). Therefore, given the types of organizational structures that are known in practice, namely: bureaucratic organizational structures, functional, divisional, matrix, conglomerate, centralized and decentralized (Donnelly, 1997), the specific principles according to the organizational structure they build, can be classified as: *linear, functional, staff, purpose-built and team principles* (Aleksiev, 1981). These principles do not apply to the control process, their purpose is to build the correct hierarchical framework on the basis of which an organizational structure should be built.

The specific (derivative) principles of financial control can be classified on various grounds, namely:

- according to the selected control technology – *immediacy, publicity, legality, competence, comprehensiveness, heuristics, retrospectiveness, reconstructiveness, etc.* (Donev, 2002);
- according to the subjective factor and the organizational structure of financial control – *planning, coordination, subordination, perspective, operational independence, etc.* (Donev, 2002);
- according to the chosen control strategy presented in the strategic plan of the control body – *coordination, rotation, systematics, reliability, professionalism, responsibility, spontaneity, etc.;*
- according to the internal normative acts adopted by the control body – *impartiality, cooperation, efficient use of human resources, transparency, confidentiality, professional conduct, etc.;*
- according to the regulated normative acts, which are intended to be applied by the control body – *legality, professionalism, good faith, immediacy, supremacy of supranational norms, comprehensiveness, efficiency, effectiveness, credibility, expediency, equality, etc.*

M. Dinev has a radically different opinion from the one presented so far regarding the classification of the principles of financial control, according to the criterion scope of financial control, to general principles and derivative (specific) ones. According to the expert, "the principles of financial control are important both for the controllers and there are possibilities for combined application of several principles. The combinatorial application of the principles is a need for continuous improvement of the control impact" (Dinev, 1999). In other words, when applying the method of comparative analysis with other opinions, it can be assumed that the innovativeness of M. Dinev's thesis is that it does not consider the principles of financial control according to individual criteria and characteristics. The fact that they are applied in combination is sufficient to assume that the classification of principles according to different criteria and features is a subjective process initiated by its creator.

Given all this, the following main conclusions can be drawn:

1. The general (basic) control principles build the overall state management matrix of the country, consisting of separate building blocks, called subsystems, in which the state power is exercised and realized.
2. It is typical that the general (basic) principles of control give the illusion of clarity and comprehensibility, but in the process of their practical observance it is established that this is not the case. In most cases, behind their verbal presentation there is a specific content, which explains their interpretation by the executive branch.
3. The non-observance of the general (basic) control principles by the control bodies is a reason to treat such actions as procedural violations, which call into question the objectivity of the implemented control processes. If the problem is considered in a broader sense, it can be assumed that the avoidance or non-compliance with the general (basic) principles of control is a prerequisite for violating the stability and security of the entire state system.
4. The specific (derived) principles ensure the functionality of the control body. They are specific to a control body. It can be assumed that this is their specificity. These principles of financial control, as well as the general (basic) principles, are made public through a specific piece of legislation, for example: Law on the State Financial Inspection, National Revenue Agency Act, Independent Financial Audit Act, etc., as the activity of the control body always affects another party in the control process.

5. The purpose of the proposed classification is to determine the main distinctive control frameworks that make up the general control framework of our country, and on the other hand, to determine the place and importance that a particular control principle occupies not only in the control frameworks but also in the overall control framework of the country. With the presented classifications, grouped by characteristics according to the hierarchical structure of the control system of the country, according to the types of financial control objects and according to the structure of the state apparatus, a clear division of responsibilities between different control, regulatory and law enforcement bodies is achieved. All legal and regulatory requirements that affect the control practice in the jurisdiction must be in accordance with the supreme normative act of the country - the Constitution of the Republic of Bulgaria. On the other hand, the principles of state control, incl. the principles of financial control are regulated in view of their impact on the overall political and economic situation in the country.
6. Also, another main conclusion that can be drawn is that the signs presented in this way for the classification of the principles of financial control have the corresponding shortcomings. We believe that these signs do not fully reveal the causal link for the application of the principles of financial control. The classification criteria presented in this way for grouping the principles of financial control do not reveal the mechanisms for the application of the principles.

In the reference books review, which we conducted and in which we shared the opinions of various researchers, we found that each specialist, according to the goals and objectives set to study the principles of financial control, presented and grouped them according to different criteria. In our opinion, in addition to the above criteria, the principles of financial control can be grouped according to the stages of the control process itself, in which the relevant control principles should be observed. We accept these principles as derivatives of financial control and according to the stage of the process, they can be:

1. **When planning the control process,** the principles set out in the strategic plans should be observed. For the period from 2007 to 2011, PFIA has developed five strategic plans for the development and activities of the Agency. The latest strategic plan for the activities of the Public Financial Inspection Agency (PFIA) covers the period from 2022 to 2024. The

principles themselves in the development of strategic policy as the first stage of the planning of control processes are presented as rules, which include guidelines for action in accordance with the set guidelines. At this stage, we believe that the principle of multiplicity should be respected. According to this principle, pre-defined strategic control decisions must be interlinked and not contradictory. The need for strategic decisions most often arises when new opportunities arise or when serious threats to the environment arise. At this stage, the principle of realism must be applied - compliance with the recommendations of European supervisory authorities such as OLAF, the World Bank and others, and with the real situation in the country. The planning of PFIA activities with the help of these strategic plans is not to take into account the fact that such a plan actually exists, but to take into account the requirements of external control observers and achieve the desired results so as to improve the quality of the control activity.

Therefore, the planning of the control process should very precisely define the principles of its implementation, and on the other hand, should take into account the requirements of the European control institutions and only then determine the actions on the basis of which the next three stages of the control process will occur, namely: its implementation, completion and subsequent control of the already implemented and completed control process.

2. **Implementation of the control process** – At this stage, PFIA should already apply all the principles set out in The Public Financial Inspection Act, namely: *legality, objectivity, professional origin and confidentiality*. What we address as a recommendation here, in this part of the exposition, to those in power is that the Law on the State Financial Inspection itself should also regulate the principle of *independence*. We take into account the fact that the Agency itself, as a body, is directly subordinated to the Ministry of Finance, but in carrying out their control activities, the inspectors must be independent. The activities of the Agency's inspectors cannot be influenced by different political attitudes, and it is also inadmissible for other executive bodies to exert pressure on its control activities. We believe that the legal regulation of the inspectors' independence in the performance of their official duties will provide them with greater security in detecting abuses and irregularities. The independence of PFIA inspectors should not be considered at the stage of entrusting inspections, as they do not have the power to determine or refuse to entrust an inspection. This principle should be observed

during the implementation of the control process. In other words, the manifestation of this principle is in the implementation of the current form of control. The principle of independence should not be seen as the independence of the PFIA control institution itself, but as the autonomy and freedom of inspectors to carry out their control duties. In this established structure of the state power, PFIA is a dependent control body of the executive power, especially with regard to the determination of the planned inspections, as well as the methodology for the implementation of the control actions. However, if the inspectors are not given the appropriate autonomy in carrying out the already assigned financial inspections, which means ensuring independence from the influence of various political and economic factors and events, we can in no way speak and claim that the inspections are effective. On the contrary, they will be highly politicized if independence is not present at a low operational and control level to identify abuses and irregularities. In addition to the principles mentioned in this way, the rules regulated in the Law on the State Financial Inspection should be applied in the control process, namely: legality, objectivity, confidentiality and officiary start. In the stages during which the implementation of the control process takes place, namely: 1) determination of the object for control; 2) development and selection of the control norm; 3) forecasting the expected state; 4) determination of the actual condition of the object of control, the principles of financial control should be applied very well. Their application should be in line with the requirements of international control organizations such as OLAF, and not just apply control principles just to render an account for any control activity.

3. **Completion of the control process** – here the principles of financial control should be observed, with the help of which the system of impacts should be realized. The main principles to be observed are the *principles of subsidiarity and impact assessment. Subsidiarity* should be accepted as a guiding principle for differentiating the responsibilities of participants in the control process. In the control process itself, the final control decision must be taken at the most decentralized level possible, in which the central managing authority is not involved, unless this is more efficient than the actions presented by the lower levels (Consolidated version, 2012). From the point of view of PFIA, this principle, despite its non-normative, clear and precise regulation, is applied by the Agency. The central governing body in PFIA is represented by a director and a deputy director. The tasks and powers of the Director and the Deputy

Director of the Agency are presented in the Rules of Procedure of the State Financial Inspection Agency. The assignment of inspections is always accompanied by an order of the Director of the Agency for their assignment. Their amendment, revocation, suspension and resumption are unappealable and are subject to immediate implementation in accordance with their purpose (Instruction, Order N° FK-09-41/23.07.2009). Upon establishment of administrative violations, administrative acts are drawn up in accordance with the requirements of the Law on Administrative Violations and Penalties, by an inspector or the head of the team that carried out the inspection activity. The act shall be sent to the Director of the Agency. It is here, at this stage, that the principle of subsidiarity should be applied. The Director should agree with the decision taken or offer another opinion, but only in cases where this opinion will contribute to a more effective end result.

The application of the *impact assessment* principle will improve the quality of inspection activities. This principle has not been applied in the PFIA control practice so far. The proposal on the introduction of this principle in control practice will have its debates among experts. In order to assess the effect of the impact, the control bodies must compare the information and the violations that they have found and established from previous inspections, and the deviations that are found should be regulated based on the proposed system of impacts. If there is a repetition of the mistakes and violations or if it is established that despite the imposed control sanctions the controlled object has not corrected its behavior, then with the implementation of the subsequent control inspection the controller should impose stricter sanctions and measures.

4. **Subsequent control of an already implemented and completed control process** – at this stage, again, all control principles covered in the previous three stages should be applied by the control authority. The fact that this is a follow-up control of an already implemented control process does not mean that any principle from the previous stages should be ignored. PFIA carries out follow-up control of the control process that the Agency has implemented. This ex-post control may also be initiated by the Court of Auditors or by the Public Procurement Agency.

One of the ways to circumvent the control activity not only of PFIA but also of the Public Procurement Agency and the Commission for Protection of Competition is by implementing actions by the contracting authority below the set value thresholds set in accordance with the Public Procurement Act.

In accordance with the latest updates of the Public Procurement Act from 2020, the value thresholds are divided according to the procedures defined in the law, regulated in Art. 18, para. 1, item 1 to item 13, of the Public Procurement Act. These procedures are: open; limited; competitive procedure with negotiation; negotiation with a preliminary invitation to participate; negotiating with the publication of a contract notice; competitive dialogue; innovation partnership; negotiation without prior notice; negotiation without prior invitation to participate; negotiation without publishing a contract notice; project competition; public competition; direct negotiation.

1. Value thresholds for procedures with public contracting authorities: construction - BGN 10,000,000; supplies and services - BGN 271, 000 and services under Annex N° 2 of the Public Procurement Act - BGN 1 000 000.
2. Public contracting authorities working in the field of defense award public contracts with an estimated value greater than or equal to: BGN 10,000,000 - for construction; BGN 271,000 - for services and supplies, which include products under Annex No. 3; BGN 418,000 - for supplies that include products outside the scope of Annex No. 3; Annex N° 2 of the Public Procurement Act - BGN 1,000,000.
3. Sectoral contracting authorities award public contracts with an estimated value greater than or equal to: construction - from BGN 10,000,000 ; supplies and services - BGN 837,000; for services under Annex No. 2 of the Public Procurement Act- BGN 1,500,000.
4. Public and sector contracting authorities award contracts in the fields of defense and security with an estimated value greater than or equal to:
   a) BGN 837,000 - for supplies of military equipment, including parts, components and/or assembly elements for it, including equipment included in the list of defense-related products adopted on the basis of Art. 2, para. 1 of the Law on the Export Control of Defense-Related Products and Dual-Use Products and Technologies;
   b) BGN 837,000 - for supplies of sensitive equipment, including parts, components and/or assembly elements for it;
   c) BGN 837,000 - for services directly related to the equipment under letters “a” and “b” for each and all elements of its life cycle;
   d) BGN 10,000,000 - for construction directly related to the equipment under letters “a” and “b” for each and all elements of its life cycle;
   e) BGN 837,000 - for services for specific military purposes or for sensitive services;

   f) BGN 10,000,000 - for construction for specific military purposes or for sensitive construction;

5. The contracting authorities hold a tender for a project with a value greater than or equal to BGN 70,000.

We consider these changes in the Public Procurement Act, current as of August 5, 2022, from the point of view of control, to be significant, because below these thresholds, in reality, we rely heavily on quality internal audits and internal control in public sector organizations in order to implement the relevant activities. According to Nedyalkova /Nedyalkova, P. 2020/ The main task of internal audit is to give confidence to the management of the organization, through its independent and objective activity, to provide confidence that the predetermined strategic goals and tasks of the organization are achieved.

Given all that is set out in this part of the study, it can be assumed that the differentiated application of individual general and derivative principles to the stage of the control process will contribute to improving the internal regulations of PFIA, regulating in which stage of the control process which exact control principles should be applied by the inspectors. We believe that the criterion proposed in this way should be regulated, in order to have more weight and to turn itself into a rule of implementation.

CLASSIFICATION OF PRINCIPLES ACCORDING TO THE TYPE AND FORM OF FINANCIAL CONTROL

The question of grouping the principles according to the type and form of financial control is still debatable. This is due to the fact that most control specialists believe that the development and change of control principles are influenced only by the type of control (Zingals, 1997), and according to another group of specialists, not only the type of control but also the form, under which it manifests, make an impact (Monks, 2001). According to the views of the second group, all the principles related to the implementation of a particular type of control process, together build the general rules that are specific and apply only to this type of control. However, when the specific type of control process is influenced by the form in which it is implemented, then it should be assumed that there is a regrouping of all the principles that make up the specific type of financial control and the so-called derivative principles of financial control. According to M. Dinev, the criterion for determining the main forms of financial control is the time in which "the controlling processes or the object of control are located. The states of preparation, course and completion of the processes determine the main forms of control impact as preliminary, current and subsequent control" (Dinev, 2008).

Other researchers, such as William L. Brogan, believe that according to the metricification of the final control results, the forms in which financial control can manifest itself are: quantitative, qualitative and value-wise. (Brogan, 1990). In quantitative control, monitoring selection and quantitative analysis of data are performed and its main goal is to provide timely and reliable information about the controlled object. Qualitative and value control as a form is manifested when the final control results can be measured qualitatively and value-wise. According to William L. Brogan, these are the most common forms of control in practice.

Regarding the nature of the control form, there is another perception - that according to the actual condition of the object of control, the following forms can be observed: preparation for the establishment of an object; the process of creating or controlling a fully completed object.

With the statements presented in this way, we agree with the opinion of M. Dinev that the forms of financial control should be accepted as a means of organizing its control elements in the preliminary, current and subsequent stages. The differentiation of the forms of control according to the established final control results can be done at a later stage, after the control process is completed and the qualitative, value and quantitative data are established. On the other hand, interpreting and analyzing data with different substances is a complex process. Sometimes it is necessary to use different statistical and graphical methods. In the new control methods (especially in medicine), the so-called Levey-Jennings control charts are applied. The analysis data are plotted on the X-axis and the control data are plotted on the Y-axis. When comparing the analyzed data with the control ones, the deviations are also established. Precisely due to the complexity of the data substances and the complexity of the objects of control, the final result cannot be determined in advance. In the planned control actions it is difficult to determine the form of control according to the criteria: established results and condition of the control object. We believe that these are the prerequisites for which the last two features in control practice, especially with regard to financial control, are almost inapplicable.

J. Heizer and B. Render examine the principles of financial control according to the type and form of financial control. According to researchers, one of the methods for determining the optimality of the control process is by comparing the principles of financial control according to the criteria, type and form of control in a matrix (Heizer, 2008). The vertical of the matrix presents the principles of financial control according to the type of control that is implemented, and the horizontal presents the principles according to their form. The matrix is presented using Table 1.

Table 1. Matrix of the types of financial control and their form of manifestation

Form of financial control / Type of financial control	Preliminary control	Current control	Follow-up control
Tax and social security control		+	+
Insurance control		+	+
Currency control		+	+
Customs control		+	+
Internal control	+	+	+
Independent financial audit	+	+	+
Control over financial discipline		+	+

According to J. Heizer (Heizer, 2010) and B. Render (Render, 2010), optimality is achieved at the moment when the rules (principles) for the implementation of the type of control and the rules (principles) for the implementation of the form operate simultaneously in the control process. That is why these experts believe that of all the types of control the most optimal are internal control and independent financial audit. As a result of the simultaneous action of the rules of conduct for the implementation of both the type of control and the form of control, the derived principles of control are formed, and they are: *sequence of processes, operations and procedures; the principles of comprehensiveness and perseverance; strong influence of the principles of efficiency and effectiveness.*

We believe that a simultaneous matrix comparison of the rules, on the basis of which the form and types of control are implemented, is not the most appropriate way to categorically determine the optimality of the control process. The comparison of quality rules for the implementation of the type of control and respectively its structural formation as a substantive process cannot be a guarantee for determining the closest and desired control result. By comparing the rules themselves, it is possible to determine the extent to which a rule is simultaneously applicable to a given type of control and the extent to which it is simultaneously applicable in the implementation of the preliminary, current and subsequent control.

According to K. Donev (Donev, 1988) "the types (content) and forms of control are in a certain connection and dependence. The connection and dependence, the dialectic of the types and forms of control are determined in the following more significant directions: 1. The form of control is always meaningful, ie. it has no independent significance without the specific species; 2. The content (types) determine the form of its manifestation; 3. The form of control actively influences the content (types), which helps its establishment and increases the efficiency; 4. Depending on the object of control, the environment, and other factors, the same type can appear and develop in different forms; 5. The forms and types of control at certain stages and under specific conditions may be in conflict. The resolution of the contradiction is achieved through changes in the form of control, and exceptionally by improving its content".

In recent years, the EU has sought to avoid inconsistencies in control processes, especially with regard to funds allocated to a specific operational program. The aim of the EC is to clearly and precisely regulate the types and forms of control over the allocated funds under the operational programs. The direction in which the EU is working towards this goal is the adoption of a single framework program, uniting the funds under a specific operational program, as well as the clear and precise definition of the coordinator of the respective program. By designating the appropriate coordinator, the EU clearly and precisely defines not only the control body that should control these funds, but also the form of control and the type of control. This is the case with the Operational Program "Solidarity and Management of Migration Flows", adopted by Decisions of the European Parliament and the Council in 2007. The program covers the European Refugee Fund, the European Return Fund, the External Borders Fund and the European Fund for the Integration of Third-Country Nationals.

These funds are aimed at supporting Member States' efforts to protect and control the EU's external borders, return illegally staying third-country nationals, integrate legally staying third-country nationals, refugees, and asylum. In other words, the aim of the program is to create a sufficiently stable, secure, and fair European area by overcoming a number of cross-border issues - illegal immigration, human trafficking, terrorism and organized crime.

What distinguishes it from other operational programs is that in the program "Solidarity and Management of Migration Flows" in addition to PFIA, as a control body, the Ministry of Interior has direct participation in the control process of the implementation of EU funds. The Minister of Interior has been appointed as a coordinator for Bulgaria's participation in the European Return Fund in the period 2008-2013 and in the External Borders Fund in the period 2010-2013. The total budget of the program is set at 5866 million euros.

For the implementation of the program, the Ministry of Interior cooperates with the Visa Information System, the Schengen Information System, the EURODAC Fingerprint System and the FRONTEX Agency.

In order to make this program as effective as possible, the EC, with the help of a number of regulations and decisions, seeks to define precisely and clearly not only the ways to implement the program "Solidarity and Management of Migration Flows", but also what rules should be applied at any stage to avoid contradictions in the control processes and to make them as effective as possible. For example, in the Commission Decision of 22.12.2011 approving guidelines on the principles, criteria and indicative rates to be applied with regard to financial corrections made by the Commission pursuant to Article 44 of Council Decision 2007/435 / EC of 25 June 2007 establishing the European Fund for the Integration of Third-Country Nationals for the period 2007-2013 as part of the General Program "Solidarity and Management of Migration Flows", in order to control the funds on the basis of which implements the program itself, the EC has set the following requirements for the control bodies to be implemented:

1. To the responsible authority / delegated authority (ies)
    - clear definition, distribution and division of functions between and within the responsible authority
    - appropriate procedures for the selection of operations
    - appropriate information and strategy for providing guidance to beneficiaries
    - appropriate management checks
    - appropriate audit environment
    - reliable systems for accounting, monitoring and financial reporting in electronic form
    - preventive and corrective measures are needed when the audit identifies systemic errors
2. To certification body / intermediate body (ies)
    - clear definition, distribution and division of functions
    - appropriate audit environment and computer system
    - satisfactory arrangements for keeping accounts of the amounts to be recovered and for collecting the undue payments made

3. To the audit authority
    - clear definition, distribution and division of functions
    - appropriate system audits
    - appropriate audits of operations
    - an annual report of the performed control, prepared in accordance with the requirements, and an adequate audit opinion

According to PFIA data for 2011 and 2012, public procurement in the Ministry of Interior and in the Municipality of Sopot was not subject to subsequent control by the Agency. According to PFIA data, during the reported 448 financial inspections and checks in 2021, 2,053 public procurements worth BGN 3,493,827,297 were checked, and violations were found in 742 cases. Of the established violations, 216 were non-executed or unfounded public contracts worth BGN 58,680,668, provided there were legal grounds for their execution.The lack of quality control, regardless of its form and type, was confirmed by the European Commission in 2008 with a report to the European Parliament and the Council, namely that the Bulgarian authorities in charge of managing funds under the General Program "Solidarity and management of migration flows" need to strengthen their administrative capacity to prepare the programs and work with the control systems. The absorption capacity needs to be improved both at the level of contracting authorities and at the level of beneficiaries. (Report of EC, 2008).

The recommendation of the EC for efficient use of these funds is to establish effective and reliable structures for management and financial control, which will promote stable implementation throughout the project cycle - from feasibility assessment and project preparation to submission of bids and conclusion of the contract, as well as with regard to the ex-ante and ex-post control and evaluation (Report of EK, 2008).

Also, according to the same EC report, Bulgaria is not able to take full advantage of this assistance due to serious weaknesses in administrative and judicial capacity at local, regional and central level. The Bulgarian state administration suffers from high staff turnover and not good enough salaries, which creates a precondition for corruption, and outdated, centralized procedures. In particular, the reluctance to use enforcement powers to rectify irregularities and fraud through the immediate recovery of funds already granted or through other safeguards and the lack of independence of the national audit authority and executive agencies raise serious concerns.

External observers also report that the lack of accountability and transparency in public procurement in Bulgaria related to EU funds is a serious problem. High-level corruption and organized crime exacerbate these problems related to a general weakness in administrative and judicial capacity.

We believe that the problems presented in this way, especially with regard to the lack of quality and timely effective control, can be overcome through the creation of a flexible regulatory regime based on regulatory principles. The paradox is that the application of the principles is a prerequisite for building trust, but the basic elements of this trust should already be built through control. The expert lady puts a sign of equality between regulatory and control principles. According to her, regulatory principles come in four forms: formal, substantive, complete, and polycentric. Have the seven paradoxes in the application of the principles. These paradoxes may be embedded in the principles themselves or may manifest themselves in their implementation:

- An interpretative paradox - although the principles may facilitate the interpretation of regulatory objectives, they may also hinder the interpretation of other control objectives.
- A communicative paradox - although principles can facilitate communication by properly expressing goals, they can hinder proper communication.
- A paradox of adherence to principles - although principles can provide flexibility to control bodies by allowing them to innovate in control processes, in practice, the lack of certainty as to what exactly the law enforcement body will adopt can lead to rather conservative behaviour on the part of the controller.
- A paradox about their control and enforcement - although the principles can provide regulators with flexibility in how to monitor and enforce regulatory requirements, it can prevent them from their own lack of foresight in the absence of such rules. In such situations, control bodies can develop quite conservative interpretations of the control situation, especially when there is little political support for sound and clear enforcement.
- Internal management - the application of the principles requires the construction of internal systems. Compliance with established systems can ensure the granting of certain powers. Research shows that problems with the application of the principles are due to improper compliance with internal control systems in institutions.
- Even if the control principles are the basis on which the ethical culture is built, they also require the control bodies to take a risk-based approach,

which, according to experts, makes the existence of such an ethical control culture meaningless.

- A paradox of reciprocity and trust - control principles can lead to the development of the control process by applying responsibility, reciprocity and trust, but these are the very elements of the control relationship that must be present in order to be effective on all stakeholders.

Some of these paradoxes can be improved or mitigated by the institutional context, while others have an inherent characteristic: they protect the state property or operate in a regime of regulatory principles.

Therefore, the principles of financial control can be classified according to the criterion type of control as follows: 1. Principles of banking control (supervision); 2. Principles of tax and social security control; 3. Principles of insurance control; 4. Principles of currency control; 5. Principles of customs control; 6. Principles of independent financial audit; 7. Principles of internal control; 8. Principles of budgetary control. In Bulgaria, under the influence of the established control structure of the state power, the classification of the principles of financial control according to the type of control is widely used. In each normative act the legislator basically distinguishes the principles of control according to the type of control, but not according to the form of control. Comparing foreign control practices, in countries such as the United States, Britain, Italy, Germany, Czech Republic, Slovenia, Slovakia, Spain, Portugal, the Netherlands, etc., it is found that the principles of various forms of control (preliminary, current and subsequent) are regulated in the internal regulations of the control bodies, as well as various derivative principles of financial control are presented, which should be observed (Tarantino, 2011). In the Bulgarian control practice, including PFIA, the internal normative acts present the principles set out in the main normative acts of the country, regulating the implementation of the respective control process. They clarify the technology of application of the legally defined principles, but do not specify additional principles that should be observed and applied in the implementation of the relevant form of control. In order to improve the control activity, especially with regard to the State Financial Inspection Agency, we believe that it is necessary to apply a number of additional control rules of conduct, through which to improve the control practice.

In order to achieve the proposal presented in this way, and to make it easier for the entitled persons who compile the internal normative acts of PFIA, the following classification of the control principles according to the form of control can be adopted:

1. Ex-ante control - this form of control should follow the following principles: *adequacy of perception* – the control process must be adequately perceived by the person performing it. At higher levels of management, control can be more generalized, based on management information systems, mathematical modeling, complex detailed analytical reports containing well-designed graphs and charts. *Timeliness* – according to this principle, approved ex-ante control mechanisms should identify deviations immediately, i.e. without delay. The purpose of this principle is to detect shortcomings in a timely manner of the controlled site, so as not to subsequently allow significant irregularities and more serious abuses. *Expediency and moderate economy* – clear and precise definition of the goal in advance. The achievement of the set goal should be achieved at moderate costs, the costs should not be too high, nor should the obligatory minimization be sought. Last but not least, is *the independence of controllers.*
2. Current control – the basic principles under which this control should take place are: *reliability, accuracy, throughput* – it is necessary to make a comparison of the results obtained at the output of the control process and these results obtained at the input of the control process. It is necessary that the current control process allows to obtain a control result at predetermined parameters. The next principles are *independence of controllers (inspectors) and systematicity* – in performing the control actions, not only all aspects of the controlled object should be considered, but also the whole system of relations on the vertical and horizontal management structure.
3. Ex-post control – the following basic principles should be observed in this form of control: *principle of continuity* – it means that all objects of control are always subject to constant control, except current, but also subsequent control. In the implementation of the different forms of control, especially with regard to the same control body, it is necessary to have continuity of information between the different formed working inspection groups; the principles *systematicity and independence* are again present in this form of control; the principle of *flexibility and adaptability to changing conditions*; the principle of *moderation* - to assess the need for follow-up control, especially for the same controlled

site, as it is possible to spend too much budget money and the end result to be zero.

According to a study conducted by Christopher G. Lynch and Cory Mchale (Lynch, 2012), in 24 countries, on the basis of data provided by the respective national courts of auditors, as well as on the basis of information provided by the relevant agencies in the countries implementing control over financial discipline, a number of irregularities are found in all forms of control, one part of which is due to non-compliance with the principles

Table 2. Data on the implemented control actions according to the different forms of control for the period from 01.01.2010 to 30.09.2010

Nº	Country	Omissions and irregularities identified during the preliminary control	Omissions and irregularities identified during the current control	Omissions and irregularities identified in the ex-post control	Total number of irregularities and omissions (3к. + 4к. + 5к.)	Relative share of irregularities and omissions due to non-compliance with the principles, in %	Relative share of irregularities and omissions due to non-compliance with the norms, in %
1	2	3	4	5	6	7	8
1.	The USA	1354	2987	1952	6239	64%	36%
2.	Canada	2221	2897	2457	7575	53%	47%
3.	Italy	1119	3716	2921	7756	38%	62%
4.	Germany	1883	1753	1942	7520	41%	59%
5.	France	2003	2663	2877	7543	37%	63%
6.	Britain	2991	1753	1994	6738	65%	35%
7.	Spain	1003	3441	1661	6105	48%	52%
8.	Netherlands	891	2325	1453	4669	49%	51%
9.	Russia	947	4856	3622	9425	47%	53%
10.	Poland	1571	5027	2772	9370	34%	76%
11.	Belarus	736	3331	2888	6955	37%	63%
12.	Ukraine	665	4911	3222	8798	31%	69%
13.	Switzerland	1002	2316	1851	5169	43%	57%
14.	Greece	594	4865	3498	8957	58%	42%
15.	Moldova	763	4155	2288	7206	49%	51%
16.	Serbia	471	4999	1866	7336	47%	53%
17.	Romania	331	3332	1055	4718	48%	52%
18.	Slovakia	1077	4 212	951	6240	44%	56%
19.	Macedonia	547	3 666	329	4542	51%	49%
20.	Spain	1996	3141	963	6100	39%	61%
21.	Estonia	1104	2 787	1446	5337	40%	60%
22.	Lithuania	851	3 002	1333	5186	45%	55%
23.	Latvia	773	4111	1022	5906	48%	52%
24.	Czech Republic	602	2223	1887	4712	49%	51%

of financial control, and another part due to the incorrect application of the relevant norms. Table 2 presents the results of the survey for the period from 01.01.2010 to 30.09.2010. The data from Table 2 relating the ex-ante, current and ex-post controls for the respective countries are presented by the implemented control processes on different control sites.

From the data presented in Table 2, it is established that in the 24 surveyed countries the admitted omissions and weaknesses are due to incorrect application of the principles and are a result of non-compliance with the legally defined norms. As a result of the study presented in this way, it is also established that the percentage ratio of non-compliance with the principles and norms is almost equal. This ratio can be justified by the fact that non-compliance with the relevant rule, which is regulated in the relevant legislation and which is a prerequisite for the implementation of this regulation, is in fact a major prerequisite for its violation.

Similar studies on the quality of law enforcement, and hence the results on the application of control principles, have been conducted by the World Bank. The survey covers all countries, and the results regard the main indicators: publicity and accountability; political stability; efficiency of public administration; regulatory quality; law enforcement and corruption control. In this part of the study, we present data that apply only to our country.

The individual indicators that the World Bank has used to construct the graph so presented are shown in Table 3.

Figure 4. The indicator "Compliance with the laws in Bulgaria" for the period from 1996 to 2009

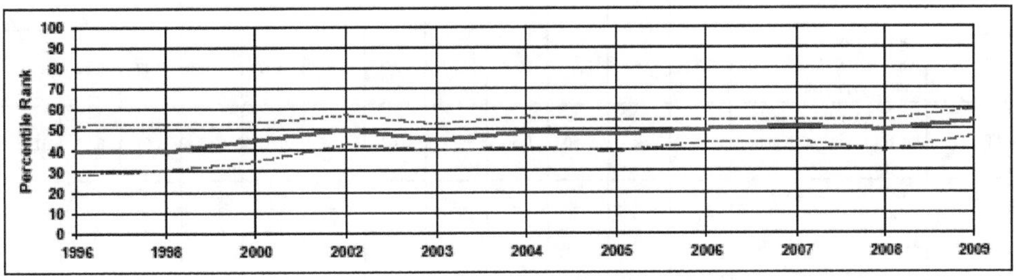

Table 3. Indicators involved in Figure 4

Code	Source	1996	1998	1999	2000	2002	2003	2004	2005	2006	2007	2008	2009
ADB	African Bank for Public Policy Development and Institutional Assessments	–	–	–	–	–	–	–	–	–	–	–	–
AFR	Autobarometer	–	–	–	–	–	–	–	–	–	–	–	–
ASD	Asian Bank for Public Policy Development and Institutional Assessments	–	–	–	–	–	–	–	–	–	–	–	–
BPS	Business research of the cooperative environment	–	–	0,47	0,45	0,45	0,45	0,48	0,48	0,48	0,43	0,43	0,43
BTI	Bertelsmann Transformation index	–	–	–	0,50	0,80	0,80	0,87	0,87	0,87	0,87	0,87	0,87
CCR	Research of „Freedom House Countries at the Crossroads"	–	–	–	–	–	–	–	–	–	–	–	–
EIU	Research of „Economist Intelligence Unit"	0,34	0,41	0,56	0,59	0,56	0,56	0,56	0,56	0,56	0,53	0,53	0,53
FRH	Research of „Freedom House"	0,46	0,54	0,58	0,58	0,63	0,63	0,67	0,71	0,71	0,67	0,67	0,67
GCS	Research of World Economic Forum Global Competitiveness Survey	–	–	0,34	0,36	0,36	0,35	0,35	0,35	0,40	0,37	0,37	0,40
GII	Index of „Global Integrity"	–	–	–	–	–	–	–	0,78	0,76	0,77	0,77	0,70
GWP	Research of „Gallup World Poll"	–	–	–	–	–	–	–	0,57	0,57	0,57	0,57	0,51
HER	Research of Economic Freedom Index Foundation	0,50	0,50	0,50	0,50	0,30	0,30	0,30	0,30	0,30	0,30	0,30	0,30
HUM	Research of Cingranelli-Richards (CIRI) Human Rights Database	1,00	0,50	0,50	0,50	0,50	0,50	0,50	0,50	0,50	0,00	0,50	0,00
IFD	IFD study to assess the development of the rural sector	–	–	–	–	–	–	–	–	–	–	–	–
IPD	Research of Institutional Profiles Database	–	–	–	–	–	–	–	0,44	0,44	0,44	0,59	0,59
LBO	Latinobarometro	–	–	–	–	–	–	–	–	–	–	–	–
PIA	World Bank - Government Policy and Institutional Assessments	–	NP	NP	NP	NP	NP	NP	NP	NP	NP	NP	NP
PRS	Political Risk - International Handbook of Government Risk	0,83	0,67	0,67	0,67	0,67	0,67	0,67	0,42	0,42	0,42	0,42	0,42
TPR	U.S. Department of State for Trafficking in Human Beings	–	–	0,50	0,50	0,67	0,67	0,67	0,67	0,67	0,67	0,67	0,67
VAB	Vanderbildt University study	–	–	–	–	–	–	–	–	–	–	–	–
WCY	Yearbook of the Institute for Management and Development of Global Competitiveness	–	–	–	–	–	–	–	0,32	0,36	0,30	0,34	0,25
WMO	A study on the global insight into business conditions and risk indicators	0,44	0,44	0,44	0,50	0,50	0,53	0,50	0,63	0,56	0,56	0,56	0,56

Focusing on the empirical data presented in this way from foreign sources which have studied the implementation of the principles and legal norms in Bulgaria, as a final stage of this part of the presentation, the following main conclusions and recommendations can be drawn:

1. The lack of clear criteria for the classification of the principles of financial control according to the type and form of control is one of the main prerequisites for a number of practical problems that arise in their application. In the normative acts of the country the emphasis is placed on the principles according to the type of control, but not according to its form. The main recommendation we make is to pay due attention in the normative acts to the principles for the implementation of the respective form of control.
2. From World Bank data, presented in Figure 4, it is established that the observance of the laws is in the range of 40 to 50%, therefore the observance of the respective principles, regulated in the normative acts, is also between 40 and 50%. The recommendation that can be made on the basis of the data presented in this way is to strengthen the restrictive measures on the implementation of the law, for this purpose it is necessary to impose higher sanctions on the perpetrators of non-compliance with the law. In addition, in order to prevent financial fraud and abuse, the precondition for the emergence and development of which is precisely the violation of legally defined principles and norms, it is necessary, on the one hand, to encourage control bodies to detect such crimes, so that they are not subject to the corruption factor. On the other hand, it is necessary for the specialized administrative directorate "Financial Intelligence" at SANS (State agency for National Security) to strengthen its joint work with the public in order to provide timely, accurate and reliable information on suspicions of financial abuse and irregularities. PFIA needs to focus its efforts on unscheduled control actions, not to rely only on the instigator of these actions to be a third party who submitted a signal to the Agency, but more to be self-initiated actions by PFIA.
3. According to the new World Bank report published in 2020, for the period of 2017 to 2018, problems with the implementation of the principles still exist, especially in the application of the legal anti-corruption rules. According to the mentioned report Competition laws generally permit action against anticompetitive practices that have effects on the domestic market, but developing countries may not have adequate capacity or jurisdiction to act. The effectiveness of this "effects doctrine" depends

on the capacity of authorities to identify, investigate, and if necessary fine foreign firms for anticompetitive behavior. Small or low-income countries may not be able to do so. Competition law enforcement capacities are widely across developing countries.

4. A significant problem in the inspection of public procurement is to emphasize the content of the legal-organizational form, ie. inspections to focus on the search for damage and not on the appropriateness of public procurement. The emphasis is on its lawful implementation, in most cases, formal features are not taken into account such as deadlines, the persons engaged in the implementation of the public procurements, their competence, qualification and experience, etc.

REFERENCES

Alekseev, S. S. (1981). *The General Theory of Law: In 2 vols* (Vol. 2). Legal Literature.

Alexandrovich, B. (2008). *Political Science*. Business and Educational Literature.

Consolidated version, (2012). Consolidated version of the treaty establishing the European Community. Available from: http//www.eur-lex.europa.eu [seen on 10.07.2012]

Corcuff, Ph. (1973). *Les nouvelles sociologies*. Nathan.

Dinev, M. (1986). *Kontrol i regulirane na ikonomicheskite sistemi*. Profizdat.

Dinev, M. (1999). Kontrol v sotsialnoto upravlenie. Sofia: Trakia-M

Dinev, M. (2008). *Obshta teoria na schetovodstvoto*. Trakia-M.

Dochev, D. (1997). Izsledvane na operatsiite. Varna: Universitetsko izdatelstvo na IU

Donev, I. (1984). *Istoria na matematikata. V. Tarnovo: UI „Sv. sv*. Kiril i Metodiy.

Donev, K. (2002). Darzhaven finansov kontrol – teoria i praktika. God. na IU Varna, 74.

Hadjolyan, M. (2012). The Bulgarian Judiciary in the System of Separation of Powers. http://ejournal.vfu.bg

Heizer, J., & Render, B. (2011). *Principles of Operations Management* (8th ed.).

Hirsh, S. (1990). *Introduction to Type in Organizations*. Consulting Psychologists Press, Inc.

Italy – Constitution. (2012). Available from: http://www.servat.unibe.ch/icl/it00000_. html [seen on 10.04.2012]

Lazarov, K. (2009). *Administrative law*. Fenea.

Lynch, Ch. (2012). *The Budget Control Act of 2011: Elements and Options (Economic Issues, Problems and Perspectives)*. Nova Science Pub Inc.

Monks, R. (2001). *Corporate Governance* (2nd ed.).

Report of the EC, (2008). Report of the European Commission on the management of EU funds in Bulgaria, July 2008.

Tarantino, A. (2011). *Financial Internal Controls Best Practices*. WILE Global Finance.

The 6 Basic Principles of the Constitution. Available from: http://voices.yahoo.com/ the-6-basic-principles-constitution -1608845.html [seen on 8.04.2012]

Zingales, L. (1997). Corporative Governance. Working Paper 6309. National Bureau of Economic Research.

Zlatarev, E. (2007). *The State Financial Inspection and Property Liability*. Ciela.

Zlatarev, E. (2007). *The State Financial Inspection and Property Liability*. Ciela.

Chapter 3
Normative Regulation of the Principles of Financial Control in Bulgaria

ABSTRACT

The normative regulation of the principles of financial control is also an important and topical issue for the control practice. In order to study the specifics of the principles of financial control in relation to the normative act which regulates them, it is necessary to determine in which normative acts the basic principles of financial control are regulated. With the help of the normative review, the essence of each principle and its purpose are presented. Each principle has its own specifics, but its applicability does not contradict any of the other principles of financial control. In addition, the principles determine the direction in which the control process itself should take place. Deviation and non-compliance with some of the principles of financial control means that the predetermined conceptual framework of the financial control process itself has been violated.

The normative regulation of the principles of financial control is also an important and topical issue for the control practice. In order to study the specifics of the principles of financial control in relation to the normative act which regulates them, it is necessary to determine in which normative acts the basic principles of financial control are regulated. With the help of Table

DOI: 10.4018/978-1-6684-8883-6.ch003

4, an attempt was made to present the principles of financial control, as well as the normative acts, which reveal the legal interpretation of each principle:

The following more important conclusions can be drawn from the data presented in the table:

1. The basic principles by which the financial control process is carried out are not regulated in a single normative act. Regardless of the fact that they are presented in different normative acts, they complement each other and act in combination to achieve the previously set goal of control.
2. In carrying out their activities, the control bodies are not guided only by the requirements and prescriptions presented in one normative act. The specific nature of the activity allows them to be guided and to combine in their work different legislative norms. Also, regardless of the circumstances and reasons, the control bodies during their control activity are always obliged to observe the certain constitutional principles, namely: democracy, equality of citizens and justice. Failure to comply with these basic principles shall be deemed to have violated the constitutional rights of the sites to be inspected.

The first principle presented in Table 1 is the *independence of financial control*. This principle has proven over the years its important place and importance in the control process. It turned out that the legislative regulation of the principle presented in the Lima Declaration is not enough for its proper practical application. This is the reason why the European Commission, in its notified decision No C (2006) 4026 of 29 September 2006, concerning the definition of audit criteria in accordance with the requirements of Regulation (EC) N° 882/2004 of the European Parliament, to further develop the legal definition of the principle of "independence of control" and its implementation. Decision C (2006) 4026 stipulates that the independence of control will be manifested only when, during the control process, the control bodies must be free from any commercial, financial, hierarchical, political or other pressure which could affects their assessment or the outcome of the control process.

In our legislation, this principle is legally presented in the Independent Financial Audit Act, in the Tax and Social Security Procedure Code, in the Law on the National Audit Office and in the Law on Financial Management and Control in the public sector. It can be assumed that in the four normative

*Table 1. Presentation of the basic principles of financial control, regulated in the normative acts of the Republic of Bulgaria **

By N°	Name of the principle	Independent Financial Audit Act	Tax and Social Security Procedure Code	Law on the State Financial Inspection	Law on the National Audit Office	Public Financial Management and Control Act sector
1	Independence	YES (in art. 2)	YES (in art. 4)	It is not regulated	YES (Article 2, paragraph 1)	It is not regulated
2	Transparency of control	YES (in art. 40m)	It is not regulated	It is not regulated	Yes (Article 2, paragraph 2)	Yes (Article 3, paragraph 1)
3	Effectiveness of control	Yes (Article 6, item 4, and in Article 40h)	It is not regulated	It is not regulated	Yes (Article 4 and in the Additional Provisions, § 1, item 2b)	Yes (Article 5, paragraph 2, item 3)
4	Legality	Yes (Article 35, paragraph 2)	Yes (Article 41, paragraph 3 and Article 160, paragraph 2)	The term "legality" in Art. 3	Yes (in Article 4)	Yes (in the Additional Provisions, § 1, item 2)
5	Expediency	Yes (Article 35, paragraph 2)	It is not regulated	It is not regulated	It is not regulated	It is not regulated
6	Official start	It is not regulated	Yes (in Article 5)	Yes (in Art. 3, as well as in the Additional provisions, § 1, item 7)	It is not regulated	It is not regulated
7	Good financial management	It is not regulated	It is not regulated	It is not regulated	It is not regulated	Yes (Article 3, paragraph 1)
8	Confidentiality	Yes (in art. 7, item 4)	It is not regulated	Yes (in Article 3, as well as in the Additional Provisions, § 1, item 4)	It is not regulated	It is not regulated
9	Objectivity	Yes (in Article 7, item 2, Article 21a, item 2, and Article 33)	Yes (in Article 3)	Yes (in Art. 3, as well as in the Additional Provisions, § 1, item 6)	Yes (in Article 11)	It is not regulated
10	Responsibility	Yes (in Article 33a, Article 34, Article 35)	Yes (in Article 17, paragraph 6, Article 18, Article 19, Article 21)	Yes (in Article 18, Article 21, Art. 22, art. 23, art. 27, Art. 28 and Art. 29)	Yes (Article 35, paragraph 5, and Article 51, paragraph 1)	The principle of "Management responsibility" is considered

* * *Note:* In the control practice there are known principles that are not regulated in a specific normative act, such as the principles: *transparency, democracy, immediacy, independent scrutiny and a systematic approach.* It can be assumed that these principles of financial control are a priori.

acts the essence of the principle overlaps with the requirement presented in Decision C (2006) 4026.

The principle of independence presented in Art. 4 of the Tax and Social Security Procedure Code, regulates the non-interference in the activity of the tax authorities with regard to the precise determination of the tax liabilities and the sanctioning of the tax subjects on the basis of the established violations of the tax legislation. In our country, this is the most common principle that is violated during the control process. A large part of the taxpayers are trying to use various illegal actions to avoid their obligations to be identified accurately and to prevent budget abuses from being detected. It can be assumed that this is one of the reasons for the presence of corruption at all levels of the tax administration. An analysis by the Center for the Study of Democracy found that more than 65% of businesses pay tax bribes to cover up VAT fraud. Most often the attempts for falsifications are under the VAT Act and are 81.1% of all cases (Grozdev, 2005).

Another characteristic feature of Decision C (2006) 4026 is that it sets out three other principles on the basis of which the control process should take place, namely: *transparency; independent verification and systematic approach.*

The second basic principle, which is presented in Table 4, is *transparency of financial control*. Historical evidence shows that the problem of transparency has been addressed in the 1957 Treaty establishing the European Community. In Art. 255 of the Treaty, the principle of "transparency" is determined by the ability of every citizen of the Union, as well as of any natural or legal person residing or having its registered office in a Member State, to have access to European Parliament documents, The Council and the Commission, when observing certain principles and conditions. The Treaty establishing the European Community, signed in Rome on 25 March 1957, defines"transparency" only as the possibility for any interested person to have access to European Parliament, Council and Commission documents, i.e. the question of transparency of the control process is not raised in any way as a requirement.

Years after the adoption of the Treaty, the requirements of society regarding the responsibility and transparency of the actions of the entire state apparatus, as well as the activities of the European Union, are becoming increasingly important. The reasons for this should be sought in the increased rate of movement of private investment capital flows to countries with emerging markets. The investment risk faced by investors, namely the non-reversibility of the investments made, as controlling shareholders and managers would keep it to themselves, has given a new task to control (and especially corporate control). Therefore, through its activities, control must cover all socially significant processes, and on the other hand, it must provide and present the information that other social processes cannot provide to society (and especially to investors). Every process must be presented and disclosed. According to the Anglo-Saxon system, this is the principle of "transparency of control". This principle is one of the main and important principles for determining the effectiveness of financial control.

A wide range of international organizations are involved in the process of promoting the principle of "transparency". For example, in 1999, the Organization for Economic Cooperation and Development developed and adopted a set of Principles for Corporate Governance of the member countries of the Organization. It can be assumed that the principle of "transparency" is the main principle to which special attention is paid is. And that is because it is considered that it will be complied with only when the control activity ensures timely and up-to-date disclosure of information on all material issues affecting the corporation, including financial, performance, ownership and management and control of the company.

There is no precise definition of the principle of "transparency" in the State Financial Inspection Law, the Rules for implementation of the Law on the State Financial Inspection and in the internal normative acts of PFIA. In Art. 10, para. 9 of the State Financial Inspection Law indirectly the legislator has regulated one of the ways to comply with this principle, namely: the director of the Agency, or officials authorized by him, inform the public about the activities of the Agency and the results of financial inspections only after their completion. Also para.10 of the same art.10 stipulates that by the 10th day of the month following the quarter, a list of the sites where the financial inspections have been completed shall be published on the Agency's website, as well as information on the results thereof. The Agency is committed to submit an annual report on the results of its activities to the Council of Ministers through the Minister of Finance by May 31 next year. The report is sent for information to the National Parliament. PFIA also prepares an annual report on its activities for the current year, which is published on the Agency's website.

In addition, according to the Law on Electronic Government, an important strategic task is the implementation and / or adaptation of electronic document management systems to minimize paperwork in and between administrations. PFIA has improved the record-keeping system with a module for receiving and processing electronic documents received through the website with an interface with the PFIA document management system. This provides greater transparency and accessibility of administrative services to citizens and organizations and better efficiency in receiving signals, complaints and requests for financial inspections and other administrative documents.

The actions of PFIA listed so far affect the quality of inspections and have an impact on the final result. In addition, the disclosure of certain information to external stakeholders is somewhat limited and also follows the sequence of stages of the control process. For example, when performing their official duties, the inspectors, on the basis of the facts and circumstances verified by them, are obliged to objectively and accurately reflect the established results of the inspection activity, the established violations and damages, and the reasons for their occurrence and the perpetrators, but they must not disclose facts and circumstances which have become known to them during or on the occasion of the performance of their official duties, except in the cases provided by law.

The legislator has minimized the possibility of full compliance with the principle of "transparency". The purpose of this restriction is not to disseminate information in the public space that has not yet been confirmed and verified. After the completion of the inspection activities, any interested person, according to the Access to Public Information Act, may request the provision of information that is created and stored in the State Financial Inspection Agency, and as a successor to the Agency for State Internal Financial Control, this information is public within the meaning of the Access to Public Information Act. In 2021, 79 applications for access to public information were submitted. Of these, 52 were granted free access, 5 – partial access to information, 21 applications were denied access to information. On 1 of the applications in 2021, the respective applicant was notified of the lack of the requested information. In 2011, PFIA received 58 applications for access to public information, of which 33 were from citizens, 17 were from journalists, 5 were from managers of companies and 3 were from non-governmental organizations. In 2010, the Agency received 51 official applications for access to public information. Of all the applications, 19 were from citizens, 18 from journalists, 10 from company managers and 4 from non-governmental organizations. According to the requirements of the Law on Access to Public Information and the State Financial Inspection Law, information was provided to 45 applications and inquiries, partial access to such information was provided to 5, and access was denied to 1, on the basis of Art. 198, para. 1 of the Code of Criminal Procedure. Information on 156 journalistic inquiries was prepared and provided.

Given all the above so far as facts and figures, it can be assumed that the principle of "transparency" of PFIA is applied correctly and accurately, without violating the established regulations.

The principle of *effectiveness of financial control* was first regulated by the Lima Declaration of 1977. The Declaration assumes that control will be effective only when there is an effectively established and robust control system.

The rapid development of the private sector and the inflow of foreign capital and investments in Bulgaria have posed new requirements and challenges to financial control. Today, its main task is to ensure the security and stability of the country's financial market, relying on its methodological control apparatus. The effective solution of this task will be achieved only when all the prescribed legal control norms are observed and all the principles of control have been correctly applied.

The main and important question that exists in the theory and practice of control is to determine its effectiveness. In the research he has done, that with the help of two indicators the effectiveness of control can be determined:

1. The level of quality performed organizational functions
2. Proper application and compliance with professional standards and the code of ethics.

According to M. Dinev, the effectiveness of control "is defined as the degree to which the goals are achieved, as an expression of the relationship between the desired effect of the activity. The end result is considered to be the ideal result to coincide with the desired results " (Dinev, 2004).

The problem of the effectiveness of control is the subject of research by various specialists. For example, the research that has been done shows that there are still different points of view and approaches in the processes of determining the overall effectiveness of control activities. This is due to the fact that (Bogdanov, 2006):

1. There are different views on the importance of efficiency.
2. There are various effects that result from the control activity itself.

Advocating the opinion of Hr. Bogdanov, we accept that "efficiency can be used as a criterion for evaluating control activities" (Bogdanov, 2006). In other words, the importance of this principle is to present a final assessment of the control process already completed.

To explain the effectiveness of control, experts often resort to distinguishing between the concepts of "effectiveness" and "efficiency". For example, according to G. Nikolov, the effectiveness of control (in the narrower sense of the audit) should be considered as a degree of achievement of the objectives of the controlled object in comparing the actual and expected results. And efficiency should be considered as achieving maximum results from the resources used in carrying out the activities of the controlled object (Nikolov, 2011). According to the European Court of Auditors, the effectiveness of the audit process means the use of resources to achieve the objectives of the activity to provide the optimal ratio between input and output, and efficiency is the extent to which objectives are achieved and the relationship between expected and actual results.

Therefore, in order to determine whether PFIA has correctly complied with the principle of effectiveness, it is necessary to determine the degree of use of control resources in carrying out not only a specific control inspection but also to determine the degree of use of resources in the overall activity, when comparing the achieved results and the invested resources in their implementation. When the resources used are greater in quantity and value than the final results, the control is considered ineffective. And vice versa, when less resources are spent to achieve the final results, the implemented control is considered effective. This study is presented in more detail in the second chapter of the study.

Comparing the principle of "efficiency" with other principles of financial control, it is established that it has great public and social significance, as its violation is a prerequisite for the following:

1. Reduction of public confidence in the work of control bodies
2. Providing an opportunity for the formation of various corruption schemes, leading to abuse of office and favoring persons holding state control positions
3. Endangering the security and stability of our country, as non-compliance with certain principles and norms by both control bodies and society, would lead to anarchism. Control bodies should serve as an example that laws apply to everyone and anyone who violates them should be held accountable for their actions.

From the information thus presented in Table 4 it is established that for the proper course and implementation of the control process itself the principles of *expediency and legality of financial control* should be observed. There is an opinion that expediency "is contained in legality, i.e. it is accepted that if it is lawful, then it is expedient. It can be assumed that there is no expediency without legality, which means that the implementation of the law is an inevitable finding for the controllers "(Dinev, 1985). In support of this view, we believe that a more complete and accurate presentation of the specifics of the two principles needs to be considered together rather than separately.

In order to present the essence of the principles of "appropriateness" and "legality of financial control", it is necessary to study, first, the very concepts of "appropriateness" and "legality" and then, to present their practical application.

From a philosophical point of view, expediency is defined as "a kind of sequence of phenomena. There is completely real expediency when it is in opposition to the causal relation, where the previous event determines a later event" (Steiner, 2007).

The very concept of 'appropriateness' (the Bulgarian word) is made up of two separate words, namely 'purpose' and 'compliance'. The goal set to be achieved in the control process is not always sufficiently specific and clearly defined, but nevertheless, it is always specified (compliant) with regulations. The conformity of the set goal to the framework of the law can be done either by defining it, or during the control process. This is a common practice, especially in cases when during the control process, in order to achieve the pre-set main goal, separate sub-goals arise. These sub-goals must also, on the one hand, be consistent with the main pre-set main goal, and, on the other hand, must not be in conflict with the legal regulations presented in the regulations of our country. It is assumed that if one of these conditions is violated, the set goal will be inexpedient.

It should be taken into account that there is a difference between the principles of "legality" and "conformity with the law". The principle of "legality" requires that each control action of the participants in the control process be in accordance with the regulations of our country. On the other hand, the principle is also reflected in the processes of issuing administrative acts by the control bodies, and on the basis of this principle the issued administrative act is required to be fully compliant with the normative acts of the country. Adhering to this statement, it can be assumed that there is a very narrow boundary between the two definitions of "legality" and "conformity with the law". Legality is manifested during the control process itself, while from the point of view of administrative control, conformity with the law is presented during the processes of drafting administrative acts by control bodies.

The principle of *sound financial management* is relatively new. It is included in Regulation 1605/2002, which governs the general budget of the European

Communities. According to the definition presented in the Regulation, the principle requires that public funds be spent and managed economically, efficiently and effectively, i.e. the principle itself will be followed only if the principles of "economy", "efficiency" and "efficiency" are observed at the same time.

In order to properly apply this principle, it is necessary for the control bodies to be well acquainted with the following:

1. The basic rules for compiling and reading the reports of organizations
2. The mechanisms for the formation and use of the coefficients for financial analysis of the activity of the organizations
3. The possibility to organize adequate financial control not only over the individual overall activities of organizations but also over all industries, sectors and units that make up the overall economic unit of the country.

This principle, as well as the principle of "transparency", has begun to gain more and more importance, especially with the country's prominent participation in the European Union's structural funds. The sensitivity of the European Union to the funds it provides to Bulgaria is the main reason for imposing various measures to ensure the correctness of spending the funds provided. It can be assumed that one of these measures is the introduction of the European control principle "sound financial management" in the Bulgarian legislation. The purpose of this principle is to enable the European Commission to control the proper use of the funds provided to the country.

The requirements of the European Union were met with the Law on Public Internal Financial Control (LPIFC) adopted in 2000 and repealed in 2007. The principle of sound financial management raised the following issues in the then LPIFC: the application of financial management and control systems should be the responsibility of authorized officers with budget credits; ex-ante control should be carried out mainly by these units - ministries and government agencies, but may also be carried out by the Public Internal Financial Control Agency on its own initiative, based on risk assessment.

1. When implementing these systems, the line minister should follow the instructions of the Agency and follow its recommendations.
2. The PIFC Agency should check/audit the proper implementation and functioning of the financial management and control systems of the ministries/agencies through systems audit (compliance and substantive

verification), performance audit, information technology audit, etc. The Agency is responsible for conducting ex-post audits.

3. The PIFC Agency is responsible for the harmonization of control/audit rules throughout the public sector and ensuring the correct application of these rules.
4. Ministry of Finance through the PIFC Agency is responsible for the analysis and summarization of control results at all levels in the executive branch and for reporting regularly to the Council of Ministers.

Over time, it has become clear that all the above requirements to ensure compliance with the principle of sound financial management cannot be covered and adequately enforced by a single law. This led to the repeal of the Law on Public Internal Financial Control and the adoption of other, new regulations, which separately address the issues raised in connection with ensuring sound financial management in the country, namely: The Public Financial Inspection Act (PFIA), the Public Sector Financial Management and Control Act (PSFMCA) and the Public Sector Internal Audit Act (PSIAA).

The importance of the principle was emphasized at the October 2007 conference of European Ministers for Local and Regional Development. The Strategy for Innovation and Good Governance at the Local Level was formally adopted during the conference. The aim of the Strategy is to influence the local authorities of each Member State of the European Union in order to constantly renew and improve their governance, respecting the principle of sound financial management, as well as existing commitments under the European Charter of Local Self-Government and other Council of Europe standards. At a later stage, the Strategy was supported by the Congress of Local and Regional Authorities of the Council of Europe with Resolution (2007-239), as well as by the Parliamentary Assembly and the Conference of International Non-Governmental Organizations. In February 2008, the Strategy was formally approved by the Committee of Ministers of the Council of Europe. Another important principle for financial control is the *official start*. What is specific is that this principle is of particular importance for the current control process. Its introduction into the control practice of the country is in response to the requirements set by the European Union and presented in various European regulations. It is noteworthy that this principle is regulated not only in the adopted Law on the State Financial Inspection but also in the Tax and Social Security Procedure Code. Despite the fact that in both normative acts the principle of "official start" is presented, its legal interpretation differs. For example, in the PFIA, the principle is manifested in the establishment at the initiative of financial inspectors of all facts and circumstances related to the audited financial and economic activities of the inspected organizations or persons. Comparing it with Art. 5 of the Tax-Insurance Procedure Code establishes that the tax normative act represents the principle, as the revenue authorities and public executors are obliged officially, when there is no request from the interested parties, to clarify the facts and circumstances relevant for establishing and collecting public receivables, including the application of the reliefs specified in the law. On the basis of this principle, control bodies ex officio have the right, if they deem appropriate, to move from one control procedure to another control procedure without requiring the approval of the inspected person. And this person should be informed ex officio that the control actions pass to further control procedural actions.

From the legal definitions thus presented, in relation to the essence of the principle of "official start", it is established that there is a difference between the two laws representing this principle. In the PFIA, the control bodies are the financial inspectors themselves, and in the Tax-Insurance Procedure Code, are the revenue bodies and the public executors. Notwithstanding these differences, it can be assumed that the principle of "official start" is interpreted in the same way in these regulations, namely: regardless of which control body will lead the control process itself (i.e. whether they are financial inspectors, the bodies revenue or a public executor), it is his duty with his actions to ensure the lawful and appropriate course of the control process itself.

From the examined 2450 reports on the results of the financial inspections carried out by the PFIA inspectors and from the information presented in 150 court decisions on the initiation of administrative penal proceedings related to the issued penal decrees of the NRA, the following results were found for the period 2007 until 2011 on the application of the "official start" principle (Table 2).

From the point of view of the National Revenue Agency (NRA), in one part of the administrative penal proceedings the requirements of Art. 37, para. 3 of the Tax-Insurance Procedure Code, namely the revenue authority has the right to request in writing from the person to provide evidence within the specified period. In cases where such evidence is not provided, the NRA inspectors have applied the principle of official start, according to the requirements of Art. 5 of the Tax-Insurance Procedure Code, and ex officio requested (collected) the necessary information.

Table 2. Application of the "official start" principle

Control Body	2007	2008	2009	2010	2011
PFIA	15%	32%	47%	54%	68%
NRA	35%	49%	59%	62%	73%

Source: The information is presented on the basis of the analysis of 2450 reports on the results of the financial inspections of PFIA and 150 court decisions on the initiation of administrative penal proceedings related to penal decrees issued by the NRA.

Table 3. Application of the "official start" principle

Control Body	2018	2019	2020	2021
PFIA	22%	42%	39%	48%
NRA	78%	58%	61%	52%

Source: The information is presented on the basis of the analysis of 2450 reports on the results of the financial inspections of PFIA and 150 court decisions on the initiation of administrative penal proceedings related to penal decrees issued by the NRA.

The data presented in Table 2 and Table 3 are summarized, but it is nevertheless noted that over the years, the tendency for more frequent application of the official start principle by the inspectors of the NRA and PFIA has increased. The reasons for this can be justified by the qualitative documentary substantiation of the documents prepared in connection with the collection of evidence during the financial inspections by PFIA and during tax inspections and audits by the NRA bodies. On the other hand, the application of the principle can be established indirectly, although it is not specified in the other control documents drawn up by the control bodies during the phased transition of the control process. For example, according to the PFIA internal regulations, when information is required in connection with a financial inspection or violations are found committed by officials who have left the audited organization or person, they are sent a written request to provide explanations.

The previous provisions of the Public Financial Inspection Act state that the principle of *confidentiality* should be understood according to the PFIA, that confidentiality is a prohibition for the Agency's bodies to disclose or provide to third parties information known to them during the performance of their official duties unless it is provided by law.

Practice shows a number of inconsistencies in the application of the principle of "confidentiality" and the principle of "transparency". Observance of the principle of transparency in no way means that all information about the controlled object is fully disclosed. One part of the information is protected under the Personal Data Act, and another part is confidential to third parties (competitors, ill-wishers, etc.). For this reason, it can be assumed that the application of the principle of "transparency" is limited and depends on confidentiality. Not all information can be provided and the adopted Instruction for ensuring access to public information in PFIA explicitly states the cases in which the director of PFIA has the right to refuse to provide information and data:

1. When the requested information is classified or other protected secret in the cases provided by law
2. Where the requested information affects the interests of third parties and they have not given their express written consent to provide access to the information concerning them
3. When the requested public information has been provided to the applicant during the previous 6 months.

Confidentiality is a principle that should be observed both from the beginning of the inspections to their completion and after the cessation of control activities. The information received by the inspectors as a result of their work for the specific undertaking should remain confidential and not be provided for the needs of third parties, except where provided by law.

The principle of *objectivity* - the control bodies are obliged within their competence to establish objectively all the facts and circumstances related to the inspected objects and their responsibility. According to the PFIA, objectivity is a principle that requires an impartial, complete and accurate establishment of all facts and circumstances subject to the financial inspection.

Objectivity has an impact in two ways. First, by applying this principle, the controller removes negative emotions, which allows people to act more rationally. It also allows discussions and interrogations to take place fairly during the control actions. The objective point of view is always fairer, more realistic and it is much more likely to reach the right control decision based on it.

If the principle of objectivity cannot be observed due to the fact that the inspector is in a special relationship with the inspected object, which raises reasonable doubts about his impartiality, or is interested in the outcome of the inspection, the inspector must inform his supervisor and terminate his participation in the inspection. It can be assumed that this is the most common principle that is violated. Unfortunately, regardless of the circumstances and the reasons for its non-compliance, this always leads to a violation of the control process itself, and as a result leads to the repeal of the act by which the control activity end (Slavchev, 2010a).

Another principle that should be observed during the financial control process is *responsibility*. In its specificity and manner of application, it is an ethical principle, as it applies both to control bodies and to all persons involved in the socio-economic life of society. From the control bodies' point of view, this principle is reduced to taking responsibility for the expressed opinion, which is based on the performed control process. From the point of view of all other persons involved in the socio-economic and political life of society, this principle is expressed in the taking civil, social and political responsibility. Etymologically, the term "responsibility" comes from the Greek word *ευθύνη* and means the delinquent's commitment to the harm caused by him (Cornyu, 2004). Depending on the way in which the undertaking of a particular person who has caused harm to others is regulated, the obligations (responsibilities) may be contractual, as regulated under a contract, or non-contractual obligations that are not regulated in a contract. Non-contractual obligations in law are considered to be treated as delicate obligations, and hence liability is defined as delicate liability. For example, the responsibility of the state and municipalities for the damage caused to its citizens as a result of issued illegal acts is considered a delicate responsibility.

The principle of "responsibility" is regulated in all the above laws, presented in table 4. According to the Independent Financial Audit Act, the responsibility is expressed in the personal responsibility of the auditor for the opinion expressed by him, i.e. this Act regulates the observance of the principle by the auditor/audit company. The requirements of the Tax and Social Security Procedure Code are more specific. Article 25 of the mentioned normative act defines the responsibility for the actions of the tax administration, namely that the tax administration is responsible for the damages caused to tax subjects by illegal tax acts, actions or inactions of its bodies and officials during or on the occasion of their activity, as the responsibility is performed by the order, provided in the Law for the responsibility of the state for damages, caused to citizens.

Based on all the above, it can be summarized that the presented approach reveals the practical and applicable aspects and features of the basic principles of financial control. Each principle has its own specifics, but its applicability does not contradict any of the other principles of financial control. In addition, the principles determine the direction in which the control process itself should take place. Deviation and non-compliance with some of the principles of financial control means that the predetermined conceptual framework of the financial control process itself has been violated.

REFERENCES

Bogdanov, Hr. (2006). Otnosno efektivnostta na kontrola. V: Mezhdunarodna nauchno-prakticheska konferentsia „Evrointegratsionnite protsesi i predizvikatelstvata pred stopanskata otchetnost, analiza i odita". Svishtov: AI „Tsenov".

Cornyu, Zh. (2004), Legal Dictionary, Sofia: "Sophi-R" PH

Dinev, M. (1986). *Kontrol i regulirane na ikonomicheskite sistemi*. Profizdat.

Grozdev, B. (2005). The tax officials would refuse a bribe for an 800 BGN salary. SEGA, N°19

Nikolov, N. (2011). On the nature of the performance audit and its directions in the public sector. International jubilee scientific conference "Economy and management in the 21st century - solutions for stability and growth", Svishtov

Slavchev, Z. (2010). *Tax-insurance procedural law*. Sofi-R.

Chapter 4
Influence and Importance of the Principles of Financial Control for Preserving the Financial Security and Stability of the Country

ABSTRACT

State control exercised in unitary states differs significantly from control exercised in federations, confederations and personal unions. Due to the limited development, we turn our attention to the internal control exercised in the unitary countries, such as Bulgaria. The overall internal control process in the unitary states is carried out by deconcentrating state power through the division of control activities between central and decentralized control bodies. Also, the bodies of the legislative power, the central executive and the judiciary have sufficient powers to be able to perform and implement the centralized state control order. They deal more with the established generally accepted control principles and apply the derived principles of financial control to a lesser extent. Decentralized control bodies have limited powers, they are fully subordinated to the central legislative, executive and judicial branches.

DOI: 10.4018/978-1-6684-8883-6.ch004

Preserving the country's financial security and stability is the main task facing the government. According to Garry Schinasi, in order to understand "the role and importance of public sector control, it is necessary to clarify the requirements for maintaining financial stability, which in turn is a key task of the public sector. In order for these requirements to be well accepted, it is necessary to adopt a good working definition of the concept of "financial stability" (Schinasi, 2006).

There are differing opinions on the meaning of the term "financial stability" in the reference books. Due to the scope of issues in this part of the study, we present the opinion of the European Central Bank (ECB) on the researched problem, namely that "financial stability plays a crucial role in the financial system and the economy in general" (Schinasi, 2006). Also, according to the ECB, in order to protect the financial system and ensure financial stability, it is necessary, first, to identify the main sources of financial risk, the degree of vulnerability and, last but not least, all stakeholders (who are part of the country's financial system) - for example, financial institutions and supervisors, to identify possible factors that presuppose the imbalance of the financial system.

In their study "Toward a Framework for Safeguarding Financial Stability", based on World Bank reports, as well as the experience of various experts, Aerdt Houben, Jan Kakes and Garry Schinasi found that there is still no consensus on what actually should be meant by the term "financial stability" (Schinasi, 2006). According to the authors of the study, some economists define "financial stability" by what is not, namely: it is not a situation where financial stability hinders the real economy (Crockett, 1996), especially when information problems undermine the ability of the financial system to allocates the funds to possible production investments (Mishkin, 1999).

A significant number of experts define financial stability as "a positive outlook related to: 1) an efficient allocation of resources between activities, as well as over time; 2) an assessment and management of financial risks and 3) an absorption of economic shocks " (Schinasi, 2006).

In the light of all the above, it must be assumed that:

1. Financial stability is a broad concept that encompasses various dimensions of the financial system, public sector supervisors, financial institutions and financial markets. Due to the close interrelations of the components that make up the financial system, any disruption in the

individual elements can undermine the overall financial stability of the country. Timely identification of problems in the financial system is a responsibility of control institutions. Their quality functioning is a prerequisite for the financial system to properly perform its tasks in the allocation of resources, mobilization of savings and diversification of risks. Also, the effective functioning of supervisory authorities is a guarantee that within the financial system money can adequately fulfil its role as a means of transactions, as a unit of account, and as a means of storing value.

2. The efficient and timely operation of supervisory authorities is a prerequisite for limiting or preventing a number of imbalances before they become a threat to the entire financial system and hence a threat to financial stability. The issue of financial stability has always been relevant; according to experts, a prerequisite for this is that it is the main factor for effective self-control (Schinasi, 2006). In the case of an inefficient financial system, as well as in case of uncertainty about its functioning, the emphasis is placed on strengthening the control functions of the existing control institutions, and self-control is limited. The weakened control system, the uncertain financial system, the imbalance of financial stability are prerequisites for the presence of corruption, the existence and more frequent manifestation of financial fraud and money laundering mechanisms.

For this reason, many international institutions, including the Committee of Experts on the Evaluation of Anti- Money Laundering Measures and the Financing of Terrorism (MONEYVAL)) at the EC, are empowered to monitor destabilization processes in the member states in order to prevent them in a timely manner. The purpose of MONEYVAL is to ensure that the member states have effective control systems in place to combat money laundering and terrorist financing, in accordance with relevant international standards in this area. Some of these standards and regulations, such as: the 1988 UN Convention against Illicit Traffic in Narcotic Drugs and Psychotropic Substances; The 1999 UN Convention on Transnational Organized Crime; The United Nations International Convention for the Suppression of the Financing of Terrorism; Directive 2005/60 / EC of the European Parliament and of the Council of 26 October 2005 on the prevention of the use of the financial system for the purpose of money laundering and terrorist financing are only part of measures to curb criminal activity in an uncertain and destabilized financial system.

In order to fulfil its main responsibilities, the MONEYVAL Committee requires all EU member states to provide annual information in the form of a joint consolidated report on the activities of all internal control bodies of the respective EU member state. The report is prepared by the specialized agencies (directorates) in the respective countries. In Bulgaria, the Ministry of Interior (MI) has an established State Agency for National Security (SANS), which is a specialized body for counterintelligence and security, whose main mission is to detect, prevent, suppress, and neutralize threats to national security. Every year SANS is committed to submit summary information on the state of Bulgaria's national security to its international partners, according to the signed cooperation agreements. In order to ensure the financial security, the Council of Ministers Decree from 18/2003 established a Coordination Council in the fight against offences affecting the financial interests of the European Communities (AFCOS). The Council "provides guidance, monitors and ensures coordination in the activities of state bodies in preventing and combating offences, fraud, abuse, inefficient management or use of funds and property belonging to the European Union or provided to the Bulgarian state by funds and European Union programs, including related national co-financing" (Resolution N° 18 of the Council of Ministers of February 4, 2003). In carrying out its activities, the AFCOS Council is assisted by the Directorate for Coordination of the Fight against Offences Affecting the Financial Interests of the European Communities" (AFCOS Directorate) at the Ministry of Interior, which is in cooperation with OLAF.

In order to achieve a stable, effective and efficient public administration, through which the sustainable financial stability of the country can be achieved, a very sustainable internal audit is required in public sector organizations so that the objectives of the administration are achieved. (Nedyalkova 2020, p. 49). For this purpose, the Institute of Internal Auditors in Great Britain and Ireland (The Chartered Institute of Internal Auditors in the UK and Ireland) have made a study that the main principles that should be followed in order to achieve the quality of the internal audit are:

- Leadership – providing vision and direction to achieve results.
- Fact-based decision making – decisions should be made based on accurate facts and data.
- Staff – adding value by developing their professional experience and skills.
- Suppliers and other business partners - maintaining mutually beneficial relationships.

- Building systems for a way of thinking - achieving process management through an integrated approach.
- Management of business processes - the goal is to increase efficiency.
- Focusing on the customer – planning and forecasting future needs.
- Continuous improvement – to improve the performance of the already set goal.

The importance and significance of the work of the AFCOS Council for the financial stability of the country is emphasized by the fact that the Council includes all executives (directors) of the control institutions in Bulgaria. For example, the members of the staff are the director of the Customs Agency, an official authorized by the chairman of the State Agency for National Security, the director of the Financial Intelligence Directorate of the State Agency for National Security, the director of the Public Financial Inspection Agency (PFIA), the executive director of the National Revenue Agency (NRA), etc. The main reason for the inclusion of all control bodies in the AFCOS Council is that they have one common goal and that is the fight against offences affecting the financial interests of the European Communities and compliance with action plans. Therefore, the control actions and the principles applied by the control bodies are not only targeted at the specific controlled object, but also have an impact on the prevention of financial fraud and abuse, violating the general financial foundations of the European Communities.

AFCOS Directorate reflects in its reports the importance and significance of PFIA, presenting the total number of identified cases of financial inspections of the Agency, which revealed violations and fraud for spending on EU programs and funds for the period from 2007 to 2011. Table 1 presents the violations and frauds under the respective operational programs, established by PFIA and confirmed in the reports of the AFCOS Directorate at the Ministry of Interior.

With the help of the comparative analysis between the data presented in Table 1, published by the AFCOS Directorate at the Ministry of Interior on the cases of violations and frauds in spending funds under EU programs and funds and the PFIA activity reports for the period 2007-2011, it is established that the information in the reports of PFIA and the information in the reports of the AFCOS Directorate at the Ministry of Interior are identical. The information in the reports of both control institutions is not presented in detail in the narrative. It is limited only to the digital presentation of the total number of cases of violations, without specifying the nature and preconditions for these violations. Data for 2007 are missing in Table 1. The reason for this is that

Table 1. Number of cases of violations and fraud in spending EU programs and funds

Operational programs	2011	2010	2009	2008	2007
Regional Development	21	12	8	1	–
Administrative capacity	26	12	4	–	–
PHARE	7	18	65	15	–
SAPARD	1	9	310	7	–
Environment	9	10	21	2	–
Human Resources Development	3	–	5	1	–
Rural Development	3	1	–	–	–
Development of competitiveness	1	–	3	–	–
Transport	1	–	–	–	–

Source: Reports from the AFCOS Directorate at the Ministry of Interior for the period from 2007 to 2011

this year the organizational changes in the control bodies of the public sector took place and as a result of these changes the PFIA reports were submitted to the AFCOS Directorate in a timely manner.

The main recommendation we make to the AFCOS Directorate is to request more detailed information from PFIA, and not to rely only on the reports on the activities of the Agency. We believe that the detailed information in the annual reports will be a prerequisite for the formation of the right decisions regarding the introduction of effective preventive measures against violations and fraud. On the other hand, it will be a prerequisite for determining the manner of application of the principles of financial control in control processes.

The ways of applying the principles of financial control, in order to preserve and guarantee the financial stability and security of the country, are significantly influenced by the regulated state structure. Four forms of government have been established, namely: federation, confederation, personal union and unitary government. Bulgaria is a unitary state with a unitary state structure. From an etymological point of view, the definition of "unitary" comes from the Latin word *unitas*, which means united (Milev, 1970). Therefore, unitary are all those states in which the right to exercise supreme state power over its entire territory is indivisible.

State control exercised in unitary states differs significantly from control exercised in federations, confederations and personal unions. Due to the limited development, we turn our attention to the internal control exercised in the unitary countries, such as Bulgaria. The overall internal control process in the unitary states is carried out by deconcentrating state power through the division of control activities between central and decentralized control bodies. Also, the bodies of the legislative power, the central executive and the judiciary have sufficient powers to be able to perform and implement the centralized state control order. They deal more with the established generally accepted control principles and apply the derived principles of financial control to a lesser extent. Decentralized control bodies have limited powers, they are fully subordinated to the central legislative, executive and judicial branches. One of the main obligations of the decentralized control bodies is to comply with the region and the industry in which the control process takes place, as well as with the specifics and peculiarities of the controlled object. On this basis, they are obliged to apply not only the generally accepted control principles, but also the derived control principles. The simultaneous application of the general and derivative principles during the control process aims to most fully and accurately reveal the emerging control situation, as well as the condition of the controlled object. There are various definitions of public internal financial control in the reference books. For example, V. Burtsev (Burtsev, 2001) assumes that state financial control is the legally regulated activity of state bodies and state administrations at all state levels in order to identify, prevent and counteract the following:

- errors and irregularities in the management of public funds and material (capital) resources used for public administration, as well as errors and irregularities in the alienation of assets and rights owned by the state, leading to direct or indirect damage to the state;
- non-compliance with the law;
- gaps in the organization of the control process in financial and economic public organizations (including non-governmental organizations), as well as in organizations with state participation;
- all threats to the financial security of the state.

According to other experts, "state control is exercised by specially created institutions. This is a control function with managerial significance and derives from the right of the state to manage its property and protect its interests" (Dinev, 2008).

Over the years, the essence of the concept of "internal financial control", which is used by control specialists, has not changed significantly, but its normative name has changed. In the repealed Law on the State Internal Financial Control (LSIFC) in Art. 2, para. 1 regulated that "the state internal financial control is control over the financial activity of the persons indicated in art. 4, in order to assess the legality and compliance with the principles of efficiency, effectiveness and economy". Following the repeal of the LSIFC and the adoption of the Public Financial Inspection Act (PFIA), the term "public internal financial control" was replaced in § 6 of the previous and final provisions of the PFIA with "public financial inspection". Also, the adopted PFIA presents in more detail the legal regulation of the main tasks facing the State Financial Inspection, namely: conducting subsequent financial inspections to comply with regulations governing budgetary, financial and economic or reporting activities of the organizations and the persons under art. 4; establishment of violations of the normative acts, regulating the budgetary, financial-economic or reporting activity, as well as of indicators for committed frauds; disclosure of caused damages to the property of the organizations and the persons under art. 4; bringing to administrative, penal and property responsibility of the guilty persons in the presence of the respective legal grounds; detection of fraud and infringements affecting the financial interests of the European Communities". Despite these legal changes, the requirement to comply with the rule remains: the methodology for implementation and realization of financial control should be developed by the Ministry of Finance. This rule was formulated as a result of the adopted unitary state structure of the country.

The applicability of the principles of financial control in order to preserve the financial security and stability of the country is influenced by the principles of social control. According to Jeffrey Pfeffer (Preffer, 1978), each organization is engaged in the exchange of transactions and services with other organizational groups. Organizations are never independent, they always depend on the environment, and the environment itself also depends on the proper and effective operation of the organization, based on which it receives the necessary services and products. This is the main prerequisite for the provision of external social control over organizations. With this kind of control, J. Pfeffer believes that it will be found out how the organizations have complied with the requirements of the environment, as well as whether they have tried to avoid its influence.

K. Spasov accepts that social control is "a creative activity for setting and achieving the goals of the system (organization) in the conditions of a changing environment and efficient use of limited resources. It can also be defined as the influence of the management system (subject) on the managed system (object) to achieve the set goals" (Spasov, 2003). Therefore, persons of different social status and "social groups (and emerging relationships) on the production, distribution, exchange and consumption of social products can participate in the implementation of social control" (Spasov, 2003).

Therefore, social control is part of the overall process of socialization, which is generally expressed in the process of adapting the individual or a specific social group (organization) to the social norms in society and respecting the social control principles. According to Clive Beed, there are four basic control principles that should be observed in the implementation of social control, namely (Clive, 2006): *respect for the dignity of the human person; respect for the common good; compliance with the subsidiarity requirement; compliance with the solidarity requirement.*

These principles are presented as permanent, universal and primary. They are the main parameters for interpretation and evaluation of social phenomena and processes (Clive, 2006). Therefore, the principles of control, incl. the principles of financial control, and social control principles cannot be absolute. These principles are interrelated and in an organizational system such as the state, they cannot exist separately. Their complementarity is a prerequisite for the existence of a unified state system, and, on the other hand, guarantee the financial security and stability of the country. In this regard, Engels states that in life "there are countless mutually intersecting forces, an endless parallelogram of forces that give one equivalent - the historical result" (Engels, 1963). But Engels does not take into account the fact that this rule applies to a shorter period. In the long run, we believe that the interaction of the same forces would not always produce the same result, as in the long run the time factor has an impact. It is it that places the events and processes in a certain chronology, and hence, to a certain extent, determines the final result.

In modern conditions, control bodies are faced with a new problem: based on their toolkit of control principles, they need to present not only the current state of the controlled object but also to forecast and determine the future state of the object. The solution of this difficult task can be achieved with the help of a summary of the information received from all types of implemented control processes. According to a group of American experts in the field of mathematical control modelling - P. Kaczmarek, S. T. Kent, G. A. Rus and B. A. Wade - the solution to this new problem can only be achieved with the help of the ***infinite three-dimensional linear programming technique*** (Kaczmarek, 2007). This three-dimensional linear programming is constructed by presenting the entire control process, limited to a given interval, and the beginning of this interval is determined by a point, which under the influence of various time factors changes to another point, ending the interval. The numerical results obtained using the steady-state convergence finite method are compared with each other using dynamic programming. The end result of this dynamic programming is presented in Figure 1.

This graphical representation of the controlled object from one state to another, as well as the pursuit of a future and accurate definition of the position it will occupy among other objects or systems, is achieved not only by following generally accepted control principles, based on which the control itself occurs but also with the help of mathematical principles. This three-dimensional modelling of the control process is achieved through the correct observance and application of mathematical principles presented as mathematical equations.

Figure 1. Dynamic programming of the control object

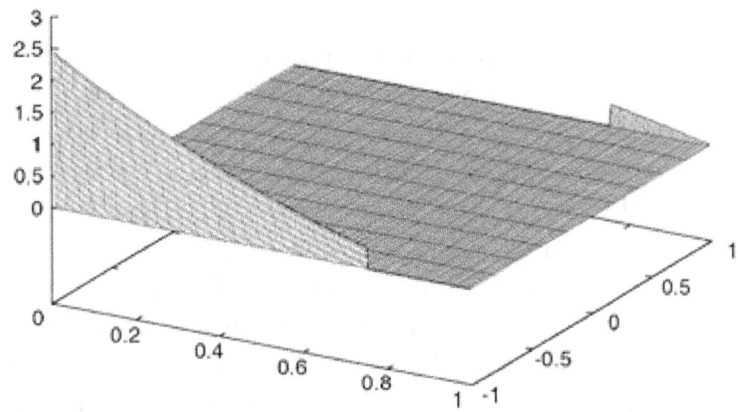

Approximate density of $\mu_{occ}^{(d)*}$, $h = 0.005$

Each state-owned structure is made up of countless objects (n – objects). According to mathematicians, the overall functioning of these n-numbers of objects is represented as a sequence of transitions. "When the transitions are made under the influence of random factors, it is said that a random process takes place in the object. A random process is called a Markov process (or a process without consequences) if its future development depends solely on its current situation and does not depend on the background of the process. When the set of states is discrete and the transitions between them are performed by jumping (instantaneously), then the Markov random process is called the Markov chain" (Georgiev, 2002).

To predict the financial stability and security of the controlled object, the American scientists P. Kaczmarek, S. T. Kent, G. A. Rus and B. A. Wade are committed to the study of the Markov chain by simulating its behaviour.

According to N. Kushner (Kushner, 2001), this approach has been applied since 1950, when economics set new requirements for mathematicians to study stochastic (natural) and non-stochastic (unnatural) processes.

Despite the many methods and models that mathematical doctrine offers to predict the future state of an object, financial professionals, economists and analysts still cannot fully trust and rely on them to predict an uncertain and overly dynamic changing event. Taking into account the words of N. Braverman (Braverman, 1974) that "control is the central concept of management of all systems", it turns out that this is its main problem, namely: to find the model that can cover and properly control all subsystems that build the general state control system of the country, so as to fully ensure the financial security and stability of the country.

Many modern analysts of the financial and economic crisis that has erupted in recent years have sharply criticized the governments of major leading countries such as the United States, Italy, Britain and others for not taking the necessary measures to preserve the financial foundations of the state society, even though there were some early signs for the crisis. One of the reasons for the emergence of the global financial crisis, according to a study in the "Bulgarian Science" journal, is the lack of sufficient effective state control over private financial institutions. This answer was indicated by 23% of the survey respondents. Other 55% believe that this is an inevitable part of the processes in the economy. The share of respondents is not small, namely 22%, who believe that this is due to the reckless desire of people to get rich.

Another interesting question that the editorial team of the Bulgarian Science magazine asks in its survey on the impact of the global financial crisis in our country is the question: "What should the Bulgarian state do to protect the country's financial stability?". A significant part of the respondents, 19%, answered that in order to protect financial stability, it is necessary for the state to attract investments in energetics. Fifteen percent of respondents believe that in order to protect the country's financial stability, it is necessary to implement better and more effective state control over private financial institutions. Eleven per cent said the problem could be solved with health and pension reforms, and 8 per cent said the state should increase its financial reserves.

Based on this poll conducted in February 2009, we find that despite the fact that a large number of respondents cite as one of the main reasons for the financial destabilization of the country the lack of sufficient effective and quality public internal financial control, still expectations of society to this state mechanism are preserved. We accept that this incorrect implementation of the state financial control, which the respondents find, is due to the circumstance for the incomplete use of the opportunities provided by the principles of financial control.

If we take into account another source of information, namely the SWOT analysis of the state of the executive power, carried out under the Operational Program "Administrative Capacity" in 2006, it is established that the emphasis is not only on the strengths and weaknesses in control and executive branch, but also on the search for mechanisms for the overall stabilization of the country. The SWOT analysis reveals a number of weaknesses in the control activities of the state executive power. One of the criticisms stated by analysts was the weak internal and interdepartmental coordination, especially at the district level and between the territorial units of the central executive and the municipal administration. The main threats facing the executive branch are outlined, and hence the growing risk to the security and stability of the country due to the ineffectiveness of anti-corruption policy. Slow reforms in the judiciary, on the one hand, delayed trends in public perceptions of the nature of the problem, and on the other hand, the lack of active anti-corruption action by previous governments, are the main reasons for destabilizing the state control policy.

Account must also be taken of the fact that, in practice, in order to apply the relevant principles of financial control, the supervisory authorities incur various expenditures related to the government of the country. According to EUROSTAT, total government revenue in 2011 amounted to 44.6% of GDP (an increase of 44.1% of GDP in 2010) and expenditure to 49.1% of GDP (a decrease of 50.6% in 2010). In the European zone, the total government expenditures amounted to 49.4% of GDP in 2011 and total revenue to 45.3% of GDP. The expenditures that the state realizes in order to implement quality and efficient government are nearly 4.5% more than GDP compared to the revenues received from governance. Also, according to the same study, in absolute terms, the total government expenditures increased at a steady pace between 2001 and 2010 in both the EU-27 and the Eurozone. In the period 2010-2011, the expenditures decreased slightly in absolute terms in both the EU-27 and the Eurozone. Revenues also increased at a steady pace until 2007 in the EU-27 and the Eurozone, remaining relatively stable in 2008, declining in 2009 and increasing again in 2010 and 2011. The distribution of general government expenditures in comparison to the GDP of the countries concerned is presented in Figure 2.

Figure 2. Expenditures of the state government sector by the function of the COFOG classification for 2010

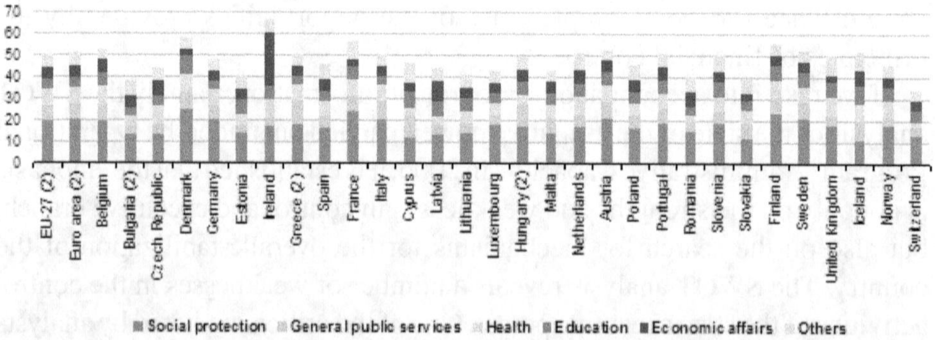

(1) COFOG: classification of the functions of government; data extracted on 23.04.2012.
(2) Provisional.
Source: Eurostat (online data code: gov_a_exp)

From the data presented in Figure 2 it is established that Bulgaria is among the countries that maintain a relatively high level of their total management costs. On the other hand, in order to determine whether the implemented government has been effective as a result of the funds and resources spent, we believe that it is necessary to give a real effective assessment of the regulatory impact itself, as well as to assess the manner of application of the principles of financial control. Both evaluation processes are very complex and specific. For this reason, back in 2008, the Council of Ministers in cooperation with the consortium "Sema-Agrer-ENA" developed a "Guide to Assessment of Impact in Bulgaria". Regulatory impact assessment is considered to be defined as a set of logical steps that structure the preparation of policy proposals. It includes building on and developing practices that already accompany the policy development process by deepening the analysis and formalizing the results in an independent report. In general, the ministry drafting the proposal is responsible for preparing the impact assessment. Therefore, the role of the impact assessment is to give a detailed assessment of the potential impact of a normative act (or amendments to the current act), so that an assessment can be made as to whether the act will achieve the desired objectives.

As a result of all the above about the impact and importance of the principles of financial control in maintaining financial security and stability of the country, the following main conclusions and recommendations can be drawn:

1. The principles of financial control have a significant impact on the financial stability of the country. Their direct influence is most noticeable first on the control body itself, and subsequently on the controlled object. Also, their influence on the state and change of the financial security and stability of the country is very abstract. In order to comprehend and illustrate this impact, it is necessary to use three-dimensional linear programming.
2. In order to determine the assessment of the regulatory impact, and hence the impact of the applied principles, a number of methods need to be applied. The main recommendation that can be addressed to the regulatory authorities is to formally post the data of the identified regulatory impacts, as well as the approaches to the application of the principles of financial control. So far, such officially disclosed information is lacking, which makes it difficult for external observers and analysts to determine the extent to which the principles have an impact on ensuring the country's financial security.
3. The legislative framework is one of the mechanisms for ensuring financial security. Therefore, it is necessary to analyze and evaluate the quality of the application of the normative acts by the control bodies, and hence - to determine whether the rules, which are regulated in the respective analyzed acts, are observed by the controllers. This analysis is aimed at assessing the objectives set during the adoption of the normative act, whether they have been implemented and how effective the normative act is.

REFERENCES

Braverman, H. (1974). *Labour and monopoly capital: The degradation of work in the twentieth century*. Monthly Review Press.

Burtsev, V. V. 2001. Basic principles of state financial control organizations in modern conditions. Financial management, N° 2.

Clive, B. 2006. Managing As If Faith Mattered: Christian Social Principles in the Modern Organization. Review of Business, Spring, 27, No. 2.

Crockett, A. (1996). The Theory and Practice of Financial Stability. *De Economist*, *144*(4), 57. doi:10.1007/BF01371939

Dinev, M. (2008). *Obshta teoria na schetovodstvoto*. Trakia-M.

Engels, F. 1963, Writings. T. 37

Georgiev, G. 2002. Modeling Markov Chains in Ms Excel. Scientific works of the University of Ruse, 47.

Kaczmarek, P., Kent, S. T., Rus, G. A., Stockbridge, R. H., & Wade, B. A. (2007). Numerical solution of a long-term average control problem for singular stochastic processes. *Mathematical Methods of Operations Research*, *66*(3), 456. doi:10.100700186-007-0166-9

Kushner, H. J., & Dupuis, P. (2001). *Numerical Methods for Stochastic Control Problems in Continuous Time* (2nd ed.). Springer. doi:10.1007/978-1-4613-0007-6

Milev, A. (1970). *Dictionary of Foreign Words in the Bulgarian Language*. Science and Art.

Nedyalkova, P. (2020). Specifics of the Assessment as a Process of Internal Audit Activity. In *Quality of Internal Auditing in the Public Sector. Contributions to Management Science*. Springer., doi:10.1007/978-3-030-29329-1_4

Nedyalkova, P. 2020. Quality of internal auditing in the public sector perspectives from the bulgarian and international context. pp. 1-151 ID: 57204010473

Nedyalkova, P. (2020). Empirical Study of the VAIA Metric (Value Added of Internal Audit) and Determination of the Internal Audit Quality for Shumen Municipality for the Period 2011–2016. In *Quality of Internal Auditing in the Public Sector. Contributions to Management Science*. Springer., doi:10.1007/978-3-030-29329-1_11

Nedyalkova, P. (2020). Presentation of the Dependence Between the Chosen Internal Audit Approach and the Methods for Assessing the Quality of the Internal Audit in the Public Sector. In *Quality of Internal Auditing in the Public Sector. Contributions to Management Science*. Springer., doi:10.1007/978-3-030-29329-1_8

Nedyalkova, P. (2020). Specifics of the Assessment as a Process of Internal Audit Activity. In *Quality of Internal Auditing in the Public Sector. Contributions to Management Science*. Springer., doi:10.1007/978-3-030-29329-1_4

Preffer, J. (1978). *The external control of organizations: A Resource Dependence Perspective*. Harper & Row Publishers.

Schinasi, G. (2006). *Safeguarding Financial Stability: Theory and Practice*. International Monetary Fund.

Spasov, K. (2003). *Social Management*. Apis.

Chapter 5
Factors Influencing the Implementation of the Principles of Financial Control:
Graphic Design of the Control Environment

ABSTRACT

the control environment where the control process takes place has a significant impact on the correctness and applicability of the principles of state internal control, including the principles of financial control. When the control environment is known, it will be much easier to determine from all legally regulated rules which will be the most vulnerable and easily violated during the control process. In this way, the principles predisposed to violation will be subject to monitoring not only by the participants in the control process, but also by third parties not participating in the control process, but interested in the proper and effective implementation of state internal control, including financial control.

The theory of control has not yet fully explored the factors influencing the application of the principles of control, including the principles of financial control. Therefore, in this part of the study we examine the main factors that affect not only the applicability of control principles in a particular control

DOI: 10.4018/978-1-6684-8883-6.ch005

process, but also affect this process. Following the prescriptions of I. Stengers (Stengers, 1994) (she puts the subject of the study of the principles of financial control in a new perspective, namely entering into a new relationship with them, creating another version or another story), in fact, the principles and mechanisms of cognitive control are formed.

The correct application of the principles of financial control is essential not only for the effective implementation of the overall control process, but also essential for maintaining the security and stability of the country. We believe that the realization of this task is influenced by the following factors:

The specifics of the subject and the object in the formed control relations. This main factor, which has a significant impact on the applicability of the principles of financial control, includes (Mladenov, 2009):

- *The will and motivation of the control body (the subject)* – will and motivation refer to psychological and behavioral factors. The theory developed by the American psychologist W. James in 1897, presented in his collection of essays "Will to Faith", reveals the thesis that in certain situations the individual is given the opportunity to choose between two possible alternatives, one of which is the situation to be resolved on a non-intellectual (emotional) basis, and the other alternative is to solve the problem on an intellectual (legal) basis (James, 1897). The volitional character of the control bodies is presented most strongly in the planning of the control actions and in the imposition of certain legally regulated behavior on the controlled object. The presence of motivation for effective implementation of the control process, combined with the strong-willed nature of the controller, are the two main prerequisites for the proper application of control principles during the control process.
- *Features and specifics of the controlled object* – the different substance of the objects is a prerequisite for them not to object of control in the same time period (Alekseev, 1981). From the point of view of the applicability of the principles of financial control, the specifics and peculiarities of the objects have a significant influence. Mathematical science examines each object as unique, different from all the others. According to the number of constituent elements that make up objects, mathematicians subdivide them into two main types - simple and complex (Georgieva and others, 1987). From the point of view

of control, it is very difficult to determine in practice which control objects are simple. Rather, we assume that they are complex, presented as control operations. An operation should be understood as "any activity or system of activities and events that are aimed at achieving a certain goal" (Dochev, 1997) according to:

- *The type of control situation*: The control situation also affects the applicability of the control principles, incl. the principles of financial control. Therefore, it is essential to specify the control situation that has developed between the controlled object and the controlling body. From a practical point of view, we assume that determining the nature of the control situation, its pragmatism and peculiarity can not be done without recognizing and separating the specific type of control situation from all other types. This is necessary when another control situation for the same controlled object has arisen simultaneously or in the near future. "Complexity increases if the situations are close to each other or intersect in their initial state and in the nature of the evolving process" (Bakardzhieva, 2006).
- *The type of control and the selected control technology*: The technology of control should be considered as a set of methods and tools for achieving a desired result (Dinev, 1986). Depending on the type of control, different control methods and tools are applied in practice. By choosing the control method and tools, with the help of which the control process will be implemented, indirectly, almost unconsciously, the rules (principles,) that should be followed in order to apply the chosen method and tools correctly, are determined.
- *The state of the environment in which the control process takes place:* The environment in which the control process takes place is essential, as it not only affects the work of control bodies, but also affects the applicability of the principles of financial control in the control situation.

Audit Standard 55 / SAS 55 - "Consideration of the Internal Control Structure In a Financial Statement Audit" stipulates that the control environment is a set of those factors that affects the implementation of the approved policies and procedures of the organization. The factors that make up the control environment are divided into internal and external. The internal factors include the adopted organizational structure, the established management philosophy and style of work, as well as the managerial relationships. External factors include the legal and normative rules, as well as the unwritten generally accepted norms. Therefore, external and internal factors influencing the development of a particular organization are the main building blocks of the structure of the control environment. Depending on the interaction between these two structural elements not only the specifics are determined but also the type of control environment. According to this feature, we assume that the control environment is divided into active, passive, and corrupt control environment.

An active control environment is one that changes rapidly and it is very difficult for the controller to determine exactly which control situation the control process is in. It is assumed that the environment is so active that it opposes the achievement of the most effective control solution. The selection and application of control principles, which help to perform an effective control process, is very often impulsive. This, in turn, is a prerequisite for finding out at a later stage that the choice made in determining the final control decision is incorrect. This error is the main reason why most of the control processes do not correctly reveal the condition of the controlled object, and on the other hand, is a prerequisite for the revocation of the acts issued by the control authorities. Considering that the principles are a constructive element of the substantive legal provisions, it follows that by violating them (the principles) we violate the legally regulated substantive legal provisions and vice versa - violating the substantive legal provisions violates the legally established principles.

According to Z. Slavchev (Slavchev, 2010b) one of the grounds for judicial revocation of acts issued by administrative bodies is the contradiction of the issued act with the substantive provisions. This contradiction of the issued individual administrative acts with the substantive legal provisions is characteristic of the active control environment. Moreover, in these cases other control bodies are involved, incl. of the judiciary (prosecutor's office). This reflexively has a negative impact on the effectiveness of the issued acts.

In such a control environment, the aim and aspiration of the control bodies should be to achieve the maximum efficiency of the control process and the control solution that is formulated to be the most optimal. Applying these rules, we believe that the individual control acts issued by the control bodies will fully meet the requirement of expediency and legality. There are still many examples in practice in which the control bodies, under the influence of the dynamic control environment, issue individual administrative acts that do not comply with the legally defined provisions and are subsequently appealed in the respective administrative and judicial order.

We assume that the passive control environment is radically different from the active one, as it favors the achievement of the optimal control solution, and it is also not too dynamically changing. The controller goes through each stage of the control process sequentially, there is no significant influence of external and internal factors that have a significant impact on the control activity. Usually the control process, which takes place in a passive control environment, ends with a protocol, except in cases when another normative act is provided. For the passive control environment, it is more typical for the control process to take place in the form of a check-up rather than in the form of inspections and audits.

We believe that the differences between the active and passive environment are also observed in the applied theories, with the help of which the processes and phenomena are studied. The passive environment is more favorable for the application of quantitative theory, which is used to study objects and phenomena, applying mathematical modeling. The change in the state of the controlled objects is much easier to interpret and explain, using the linear and dynamic programming, the simplex method, as well as applying the theory of queuing. The security provided by the passive environment not only for the control bodies, but also for the controlled objects, is a prerequisite for the correct and accurate analysis of the formed control situation. On the other hand, the correct application of mathematical methods and models in the passive control environment is a prerequisite for the correct modelling of the control process and presentation of the influence that exists between the control principles on the basis of which the control process and the legally regulated principles are performed. The controlled object should have observed these principles during its economic activity. The dynamics of the active environment does not allow this influence to be fully revealed. Figure 1 clearly shows the applicability of the principles of financial control in a passive environment.

Figure 1 shows that the principles of financial control applied by the control bodies during the control process, in addition to aiming to present the specifics and condition of the controlled object, seek to reveal ways to apply and implement the prescribed and established state and social rules, requiring a lawful and expedient course of the economic and social activity of the controlled object. Improper application of these rules is the main prerequisite for the violation of the established state order, and on the other hand, is the main reason for the threat to the financial security and stability

Figure 1. Applicability of the principles of financial control in a passive environment

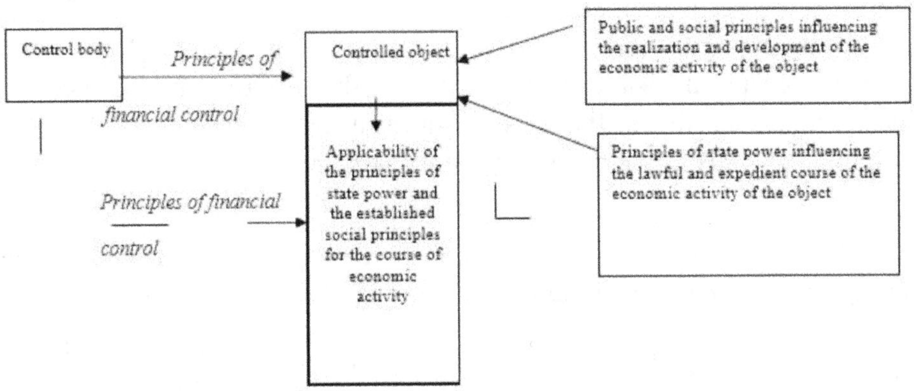

of the state. For this reason, the control bodies are assigned several tasks for resolution in one control process.

The corrupt control environment is the one in which one of the factors influencing the development of the respective controlled organizational unit is corruption. The question of whether an effective control process can be properly and accurately implemented in a corrupt environment is still controversial. The survey, conducted by the leading audit company Ernst & Young in 2008 among 1,186 companies, found that despite the corruption factor, 72% of respondents believe that the work of control bodies is sufficiently effective, as the control activity has facilitated the detection of bribes and corrupt practices. The remaining 22% believe that the control bodies do not cope well with their pre-set tasks and goals and the control activity is influenced by the corrupt environment in which the control process develops.

A study by Ernst & Young found that there was no consensus on the issue among respondents in different geographical regions. For example, of the surveyed companies in Latin America and Japan, the percentage of dissatisfied with the implemented control activity is very small, this percentage is only 7% and 8%. Respondents from the Far and Middle East, as well as India and Africa, give an excellent assessment of the effectiveness of the control activity, as only 11% of respondents believe that the control process is strongly influenced by the corruption factor, and accept that the applied control principles and rules for the implementation of the control process were ineffective. The share of respondents from Central and Eastern Europe is significant - 44%, followed by Australia and New Zealand - 32%, Western

Europe - 25%, and North America - 19%, who believe that the implemented control processes were ineffective.

The survey, conducted in 2009 by the Center for the Study of Democracy, presents corruption not as a factor influencing the control activities of control bodies, but as a problem that arises as a result of abuses by control bodies with their administrative powers, done for personal gain.

Table 1. The respondents believe they are most often forced to bribe the revenue inspectors for the following types of services

Types of services provided by the tax administration in exchange for bribes	%
Avoidance of fines and sanctions	55,1%
Acceleration of tax procedures	44,6%
Faster tax credit recovery	44,1%
Failure to establish a violation	40,9%
Illegal VAT refund	33,9%
Evasion of tax and social security liabilities	23,5%
Delay in revision proceedings	17,2%
Admission of document fraud	14,4%
Providing external information	11,3%
Not having knowledge and not giving answers to questions	15,6%

Source: Konstantin, P. Corruption in Taxation. Challenges for tax policy and administration, 2012. Available at: www.csd.bg

The survey covers the analysis of tax fraud and corruption, carried out by inspectors at the National Revenue Agency. Table 1 presents the most common services for which the tax authorities are willing to accept bribes.

Analyzing the data presented so far, the following main conclusions can be drawn:

1. An infringement is never the result of incorrect application and non-compliance on a single principle; it is a consequence of the compiled non-compliance with several principles.
2. The corruption factor can be investigated in various aspects. The first aspect is to look at the factor as caused by external preconditions for the control institution. The preconditions for the existence of corruption are people's mentality (lack of ethical and moral norms, low level of public self-awareness, etc.), socio-economic factors (low income, social environment, the desire for a better life, etc.), as well as the lack of

sufficient political will for the adoption of counteraction mechanisms by the state authorities. The second aspect of research is when corruption is carried out by persons employed in the control institution for personal gain. The admission of a number of omissions, weaknesses, irregularities on the part of the controllers, and on the other hand - the use of official position for personal gain, favor the presence of corruption.

Preventive measure against corruption by PFIA is the effective application of the principles of legality, objectivity and efficiency. According to a study by the Institute for Economic Policy, together with the Association for Governance Monitoring in 2009, on "Combating Corruption in Public Procurement - Indicators for Assessing the Effect of Policy", the indicator of the effectiveness of control in public procurement is the application of control principles in the implementation of the subsequent and preliminary control. In the mentioned research it is established that it is very difficult for PFIA to establish which of the established violations are for the purpose of undue personal gain and which are omissions and mistakes without intent. PFIA reports distinguish between "culpable damages" (20.6% of all damages found in value terms in 2008) and other damages found. But this distinction is for the entire activity of PFIA. It is not clear in the PFIA activity reports the nature of the culpable damages, whether they are the result of the impact of the corruption factor (bribery or other due benefits), or the result of the impact of another factor (errors, inaccurate application of regulatory requirements due to insufficient competence and knowledge, etc.). The recommendation we address to the activity of PFIA is to apply the principles of "legality", "objectivity" and "effectiveness" and to specify in their activity reports what is the nature of the culpable damages. In this way, indicators will be established on the basis of which to determine the effectiveness of financial inspections.

With the help of the results of various surveys of non-governmental organizations it was proved that there are a number of violations by the control bodies in the implementation of their control activities, which are due to the manifestation of the corruption factor.

The presented Eurobarometer survey (Table 2) shows that for 2011 compared to 2009 "the subjective prerequisites of citizens for corrupt practices in the period 2009-2011 are improving. The level of corruption in Bulgaria in 2011 in all areas is higher than the average for EU countries. The distrust of the surveyed citizens towards the inspection activity, including PFIA, is also confirmed in this study by the data presented in Table 8. Fifty-two percent of respondents in 2009 indicated their distrust of the work of inspectors in

Table 2. Perceptions regarding corruption in Bulgaria and in the EU

	Bulgaria		EU27	
You are personally affected by corruption in your daily life				
	2009	2011	2009	2011
Total "Agree"		45%		29%
Total "Disagree"		48%		67%
Don't know		7%		4%
Do you think that giving and taking bribes and using power for personal gain in Bulgaria is common among some of the following groups?				
People working in the customs	87%	77%	36%	31%
People working in judiciary	82%	76%	37%	32%
People working in police	80%	70%	39%	34%
People working in public healthcare	65%	63%	32%	30%
Politicians at the national level	76%	60%	57%	57%
Officials issuing company licenses, permits, etc.	61%	54%	38%	33%
Inspectors	62%	52%	39%	35%
People working in the educational system	45%	34%	19%	17%
The government's efforts to fight corruption give result				
Total "Agree"	28%	29%	23%	22%
Total "Disagree"	63%	65%	71%	68%
Don't know	9%	6%	6%	10%

Source: Eurobarometer 76.1 (September 2011) and Eurobarometer 72.2 (September 2009)

Bulgaria, and in 2011 their share increased significantly - to 62%. For the EU countries, the respondents present relatively good results, namely 39% for 2009 and 35% for 2011, which means that there is more confidence in the activities of control institutions.

The distinction between the control environments as active ones, passive ones and corrupt ones is only in a theoretical aspect. This is due to the fact that the factors that affect the environment are constantly changing.

In a shorter time interval, the dominance of a particular factor can be observed, and in the next moment the control situation can be under the influence of another factor. For this reason, from a practical point of view, the active, passive and corrupt control environment are almost impossible to distinguish. Graphically, Fig. 6 presents the interaction between the three control environments and the formation of the so-called mixed control environments. We assume that the mixed control environments are of the type:

active-passive control environment; active-corruption control environment; passive-corruption control environment. In a longer period, a change in the control environment can be observed, i.e. the control process has started in an active environment, then it has turned into a corrupt one, and finally, a passive environment can be reached. Of course, this distinction of control environments is too hypothetical and can be demonstrated by Figure 2.

Figure 2. Interaction between active, passive and corrupt control environment

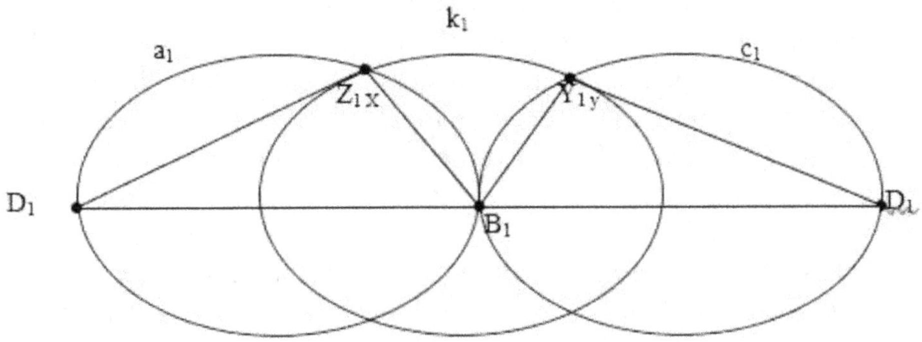

Figure 2 shows that the transformation of the active environment into passive and vice versa is influenced by the corruption factor, i.e. the corrupt environment. If the control environment is too dynamic, for example, if the country's regulations change too quickly, and at the same time there is corruption pressure from one of the two participants in the control process, then it is the control environment that is in state "x", which is seen from Figure 2. When the environment is passive, i.e. the control process is not limited in time, nor do the regulations change too fast, but again the influence of the corruption factor is observed, then we assume that the control environment is in state "y", indicated in Figure 2. With "a1" we denote a specific active control environment, with "c1" - the passive control environment, and with "k1" - the corrupt environment, which affects both the active and the passive control environment.

We believe that in order to study the control environments, it is necessary to test how the same control process will take place simultaneously in the active environment and in the passive control environment. For a more complete and accurate study of the selected active control environment (a1) and also to study the selected passive control environment (c1), we have accepted to perform the control process, denoted by D_1B_1, in these control environments. When testing the environments, we assume that: 1) the active (a1), the passive control environment (c1) and the control process D1B1, which takes place in both control environments, are influenced by the corruption factor and especially the corruption environment (k1); 2) the corrupt environment (k1) evenly affects both the active environment (a1) and the passive environment (c1).

In the presented figure we have developed the following hypotheses:

First hypothesis – if the active environment a1 is significantly affected by the corrupt control environment k1, i.e if a1 <k1, then we assume that there is a change in the control process. According to initial data, the process is planned to flow from point D1 to point B1. However, due to the strong influence of the corrupt environment k1, the planned process proceeds from point D1 to point Z1. The end result obtained in this situation is Δ D1B1Z1. Side D1Z1 of Δ D1B1Z1 represents the actual control process, and side D1B1 is the pre-planned control process.

Second hypothesis – if the active environment a1 has a significant impact on the corrupt control environment k1, ie. a1> k1 then we assume that the control process proceeds in the desired direction, ie. from point D1 to point B1, and the desired result D1B1 is achieved.

Third hypothesis - (it is from the point of view of the passive environment) - if the same selected control process, i.e from item D1, we want to reach item B1, but achieved not in an active control environment, but in a passive c1, which environment is strongly influenced by the corruption factor, i.e. c1 <k1, then the control process changes from endpoint B1 to endpoint Y1. The end result is not D1B1, but B1Y1.

Fourth hypothesis - (it is again from the point of view of the passive control environment) - if the passive control environment cannot be influenced by the corrupt environment, i.e. c1> k1, it is in this situation that the desired control result D1B1 is achieved, i.e. the control process proceeds according to the pre-planned stages.

Taking into account mainly the first and third hypotheses, a deviation of the control process from the previously planned one is established. Regardless of whether the environment is active or passive, whether it is influenced by the corruption factor, all the processes that take place within it change. Geometrically, this change is shown in Figure 2 by Δ D1B1Z1 for an active environment and Δ D1B1Y1 for a passive environment. Also, the two triangles, namely Δ D1B1Z1 and Δ D1B1Y1, although located in two different control environments, represent the range in which the control authorities apply the principles of state internal control, incl. financial control. They also present the perimeter in which the principles of state power and the social principles governing the preservation of the security and stability of the state by the control objects are applied.

Research in the field of the control environment had its high achievement with the discoveries that Mary Parker Follett made in 1937. During his time, Follett came to concrete conclusions, but these findings remained unexplored and at times even misunderstood, as they were sharply criticized. With her numerous scientific works, M. Follett also managed to outline the answers to many of the control problems and laid the foundations on which all her followers should continue their research processes. According to the specialist, the control environments (models) are of two main types: behavioral and holistic (Fayol, 1937). Mary Follett's behavioral environment is shown in Figure 3.

Figure 3. Behavioral control environment

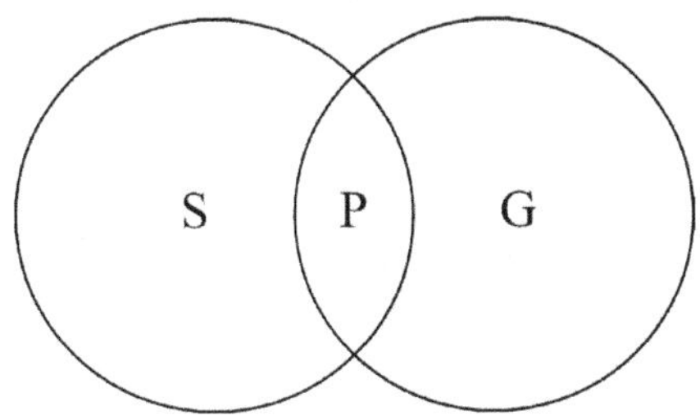

In the study of control environments Mary Follett also came to the conclusion that it is necessary to assume specific hypotheses and examining them, in fact, the study of the control environment itself will be achieved. Follett's behavioral control environment assumes that it is built on the self-control exercised by the individual (S) and on the control of the whole organization (system) (G). The impact that the organization (system) has on the individual, and on the other hand, the control that the individual has on the activities of the organization (system) are a prerequisite for the formation of a strong control environment (power-sharing control (P)). It is this power-sharing control that reveals the real possibilities of control, which covers all levels of an organization, in contrast to previous management claims that control is centralized only at the top of the management hierarchy (Parker,1984).

The overall control environment, according to M. Follett, presents an organization as a set of countless groups that interact with each other. The control is not only inside the organization itself, but also outside the defined control system. This complex relationship between the self-control that the individual exercises, the control impact of the environment and the control influence of an organizational structure form the overall control environment. In Follett's view, in this overall control environment, there is no authoritarian control regime, but mutual control works, which demonstrates it as follows (Parker, 1984).

From the types of control environments proposed by M. Follett and the way of their graphical representation we find that the interaction between the individual controlled environments, building the overall control system, is not fully revealed. We accept that this interaction, especially between the active, passive and corrupt environment, can be achieved by applying the methods of correlation analysis.

Each system (such as the control environment, as it is a set of interconnected building blocks) depends on many and often changing factors.

Figure 4. The overall control environment according to M. Follett

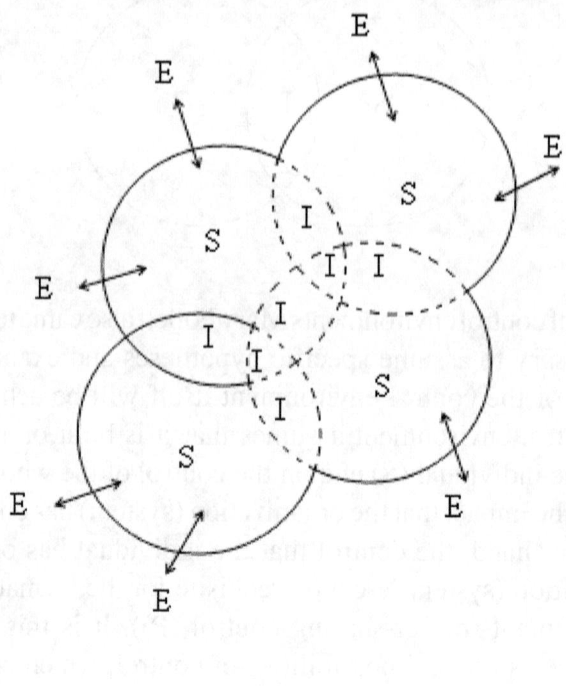

Over the years, it has been proven that functional and correlation dependencies play a decisive role in state control. Functional dependence, as it is known, is a concept from mathematical analysis, which "shows the unambiguous correspondence between quantities, when one quantity, called an argument, corresponds to a strictly defined meaning (value) of another quantity" (Golikov, 2003). It has been proven that functional dependence can be observed only in natural doctrines and most of all their action is revealed only in laboratory military field conditions. In real living conditions, under the influence of various conditions and factors, this pure functional dependence is not observed. What the real world around us offers, and hence what we see in the state activity of the country, is the correlation dependence, also called "empirical dependence". Correlation dependence never puts the studied processes and phenomena in the same meaning (value). The study of variables (i.e. of processes and phenomena) is performed with the help of the correlation coefficient. The correlation coefficient describes the extent to which the two variables are linearly related. It is accepted that the correlation coefficient accepts values only in the interval [-1; 1], as the sign "+" or "-" indicates the direction of the relationship (dependence), and the value of the coefficient itself shows the size (magnitude) of this dependence (Golikov, 2003). Also, the obtained value should be interpreted as follows (Golikov, 2003): 0 <r <0.3 - weak correlation; 0.3 <r <0.5 - moderate correlation; 0.5 <r <0.7 - significant correlation; 0.7 <r <0.9 - large correlation; and if *r* is in the range from 0.9 to 1 there is a strong correlation between the two studied variables.

For the needs of the research we assume that the correlation coefficient between the variables X and Y for a given financial control sample is obtained by the formula (Figure 5).

Figure 5.

$$r = \frac{n\sum XY - \sum X \sum Y}{\sqrt{\left[n\sum X^2 - \left(\sum X\right)^2\right]\cdot\left[n\sum Y^2 - \left(\sum Y\right)^2\right]}}$$

Where:

X – the active control environment we study

Y – the passive control environment
n – the number of continuous control processes that can be realized under the influence of both the active and the passive control environment.

To illustrate the correlation between the active and passive control environment, we apply the following example: for the period from 01.01 to 31.01.2008, 12 inspections were performed by PFIA (i.e. 12 control processes were carried out in January) out of 496 inspections for the year. For the study of the control environments, with the help of the correlation analysis, we accept the following rule: the control object, which is examined by the respective control process in active control environment, has different significance in comparison with the process realized in passive control environment. In this way, we keep the rule of correlation dependence, namely that the studied phenomena and processes are not examined in the same meaning. The results of the correlation analysis are presented using Figure 6.

Figure 6. Correlation between active and passive control environment

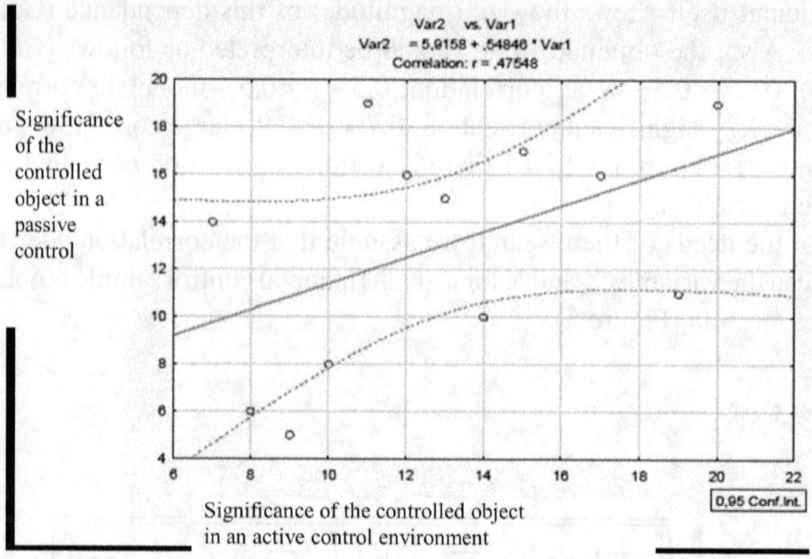

From the presented diagram 1, developed with the help of the software program “StatSoft”, it is established that in their interaction, the two control environments have a correlation coefficient of 0.47548 for the period from 01.01 to 30.01.2008. This means that there is a moderate correlation between the active and passive control environment. It should also be assumed that the control principles that the controller has applied in an active control environment to reveal the nature and characteristics of the controlled control object are applicable in the passive control environment, as the impact of both variables on the same control object is significantly moderate.

We believe that the most unfavourable situation is if, with the help of correlation analysis, it is established that the observed control variables are highly dependent, i.e. when the correlation coefficient is in the range of 0.9 to 1. When studying the correlation between the active control environment and the corrupt control environment, it is established that the correlation coefficient is 0.97980, and the correlation coefficient between the passive control environment compared to the corruption control environment is 0.82161. The correlation dependences are presented using the following diagrams.

From the data presented in Figures 7 and 8, we came to the following main conclusions:

Figure 7. Correlation between the active and the corruption control environment

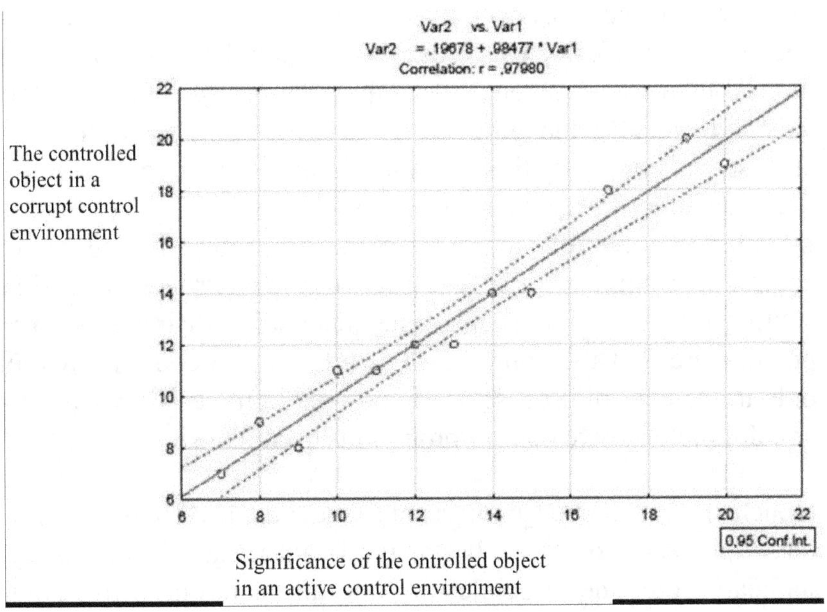

Figure 8. Correlation between passive and corrupt control environment

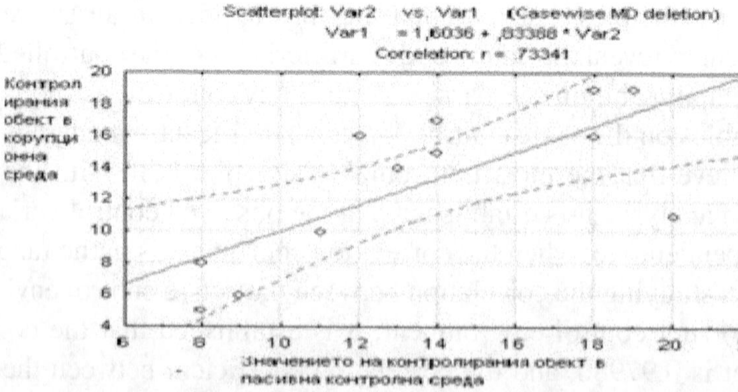

- The corruption factor strongly influences both the active and the passive control environment;
- The difference in the values of the correlation coefficients testifies to the different degree of dependence of the environment on the corruption factor. It turns out that this dependence is too strong in the active control environment, because the correlation coefficient is 0.97980, in contrast to the passive control environment, where the dependence coefficient is 0.73341. This proves once again the thesis that it is much more difficult to overcome the impact of the corruption factor in a very dynamically changing control environment; according to some analysts, it is precisely this dynamics in the environment itself that is a prerequisite for the existence of corruption (Wheatley, 2009);
- In order to solve all control problems in highly dependent corrupt control environments, it is necessary for the controller to use different control methods and means. The tendencies that are observed in practice are that the control bodies analyze the control environment only in the control process itself and only in the cases when a serious and difficult to solve control problem is established.

In conclusion, it can be summarized that the control environment where the control process takes place has a significant impact on the correctness and applicability of the principles of state internal control, including the principles of financial control. When the control environment is known, it will be much easier to determine from all legally regulated rules which will be the most vulnerable and easily violated during the control process. In this way, the principles predisposed to violation will be subject to monitoring not only by the participants in the control process, but also by third parties not participating in the control process, but interested in the proper and effective implementation of state internal control, including financial control.

REFERENCES

Alekseev, S. S. (1981). *The General Theory of Law: In 2 vols* (Vol. 2). Legal Literature.

Bakardzhieva, M. (2006). *Quantitative methods in management, Svishtov*. Tsenov Academic Publishing House.

Dinev, M. (1986). *Kontrol i regulirane na ikonomicheskite sistemi*. Profizdat.

Dochev, D. (1997). Izsledvane na operatsiite. Varna: Universitetsko izdatelstvo na IU

Fayol, H. (1937). The administrative theory in the state. In: L. Gulick & L. Urwick (Eds.). Papers on the science of administration. New York: Institute of Public Administration. Golikov, A. P. (2003). Эkonomiko-matematicheskoe modelirovanie mirohozyaystvennыh protsessov. Harykov: Harkovskiy natsionalynыy universitet im. V. N. Karazina.

Georgieva, P. I., & ... (1987). Mathematical-Statistical Methods in Technological Research. *Agricultural Science*, *XXV*(1).

James, R. (1951). Some aspects of a Governmental Audit. *The Accounting Review*, *26*(3).

Mladenov, M. (2009). Conflict Management. Alternative dispute resolution methods in the tax process. www.eprints.nbu.bg/408/ [seen on 24.05.2009]

Slavchev, Z. (2010b). *Appeal of revision act*. Nova Zvezda.

Stengers, I. (1994). (ed.). L'effet Whitehead. Paris: Vrin.

Chapter 6
Stages for Implementation of the Principles of Financial Control by the Public Financial Inspection Agency

ABSTRACT

The proposed structure and content of the report of findings is not based solely on the documentary findings regarding the committed violations found by the inspectors. In the proposal made by us regarding the amendment of the findings protocol, we believe that by indicating the degree of application of the principles in the control process, the inspector will be able to express his objective opinion about the way the inspection was conducted, not directly, but indirectly. In our opinion, the adoption of this new form of the protocol of findings, in order for it to be actually implemented, should be legally approved, imposing appropriate sanctions on inspectors in case of non-compliance.

INTRODUCTION

Each principle has its own specific features regarding the method of application. The application of the principle is determined by the control environment, by the powers of the control body, as well as by the goals and tasks set in the control process. The general requirements for compliance with the principles of financial control apply to all control bodies. For example, the application

DOI: 10.4018/978-1-6684-8883-6.ch006

of the principle of "legality" requires all inspectors to comply with the requirements of the law, as well as to prepare their findings on the basis of current regulations. The application of the principle of "objectivity" requires controllers to be impartial and also not to be subject to the conviction of others. Compliance with these principles, as well as with the principles of "efficiency" and "official start", requires not only adherence to the substantive side of the established control rules but also inspectors must follow the accepted control technology for the relevant control institution.

The phased application of the principles we propose in this part of the monograph is designed to address the shortcomings we have identified in the course of our observations on the final inspection reports. The development of the stages takes into account the negative results that the Prosecutor's Office of the Republic of Bulgaria reports on the activities of the Public Financial Inspection Agency (PFIA), and on the other hand, the proposed stages aim to improve the results of the financial inspections, which are also under OLAF surveillance. The purpose of the control stages thus proposed is to improve the quality of the application of the principles of financial control. We believe that with the help of the proposed stages of the application of the principles of financial control all shortcomings that PFIA allows in its control activity will be eliminated.

***The first stage* is the development of a control policy.** In fact, the control policy must also be a policy for the application of the principles of financial control. It should be adopted as an internal normative act for PFIA, with the respective structure and content, and it should emphasize the manner of application and observance of the principles of financial control. It should present the essence of the principles of financial control, which are regulated both in the Public Financial Inspection Act (PFIA), but also other control principles regulated in the internal acts of the Agency should be essentially characterised. We believe that the control policy of the Agency should be in accordance with the Code of Ethics for the behaviour of the control inspectors so that it does not contradict the ethical principles and norms. It should instruct inspectors in the control process not to waste material, financial or personal resources of PFIA. The control policy should be adopted as an internal regulatory framework that determines the manner in which inspections are carried out on the basis of the application of the principles of financial control. It must regulate in great detail the control actions of financial inspectors, as well as the control technology.

We believe the control policy should be jointly developed by the Ministry of Finance (MF) and PFIA and approved by an order issued by the Director of PFIA. The policy can be presented in separate parts. All of them should be interconnected and not in conflict. These parts can be:

1. General - the purpose of the policy and the control body implementing it should be presented here. Information should be provided on the stages of its adoption and approval. In these general provisions, information can be provided that the policy thus developed is a supplement to the Code of Ethics for Inspectors and it is not in violation of its norms. It should also contain information that the policy developed in this way does not contradict the normative acts of the country.
2. Justification of the principles of financial control - in this part of the policy, information can be provided on the nature, impact and development of the principles. It can also be specified which principles are accepted as basic and which as derivatives.
3. Detailed presentation of different control situations and the principles that should be applied to them by the financial inspector - we believe that the main control situations should be selectively described and thus the policy about the application of the principles of financial control will require in advance the exact principles that should be observed by the PFIA inspectors in a given control situation. The existence of such a legal prescription will subsequently be a prerequisite for the application of a methodology for assessing their application.

This element of the structure of the control policy can very easily be built by those in power. This can be done by taking into account all inspections carried out so far by PFIA. Those control processes and situations that have been repeated most often may be reflected in the developed policy. In this way, PFIA will have an established methodology at least for repetitive control processes, although the control object may be different. Table 1 presents the most common control situations and the principles that inspectors should follow in such situations.

We believe that the control situations presented in this way are the most common and repeatable, which is why they should be detailed in the control policy. The study was made on the basis of 387 financial inspections carried out for the period from 2011 to the first quarter of 2012. In the content of the table, the use of the word "inspection" is imposed by the fact that, according to the PFIA and the Rules for Implementation of the State Financial Inspection

Table 1. Control situations and principles to be followed

Control situation	Normative acts that should be taken into account by the controller	Control principles to be applied by the controller	The controller should in turn check whether the inspected object has complied with the following principles
Verification of legality regarding the observance of the regulations in the field of public procurement in construction	Public Procurement Act (PPA) Public Financial Inspection Act (PFIA) Accounting Act (AA)	Transparency, equality, non-discrimination, legality, objectivity, professionalism and confidentiality	Publicity, transparency, freedom and fair competition; equality and non-discrimination, current accrual, cautiousness, comparability between income and expenses, the priority of content over form, preservation, if possible, of the accounting policy from the previous reporting period, independence of the individual reporting periods and value relation between opening and closing balance, documentary justification
Verification of legality regarding the conduct of public procurement procedures in connection with the implementation of projects with EU money	Public Procurement Act; State Financial Inspection Act; Accounting Act	Transparency, equality, legality, objectivity, official start and confidentiality	Publicity, transparency, freedom and fair competition; equality and non-discrimination, current accrual, cautiousness, comparability between income and expenses, the priority of content over form, preservation, if possible, of the accounting policy from the previous reporting period, independence of the individual reporting periods and value relation between opening and closing balance, documentary justification
Verification of legality related to the execution of contracts	Law on Obligations and Contracts; Law on State Financial Inspection; Law on Public Procurement	Legality, objectivity, official start and confidentiality	Good faith
Verification of the legality of an open competition held	Public procurement law; Law on State Financial Inspection	Transparency, equality, non-discrimination, legality, objectivity, official start and confidentiality	Publicity, transparency, freedom and fair competition, equality and non-discrimination
Verification of legality related to compliance with budgetary and financial discipline in the provision of financing and reporting of spent budget funds	State Financial Inspection Law; Accountancy Act; Compliance with the requirements of accounting standards	Legality, objectivity, official start and confidentiality	Current accrual, cautiousness, comparability between income and expenses, priority of content over form, preservation of the accounting policy from the previous accounting period if possible, independence of individual accounting periods and value relationship between opening and closing balance, documentary justification
Verification of compliance with the requirements of Art. 8, para. 1 of the Law on Financial Management and Control in the Public Sector to submit to the Minister of Finance information on the functioning, adequacy, efficiency and effectiveness of financial management and control systems	Law on Financial Management and Control in the Public Sector; Law on State Financial Inspection	Legality, objectivity, official start and confidentiality, reliability, efficiency, effectiveness	Reliability and comprehensiveness of financial and operational information, economy, efficiency and effectiveness of activities, protection of assets and information
Verification of the implementation of the instructions and deadlines under Art. 18, para. 1, item 1, and para. 2 of the Public Financial Inspection Act	Public Financial Inspection Act	Legality, objectivity, official start and confidentiality	Legality, objectivity and confidentiality
Verification of legality related to funds received from donations, expenses incurred and their accounting report	Public Financial Inspection Law; Accountancy Act; Compliance with the requirements of accounting standards	Legality, objectivity, official start and confidentiality	Current accrual, cautiousness, comparability between income and expenses, a priority of content over form, preservation if possible of the accounting policy from the previous reporting period, independence of the separate accounting periods and value relationship between the opening and closing balance, documentary justification

continued on following page

Table 1. Continued

Control situation	Normative acts that should be taken into account by the controller	Control principles to be applied by the controller	The controller should in turn check whether the inspected object has complied with the following principles
Verification of the legality of the spent earmarked funds	Law on Financial Management and Control in the Public Sector; Law on Public Financial Inspection	Legality, objectivity, official start and confidentiality, reliability, efficiency, effectiveness	Reliability and comprehensiveness of financial and operational information, economy, efficiency and effectiveness of activities, protection of assets and information
Verification of the legality of the incurred expenses related to the acquisition of durable tangible assets	Law on Financial Management and Control in the Public Sector; Public Financial Inspection Law; Accountancy Act; Compliance with the requirements of accounting standards	Legality, objectivity, official start and confidentiality, reliability, efficiency, effectiveness	Reliability and comprehensiveness of financial and operational information, economy, efficiency and effectiveness of activities, protection of assets and information
Verification of the legality of performed administrative actions and transactions related to the management of land and buildings, municipal property and their accounting	Public Financial Inspection Law; Accountancy Act; Compliance with the requirements of accounting standards	Legality, objectivity, official start and confidentiality	Current accrual, cautiousness, comparability between income and expenses, a priority of content over form, preservation if possible of the accounting policy from the previous reporting period, independence of the separate accounting periods and value relationship between the opening and closing balance, documentary justification
Verification of the amount of financial assistance granted and receipt of remittances	Public Financial Inspection Law; Accountancy Act; Compliance with the requirements of accounting standards	Legality, objectivity, official start and confidentiality	Current accrual, cautiousness, comparability between income and expenses, a priority of content over form, preservation if possible of the accounting policy from the previous reporting period, independence of the separate accounting periods and value relationship between the opening and closing balance, documentary justification
Verification of legality related to compliance with the requirements of the Law on the State Budget of the Republic of Bulgaria for the relevant year regarding the introduction of a Single Account, as well as the instructions of the Ministry of Finance and the BNB for its implementation	Law on the state budget of the Republic of Bulgaria; Accountancy Act; Law on Public Financial Inspection	Legality, objectivity, official start and confidentiality	Current accrual, cautiousness, comparability between income and expenses, a priority of content over form, preservation if possible of the accounting policy from the previous reporting period, independence of the separate accounting periods and value relationship between the opening and closing balance, documentary justification
Verification of legality regarding the observance of order and budget discipline when providing funds from the budget of the municipality	Accountancy Act; Law on Public Financial Inspection	Legality, objectivity, official start and confidentiality	Current accrual, cautiousness, comparability between income and expenses, a priority of content over form, preservation if possible of the accounting policy from the previous reporting period, independence of the separate accounting periods and value relationship between the opening and closing balance, documentary justification
Verification of the legality of the collection, spending, storage and reporting of cash in the cash register	Law on Public Financial Inspection; Accountancy Act	Legality, objectivity, official start and confidentiality	Current accrual, cautiousness, comparability between income and expenses, a priority of content over form, preservation if possible of the accounting policy from the previous reporting period, independence of the separate accounting periods and value relationship between the opening and closing balance, documentary justification

Act, "inspection aims to check specific objects". In compliance with the requirements of the legislator, in the Instruction on the form, order, terms and movement of the documents and acts drawn up during the performance of financial inspections by the bodies of the Agency, developed by the Ministry of Finance and approved by the director of PFIA, the term "inspection" is used again. The Approved Instruction is not in conflict with the law, but on the other hand, this explains the fact why the term "inspection", and not "control", is present in the final inspection reports.

***The second stage* is the development of Regulations for organizational technology for carrying out financial inspections.** This Regulation should describe the sequence and manner of carrying out those basic inspections, which are presented in the Policy on the application of the principles of financial control. Therefore, it must be assessed whether the norms of conduct that are prescribed are fulfilled by the inspectors and, accordingly, it should be assessed whether the financial inspector will perform compliance with the principles themselves.

The Regulations should also describe the ways of requesting the necessary information from the examiner. Also, the ways of documentary justification of the established violations should be regulated. Accordingly, the established violations, as well as the documents that prove the committed irregularities and abuses, must be presented in great detail both in the findings protocols and in the final closing reports. At the moment, in the control practice of PFIA, given the information presented in the examined 2450 reports from the financial inspections carried out for the period from 2007 to 2011, the documentary justification of the discovered violations and abuses is not presented in detail and qualitatively. For example:

- In Report No. FI5SF-0045/14.07.2011 of PFIA on the financial inspection of the state-owned enterprise National Company "Railway Infrastructure" regarding the findings of the performed inspection and analysis of the enterprise's receivables and liabilities, only the amount of the relevant receivables and liabilities for the period from 2008 to 2010 was presented.

The amounts in dispute with the counterparties of the National Railway Infrastructure Company do not indicate which documents prove the corresponding claim and liability, and which documents the inspectors checked to claim that there were outstanding liabilities or uncovered claims. As proof of the accepted statement, we present part of the written opinion of the inspectors on the report, namely: "During the analysis of the receivables from customers and receivables from suppliers for advances provided in the total amount of BGN 47,558,849.00, it was found that of the indicated amount, receivables in the total amount of BGN 36,268,304.00 have a maturity of up to 3 months; receivables in the total amount of BGN 958,834.00 have a maturity of 3 to 6 months; receivables in the amount of BGN 10,331,711.00 are over 6 months old. During the inspection, it was found that of the uncollected receivables with an origination period of more than 6 months, the largest is the receivable from BDZ Holding EAD in the amount of BGN 7,959,135.40. The collection is in connection with an agreement between "Holding BDZ" EAD, the city of Sofia, and the National Railway Infrastructure Company for the repayment of obligations of "Holding BDZ" EAD to the National Railway Infrastructure Company (NRIC) in the amount of BGN 91,065,054.00, including infrastructure fees in the amount of 79,591,234.00 BGN, incurred as of 30.11.2007. During the analysis of the claim, it was found that according to Protocol No. PD-304/03.12.2007, the Minister of Transport, as an authority exercising the rights of the state, as the sole owner of the capital of "Holding BDZ" EAD, made a decision, which confirmed the agreement between "Holding BDZ" EAD and NRIC for the repayment of obligations of "Holding BDZ" EAD and NRIC that arose as of 30.11.2007, with the repayment being carried out by 30.06.2008 with a 10% reduction of the total amount of the obligation, not being subject to the use of the railway infrastructure - public state property managed by NRIC. The only documents that are mentioned in the receivables checked in this way are the outgoing letters to the Ministry of Transport, with which NRIC notified about the dispute regarding the amount of the amount subject to discounting between NRIC and "Holding BDZ" EAD.

From the information thus presented in this report, it can be assumed that the audit carried out by PFIA does not clarify whether there is really any kind of problem with the receivables from NRIC that have arisen in this way, apart from the fact that the corresponding receivable has not been repaid. Also, the inspection does not provide an answer to the following two more important questions, namely: is this expense legal and has the price of the service between the state companies - the operator "Holding BDZ" EAD and the infrastructure company NRIC - been correctly determined?

- In Report No. FI1BP0013 dated 18.10.2011 of the PFIA for a financial inspection of the "Multispecialty Hospital for Active Treatment - Oryahovo" Ltd (Oryahovo town, Oryahovo municipality, Vratsa region, 98 "Architekt Tsolov" street), a verification of the legality of the delivery of x-ray films and consumables during the period from

> 01.01.2005 to 31.12.2007, established the following: "During the same time period from 01.01.2005 to 31.12.2007, X-ray films, developers and fixatives were delivered to the "Multispecialty Hospital for Active Treatment - Oryahovo" Ltd - Oryahovo for BGN 21,186.14 at prices including value-added tax or BGN 17,655.12 without charges from suppliers on added value".

From the information presented about these supplies, without the inspectors specifying which documents they analyzed, they found that the total amount exceeded BGN 15,000 as of 06/04/2007 (BGN 15,484.02 without VAT), as of that date the manager of the hospital should have made a decision and assigned the collection of bids for the supplies in the periods after 04.06.2007.

We believe that it is not necessary to present more similar examples to prove the need for the adoption of an internal normative act regulating the technology of financial inspections. We believe that the proposal thus presented will improve the quality of financial inspections by requiring greater documentary justification of the control opinion. Otherwise, we believe that in the absence of such an internal regulatory act, the inspections will continue to be carried out according to the established practice, only ascertaining specific facts, without having them checked in depth.

The third stage **is the regulation of a system for evaluating the effectiveness of the control process** – we believe that this element is also an important part of the policy on the application of the principles of financial control. The effectiveness of the application of the principles can be represented as a ratio between the results that are obtained at the output of the control process and the expected results at the input of this process.

To determine the effectiveness of the control process, the following groups of indicators can be used:

- structural indicators related to the conditions in which the control process takes place, including: personnel qualification, software and hardware provision of the control process, some legal requirements regarding the way the control process is implemented;
- requirements for the way and organization of performing control activities - this refers to the correct implementation of the sequence of control stages through which the control process takes place. In addition, compliance with internal regulations regarding the form, order, terms and movement of documents and acts should be taken

into account when performing a financial inspection by the PFIA authorities;

- summarizing the results presented in the findings protocols regarding the level of implementation of each individual principle. We believe that these indicators can be obtained after introducing a **system of individual assessment on how to apply the principles of financial control.** This evaluation system should be presented in detail in the Policy for the implementation of the principles of financial control.

The individual evaluation system for the application of the principles of financial control is the main stage of the proposed methodology for the application of the principles of financial control. It must be very precisely and clearly regulated in the Control Policy. Here it can be said that self-control will be performed by the inspectors on the basis of this system.

In order to implement this system, we propose additional ascertainment elements related to the application of the principles of financial control to be included in the currently effective and defined protocols of findings of the PFIA inspectors. The format and content of the new report form of the protocols look like this:

Model 1. of Protocol of Findings of the State Financial Inspection Agency

PROTOCOL OF FINDINGS

Today, 20, in the city(town/village) of..., manucipality (*date*)

district ..., the undersigned... (*full name and position of the financial inspector*) from the State Financial Inspection Agency,

and... (*full name and position of the person whose activity is being inspected*) performed an inspection of ...(*the object is indicated - the specific activity that is being inspected*)

The inspection was performed in the presence of ...(*full name and position of the person from the inspected organisation*)

Foundings of the inspection: ...(*the facts are presented as they are at the moment, without making analyses, summaries, conclusions and legal qualifications*)

The following principles of financial control were applied during the inspection:

(*Check with „√“*)

Legality...Objectivity...Official start Confidentiality...Independence... Credibility Responsibility...Expediency...Efficiency Impartiality... Effectiveness Comprehensiveness

All stated principles are applied

Table 2. The degree of application of the principles of financial control is as follows

Principles	From 0% to 35%	From 35% to 60%	From 60% to100%
Legality			
Objectivity			
Official start			
Confidentiality			
Independence			
Credibility			
Responsibility			
Expediency			
Comprehensiveness			
Impartiality			
Effectiveness			
Efficiency			

Financial inspector: (*First name, last name*) Participant: (*First name, last name*) Present: (*First name, last name*)
(*Check with „√"*)

We believe that the proposed model of the protocol of findings can have more constructive elements related to the determination of the method of application of the principles of financial control. But we take into account the fact that, until now, in the control practice of PFIA, the principles that the inspectors applied are not mentioned in the protocols.

The proposed structure and content of the report of findings is not based solely on the documentary findings regarding the committed violations found by the inspectors. In the proposal made by us regarding the amendment of the findings protocol, we believe that by indicating the degree of application of the principles in the control process, the inspector will be able to express his objective opinion about the way the inspection was conducted, not directly, but indirectly. In our opinion, the adoption of this new form of the protocol of findings, in order for it to be actually implemented, should be legally approved, imposing appropriate sanctions on inspectors in case of non-compliance.

On the other hand, based on the information in the findings report, the final opinion will be presented in the final report of the inspection activity. Therefore, the proposed change will also reflect on the final report, as it should also contain information about the principles applied by the inspector.

This information, we believe, will be useful not only for the inspected object, but also for external users. In this way, each interested party can individually determine to what extent the information in the report is presented objectively and to what extent the controller has assumed the risk of inaccurate and/or incomplete presentation of information in the final reports.

We believe that regarding the way of applying the principles of financial control, the proposed system for individual assessment should not be bound by the requirements of Art. 76 of the Civil Servant Act, as its very purpose will be undermined. The system should give an idea of how the controller himself determines the relevant control situation, whether it is risky, whether he is under the pressure of corruption factors. If this system of individual evaluation is tied to giving an evaluation for the performance of his position, then the probability of a subjective indication of 100% full and effective application of the principles of financial control is very high. Job performance evaluation must be determined by other methods and means. Thus, we believe that the inspectors will retain their sovereignty and objectively present the control situation.

Although such an evaluation system regarding the application of the principles of financial control has not been implemented to date, the Agency's inspectors have nevertheless made efforts in the fight against corruption. These results are presented by the Research Center of the Management Monitoring Association and the Institute for Economic Policy as "reducing corruption risks and introducing good practices in the management of public procurement" (Pashev, 2013). The research carried out by Konstantin Pashev found that PFIA annually found a high relative share of contracts concluded without conducting a procedure when there was a basis for this: between 9% and 13% of the procedures carried out (Pashev, 2013). According to the research presented by the Management Monitoring Association and the Economic Policy Institute, it has been found that a relatively more common practice

Table 3. Relative share of non-conducted procedures established by PFIA for the period from 2003 to 2007г

	2003	2004	2005	2006	2007
Conducted	6096	5624	6399	2130	1529
Non-conducted	820	484	641	83	202
Share	13,5%	8,6%	10,0%	3,9%	13,2%

Source: **Pashev, K.** Reduction of corruption risks and introduction of good practices in public procurement management. Available at: www.epi-bg.org/dmdocuments/work-corruption, risk.May.pdf

is to circumvent the Public Procurement Act by artificially fragmenting the value of the contract in order to avoid the limits of the value thresholds. The remaining violations are related to the conduct of the procedure for awarding and executing the specific contracts (Pashev, 2013).

Taking into account everything stated so far regarding the presented exemplary methodology for the application of the principles of financial control by the Public Financial Inspection Agency, the following conclusions and recommendations can be made:

1. The incorrect and inaccurate application of the principles of financial control by any control institution, including PFIA, is not due to unclear regulation of their essence in the normative acts but is the result of the lack of an internally approved methodology regarding the manner of their application. Therefore, the main recommendation we make to the control authorities is to develop such a methodology.
2. The proposed stages for applying the principles of financial control are tailored to the specifics, goals and tasks of the control body. They are the basis for building a methodology for applying the principles of financial control. Each stage, namely: *control policy*, the development of *organizational technology for the conduct of each control inspection* and the implementation of a *system of individual evaluation on the way of applying the principles of financial control* can also be considered as a contribution of the development to the control practice. We are mindful of the fact that in order to account for the effectiveness and efficiency of the stages thus proposed, the following is needed:
    a. The way it is proposed, the presented sequence of organizational stages in the application of the principles of financial control should be reflected in the control practice as well;
    b. Once implemented, the final results that will be realized should be reported and a comparative analysis between the results of the control actions should be done before the approval of the stages and the results that will be established subsequently after the proposed stages have been consistently followed. In this way, we believe that the effectiveness of the proposed change in financial control technology will be reported.

REFERENCES

Pashev, K. (2013). Corruption in taxation. *Challenges to tax policy and administration*. CSD. https://www.csd.bg/fileSrc.php?id=1412

Chapter 7
Methodology for Studying the Principles of Financial Control

ABSTRACT

The methodology for researching the application of the principles of financial control is dependent on the established stages of their application. The methodology consists of approaches that express the established and predetermined research tasks and are closely related to them. Through the chosen methodology, in addition to examining the efficiency and effectiveness of the applied principles of financial control, the control activity of the inspectors will also be evaluated. Due to the innovative nature of the proposed research method, the authors believe that to determine its significance and efficacy, sufficiently large and qualitative empirical studies covering a ten-year study period are needed. For such research, a good database of control practices in the country is needed, and at the moment there is no such database. This further complicates research work using the method thus proposed.

INTRODUCTION

The methodology for researching the application of the principles of financial control is dependent on the established stages of their application. The methodology consists of approaches that express the established and predetermined research tasks and are closely related to them. Through the chosen methodology, in addition to examining the efficiency and effectiveness

DOI: 10.4018/978-1-6684-8883-6.ch007

of the applied principles of financial control, the control activity of the inspectors will also be evaluated.

The proposed methodology for researching the principles of financial control, which is based on the methodology for researching the impact of the regulatory impact of the PFIA and Regulations for the Implementation of the PFIA, will contribute to the clarification of a number of control problems. The regulatory impact actually represents a simultaneous impact of both the regulatory requirements and the rules of conduct that are regulated in the relevant act. The regulatory impact on the part of those in power is manifested in the control processes, and in these processes the effect of the normative acts themselves is also manifested. It is the duty of PFIA, after the entry into force of a normative act that affects the inspection activity of the Agency, to verify the results established by the amendment or adoption of the relevant act. In the event of inconsistencies between the regulated norms and principles in an amended or adopted new normative act with the requirements of a higher-level act, it is required, according to the Act on Normative Acts, to notify the body that is authorized to cancel or make the necessary corrections in the relevant act.

Regulatory Impact Assessment (RIA) was first introduced in the UK and was originally developed to assess policy in order to present the best policy decisions, as well as to assess the impact of different policy options regarding the costs, benefits and risks of proposed policies. Initially, the aim of regulatory impact assessment was to examine whether regulatory initiatives had an impact on business, charities and voluntary organizations (Paradis, 2006).

The methodology for determining the regulatory impact, adopted according to the implementation of the Phare project BG-0103.01 “Strategic planning and coordination”, the Consortium “Sema-Agrer-ENA” and the administration of the Council of Ministers of the Republic of Bulgaria, includes the following elements:

1. SWOT analysis (strengths, weaknesses, opportunities, threats)
2. Standard cost analysis
3. Cost-benefit analysis
4. Cost effectiveness analysis
5. Multiple criteria analysis
6. Risk analysis
7. Comparative analysis

SWOT analysis was first introduced by Kenneth Andrews at the 1963 Business Policy Conference at Harvard University. Initially, this analysis was based on scoring and structuring knowledge about the current state and future trends of an organization (Ehrmark, 2011).

The abbreviation SWOT, which K. Andrews introduced back in 1963, is still an acronym for the words Strengths, Weaknesses, Opportunities and Threats. Therefore, as a rule, the SWOT analysis can be applied to study the strengths and weaknesses of the regulatory impact, and also with its help can analyze the capabilities of the control body itself and the threats from the environment that exist and can have an impact on the activity of the controllers. We also believe that the development of this method for choosing a control strategy was influenced by the scientific achievements of Heinz Weihrich, who in 1982 in his article "The TOWS Matrix - A Tool for Situational Analysis" proposed the SWOT analysis to be presented in the form of a matrix. N. Weihrich assumes that this matrix is the conceptual framework of system analysis. With its help, it is easier to compare the external threats and opportunities related to the internal weaknesses and strengths of a given organization (Weihrich, 1982). According to the researcher, the SWOT matrix is built over a certain period of time, thus making it possible to track changes in the dynamically changing environment when building and choosing strategies.

Unfortunately, in our practice, the mechanisms and methods for forming a good database, on the basis of which a good empirical study on the regulatory impact of a specific normative act can be implemented, are not yet sufficiently well developed. According to data from the Institute of Market Economy, obtained on the basis of the implementation of projects financed by the United States Agency for International Development (USAID) and the German Marshall Fund of the United States (GMF), it is established that only ten analysis have been made for the country so far for regulatory impact in the following directions:

- Assessment of the impact of the Ordinance on the markets on the territory of the Capital Municipality
- Assessment of the impact of the Ordinance on the Management and Disposal of Municipal Sports Properties in the Capital Municipality
- Analysis of the impact of the Ordinance on movable objects, on advertising, informational and decorative-monumental elements and on advertising activity on the territory of the Capital Municipality;
- Analysis of the impact of the draft Law on Amendments and Supplements to the Law on Health and Safety at Work

- Analysis of the impact of the draft law on changes to the Law on Access to Public Information
- Assessment of the impact of the repeal of paragraph 6 of the Transitional and Final Provisions of the Law on People's Community Centers
- Assessment of the impact of policies and regulation on competition
- Analysis of the benefits and costs of legislative changes in the enforcement system
- Analysis of the impact of the Ordinance on Licensing of Tour Operators and Travel Agents
- The Officially Published Handbook of the Ministry of Justice on the Integrated System for Monitoring the Implementation of Legislation in the Judiciary.

Due to the lack of qualitative empirical research on the determination of the impact of regulatory impact of the normative acts that implement state financial control, and hence the lack of research on the determination of the impact of the applied principles of financial control in Bulgaria, in this part of the development, we present the final results achieved by various foreign specialists in the implementation of similar studies (Tables 1, 2, and 3).

Table 1. Zsombor Kovacsy's SWOT analysis on the regulatory impact of regulations in Hungary (Kovacsy, 2012)

Strengths	Weaknesses
1. A solid legal system 2. Regulated legislative procedures 3. Determining the quality of the relevant impact 4. Qualification training 5. Active participation of some ministries	1. 1. Unilateral positive law operating within legislative 2. 2. In the training of civil staff, more emphasis is placed on the implementation of the policy decision, but the grammatical and technical high-quality development of an analysis of consequences remains excluded 3. 3. Functions are defined by structure 4. 4. After the development of the relevant normative act, not enough time is left for analyses
Opportunities	**Threats**
1. 1. A better EU program to regulate national legislation 2. 2. Rational development of laws in order to achieve business and economic growth	1. 1. Politicians tend to abuse legal methods to justify the benefits of their intentions, and/or believe that legislation is a useless tool that inhibits rapid implementation of programs 2. 2. Medium and long-term legal requirements do not allow to put a number of government goals on the agenda

Thus presented SWOT analysis on the determination of the regulatory impact of the normative acts in Hungary summarizes in just a few points the strengths and weaknesses, opportunities and threats that influence the regulatory mechanisms. A similar study was carried out in Croatia for the period from 2007 to 2009. The results are presented in Table 2.

Table 2. SWOT analysis of the regulatory impact of legislation in Croatia for the period 2007 to 2009

Strengths	Weaknesses
1. 1. Active state policy to promote the business climate 2. 2. Systematic harmonization of national policy in the field of small and medium-sized enterprises with European practice 3. 3. A developing culture of participation and partnership in the field of regional development, as well as in the development of a top-down planning approach 4. 4. Examples of enterprising and successful initiatives for state development 5. 5. Improving government programs in the field of science, technology and innovation	1. 1. Lack of systematic and independent evaluations of the impact of implemented policies 2. 2. Insufficiently developed administrative capacity to control and absorb the funds provided by various EU funds 3. 3. Lack of quality cooperation between the various state administrations
Opportunities	**Threats**
1. 1. Full harmonization with EU regulatory requirements 2. 2. Full and quality use of available administrative capacity 3. 3. Development of a strong base of organized business consulting, which is essential for the existence of a single European market	1. 1. Pressure to cut government spending with a negative effect on strengthening administrative capacity 2. 2. Difficult coordination, taking into account the number of institutions involved in the management of operational programs and the negative impact on the timely implementation of projects

Table 3. A SWOT analysis of the regulatory impact of UK legislation in 2006

Strengths	Weaknesse
1. 1. Strong methodological support from departmental units related to relevant procedural steps, ensuring regular quality improvement 2. During the control processes, the impact assessment is revisited iteratively and continuously to allow corrections in emerging goals or questions	1. The three types of impact assessments (initial, partial and final) are accepted as a series of procedural steps but do not materialize into concrete results or reports 2. Apart from the negative list (which allows some policy proposals to be excluded, depending on their nature), there is no formal defensive phase
Opportunities	**Threats**
1. Strong procedural embedding in the determination process of the control policy 2. Policy support in assessing the application of control policy and to support the development of inter-agency capacity building	1. A continuous and cumulative process from start to finish gives potentially much flexibility and depth to impact assessment 2. Introduction of negotiation and divergence of the adequacy between the original objectives and the achieved results 3. The weight of the structure and obligation of all policy proposals, on the basis of which the impact assessment is carried out, is the main prerequisite for simplifying the way the impact assessment is carried out

In addition to the results of the SWOT analysis on the regulatory impact of the regulatory acts in Croatia and Hungary, we present another example - from Great Britain, which also carried out a similar study (Paradis, 2006).

Although only three SWOT analyzes are presented to determine the regulatory impact of legislation in Croatia, Hungary and the UK, the following conclusions can be drawn from them:

1. The studies thus presented regarding the assessment of the impact of the normative acts that are applied in the relevant EU member countries are part of the fulfillment of the requirements of the Good Regulation Action Plan of the European Commission COM(2002)278.
2. The regulatory impact of the relevant normative acts cannot be realized without the direct influence of financial control by the state authorities.
3. The assessment represents the value expression of all processes and phenomena, on the basis of which the relevant legal acts have influenced public behavior. On the other hand, the assessment itself also provides information on the quality of the implemented control processes, and hence on the quality of application of the principles of financial control.
4. SWOT analysis presents the strengths and weaknesses, opportunities and threats of the regulatory impact. Despite the foreign practice and the results found based on the analysis, Bulgaria still lacks such a comprehensive study. We accept that the main prerequisites for this are the presence of a number of unexplained questions in our practice, namely: who should carry out this research; the lack of a database, as well as the painful question in recent years regarding the financial security of such research.
5. In order to determine the final result of the application of the principles of financial control, it is necessary: to analyze the standard costs; analyze the costs and benefits of the implemented control activity; analyze the effectiveness of control costs; analyze the control risk and to implement a comparative analysis between the assumed control risk, the effectiveness of the realized control costs and benefits.

Standard cost analysis (SCA) aims to determine the administrative burdens imposed on businesses by a given act. It is a quantitative methodology that can be applied in all countries and at different levels. The analysis can be used to measure a single law, selected areas of legislation or to carry out a baseline measurement of legislation across the country. Moreover, standard cost analysis is also suitable for measuring simplification proposals as well as the administrative consequences of a new legislative proposal.

With the help of this analysis, steps are taken to reduce the administrative burden. This is partly achieved by simplifying duties to comply with governments' regulatory requirements and partly by exploring options to remove them altogether (Weigel, 2012).

According to foreign practice data, for example in Australia, in order to determine the amount of expenses that the business generates continuously, complying with the specific normative acts, there are experts grouped in the relevant teams to each ministry, and their task is to collect data and establish the amount of the expenses the business incurs (Weigel, 2012). When applying this method, specialists have long come to the conclusion that it is necessary to distinguish between the volume of mandatory information that the business must provide to the relevant administrations. According to specialists, the logic for the division of information into voluminous, medium and insignificant is purely economic.

According to data from the analysis of standard costs in Australia, the voluminous obligations of businesses to provide information amount to 90% of the administrative burden, with 7.5% and 2.5% remaining for medium and minor information provided respectively (Weigel, 2012).

According to various American specialists, as far as the rules that will be measured using the standard cost analysis are concerned, it is necessary to distinguish between the two types of existing regulations that define mandatory and voluntary rules. Under mandatory rules, all costs incurred by the business in complying with them must be measured by applying standard cost analysis. Voluntary information requirements include the implementation of various environmental improvement schemes and some types of statistical information.

It is possible to distinguish between voluntary rules that are considered necessary in relation to the market. Voluntary rules need to be followed where they are relevant to the majority of businesses concerned, for example, requirements regarding applications for agricultural subsidies. Thus, while some rules may be voluntary in theory, in practice they often are not, such as in cases where a company wants to compete and/or enter the market through public procurement.

Although the analysis of standard costs is regulated in the Manual for the integrated monitoring system for the implementation of legislation in the field of the judicial system, it appears that even in the judicial system the analysis as a means of control is not applied qualitatively. From the point of view of PFIA, taking into account the example of the judiciary, we believe that it is also appropriate to introduce an Integrated Monitoring System for the implementation of legislation in the field of financial discipline and control over public procurement. We believe that with the help of such a system, many of the weaknesses in the control activity of the Agency will be identified. It is also essential to build a proper information system in each ministry, including the Ministry of Finance, so that it can be determined exactly what expenses are incurred by the executive and the judiciary for the implementation of the relevant normative acts, observing the principles regulated therein.

The next approach that we believe can be applied to determine the impact of the two main legal acts applied by PFIA, namely the State Financial Inspection Act and the Regulations for the Implementation of the PFIA, is ***an analysis of the realized control costs and the benefits of the control process***. Using cost-benefit analysis, governments assess the desirability of a given legislative intervention. The impact of the normative acts on the controlled objects is carried out with the help of the application and observance of the principles regulated in the relevant acts. If the impact of the normative act on the controlled object is determined, the influence and impact that the principles have on this object will also be determined indirectly.

The costs and benefits of an impact are assessed in terms of stakeholders' willingness to pay for them (benefits) or willingness to pay to avoid them (costs). The cost-benefit analysis process involves weighing the total expected costs against the total expected benefits of one or more activities to select the best or most profitable option. A measure is considered justified if it results in net benefits*.

In order to analyze the control costs and benefits, it should be taken into account that the activities of the realized financial inspections of PFIA are financed under the Program "Protection of Public Financial Interests" under the

Table 4. Expenditures under the "Protection of Public Financial Interests" Program

Program costs	Sum
I. Total Departmental Expenses	**7 351 500**
Part of them for:	
• staff	6 457 040
• maintenance	814 460
• capital expenditure	80 000
II. Administered budget expenditure paragraphs	**0**
III. Total expences (I + II)	**7 351 500**

"Sustainable and Transparent Public Finances" policy from a subsidy through the budget of the Ministry of Finance and from own revenues, according to the Law on the State Budget of the Republic of Bulgaria for the relevant year.

According to data from the Ministry of Finance, the following expenses are foreseen in the 2012 budget under the "Protection of Public Financial Interests" Program:

The "Protection of Public Financial Interests" program (Program 2) is the second of the two programs under the "Sustainable and Transparent Public Finances" Policy, formulated since 2007 in the budget in program format of the Ministry of Finance.

The objectives of Program 2 are the protection of public financial interests through:

- good financial management of public funds by strengthening managerial responsibility, building adequate and efficient systems for financial management and control and independent internal audit
- assessment of the financial management and control systems of the bodies involved in the absorption of funds from the European Union and obtaining sufficient assurance of their adequacy, reliability, effectiveness and efficiency
- subsequent financial inspections for compliance with the normative acts governing budgetary and financial-economic activity
- implementation of the procedural representation of the Ministry of Finance and of the state represented by the Minister of Finance, in the cases provided for by law in established court, arbitration and other proceedings
- prevention and fight against corruption

The results of the implementation of the "Protection of Public Financial Interests" Program, and hence the possibility of making a comparative analysis between the realized costs and revenues, can be established from the Auditor's Report No. 0300001610 of the Audit Chamber on the audit carried out in the Ministry of Finance for the period from 01.01.2008 to 30.06.2010. During the audited period, the "Protection of Public Financial Interests" Program includes activities performed by the following structural units of the Ministry of Finance: the Directorates "Internal Control", "National Fund", "State Legal Consultancy", "Finances of the Real Sector", "External Finances" " and "Audit of European Union Funds", transformed on 01.01.2009 into the

Executive Agency “Audit of European Union Funds”, as well as the Public Financial Inspection Agency (PFIA).

According to the data of the Audit Chamber, the expenses under the Program for the period from 01.01.2008 to 06.30.2010 are as follows:

From the data thus presented in Table 5, it is established that the costs, which are legally provided for the implementation of the Program, are relatively more than the actually spent and reported. The data from the Audit Chamber are summarized and based on them it is not possible to determine how real the expenses of the following are: PFIA, the Directorates “Internal Control”, “National Fund”, “State Legal Consultancy”, “Finances of the Real Sector”, “External Finances” ” and “Audit of European Union Funds”, transformed on 01.01.2009 into the Executive Agency “Audit of European Union Funds”. This fact once again proves the need for the competent control authorities to clearly differentiate the available information and for its accurate presentation in various reports external to users and reports by individual business units. Due to the impossibility of analyzing in more detail the information presented in Audit Report No. 0300001610 of 2010, the emphasis is placed on the information presented in Audit Report No. 0500001410 of the Audit Chamber on the audit of the activities of the State Financial Inspection Agency for the period of 01.01. 2008 to 30.06.2010.

Table 5. Costs under the implemented Program “Protection of Public Financial Interests” for the period from 01.01.2008 to 06.30.2010

Year	Act (BGN in thousands)	Detailed plan (BGN in thousands)	Report (BGN in thousands)	% (report/detailed plan)
2008	22 151,7	21 171,6	10 441,2	49
2009	25 352,0	27 027,2	10 698,7	40
2010 (first half of the year)	23 362,7	23 908,1	6 240,3	26

Source: Audit report No. 0300001610 on an audit of the “Protection of Public Financial Interests” Program in the Ministry of Finance for the period from 01.01.2008 to 06.30.201

According to the data from the report of the Audit Chamber, the amount of subsidies granted and absorbed for 2008, 2009 and the first half of 2010 is BGN 3,313, BGN 3,293, and BGN 1,769 respectively.

According to the data of the Audit Chamber as of 30.06.2010, the confirmed number of financial inspectors in PFIA is “117 full-time employees, of which 113 full-time employees are employed. 106 financial inspectors carry out

PFIA financial inspections, and the remaining 7 inspectors carry out the activities of reporting, analysis and taking follow-up measures, methodology and control of the inspection activity".

Regarding the expenses spent by the Agency in the implementation of the goals and tasks defined by the law, the structure and functions of PFIA should be taken into account, as well as the organization of the activity of the financial inspections. According to Art. 6, para. 2 of the PFIA, the structure, composition and organization of work of the Agency are determined by organizational regulations adopted by the Council of Ministers. It is also determined, according to the PFIA, that the Secretary-General shall carry out the administrative management of the Agency by coordinating and controlling the administrative units. This requirement of the law, according to the control carried out by the Audit Chamber for the period from 01.01.2008 to 06.30.2010, presented in Report No. 0500001410, was not complied with. According to the opinion expressed in the aforementioned Report of the Audit Chamber, the state of the Agency's administrative activity is reflected in the annual reports on the results of the activity. This can be taken as further evidence in this study that there are still a number of problems in the overall control system of the country. Control problems and unsolved problems do not relate only to the activity of PFIA, they are a consequence and result of non-compliance with specific established rules of conduct by higher-ranking persons and bodies in the hierarchical structure of the state.

According to Art. 3 of the PFIA Regulations for application, the Agency is structured in a general and specialized administration, and the structural subdivisions of the administrative units are determined by an order of the director of the Agency on the proposal of the directors of directorates. The general administration is organized in the Directorate "Financial and Economic Activities and Human Resources Management" and in the Directorate "Information Technologies and Communication", and the specialized administration is in two directorates: "Organization and Implementation of Inspection Activities" and "Legal and Methodological Insurance of the Inspection Activity". By 2009, that is before the change of the PFIA Regulations for Application, there were a total of three directorates at the Agency, namely: "Organization and Execution of the Inspection Activity", "Internal Financial Inspection" and "Legal and Methodological Insurance of the Inspection Activity". According to the Ministry of Finance, the main reason for the reduction of directorates is the reduction of administrative costs. Whether this step to reduce administrative costs was the right one, we believe, remains to be considered. At this stage, we can only welcome this decision, so much so that the objects that were under the scope of the Internal Financial Inspection Directorate are now subject to financial inspection on a general basis.

Table 6. Expenditures for wages and salaries (in BGN) of the personnel employed under employment and official relations with the Ministry of Finance for the period from 2007 to 2011

Expenditures for wages and salaries of the personnel employed under employment and official relations with the Ministry of Finance	2007 in BGN	2008 in BGN	2009 in BGN	2010 in BGN	2011 in BGN
Salaries and remuneration of the personnel employed under labor relations	13 301 214	14 755 662	15 043 021	17 387 310	18 453 929
Salaries and remuneration of staff employed under official legal relations	78 771 462	79 434 647	82 011 733	85 522 846	88 344 771
Salaries of staff in the political office	95 457	98 653	110 612	103 154	121 332
Additional material incentives and other additional remunerations	33 501 273	40 727 950	50 043 073	56 863 330	55 085 865

Source: Annual financial statements of the Ministry of Finance for the period from 2007 to 2011 – www.minfin.bg

Table 7. Breakdown of information regarding additional material incentives and other additional remunerations to the Ministry of Finance (in BGN) for the period from 2007 to 2011

Breakdown of information regarding additional material incentives and other additional remunerations	2007	2008	2009	2010	2011
Ministry of Finance	2 663 187	2 807 469	3 531 222	5 348 845	5 585 113
NRA	26 157 231	32 248 384	38 466 721	41 347 561	43 386 030
State Gambling Commission	181 872	299 177	391 017	461 289	461 324
PFIA	671 936	707 328	833 114	1 006 250 л	961 782
Association for Economic Analysis and Forecasting	86 296	116 962	188 661	209 298	221 357
Executive Agency "Audit of European Union Funds"	87 440	187 331	211 087	235 520	255 668
Customs Agency	3 653 311	4 361 299	6 421 251	8 254 567	4 214 591

Source: Annual financial statements of the Ministry of Finance for the period from 2007 to 2011

In order to evaluate the effectiveness of the financial inspections carried out in relation to the total number of inspectors of PFIA, it is necessary to make a comparison between the expenses, that the state incurs for maintaining the control activities and functions of PFIA, and the benefits received. For this purpose, we use the officially published data in the annual financial statements of the Ministry of Finance for the period from 2007 to 2011:

We analyze the benefits from the point of view of the revenues received for the benefit of the state with the help of the information presented in Table 6 and 7.

From the data thus presented in Tables 5, 6 and 7, it is seen that the revenues that PFIA receives for the respective calendar years barely cover their determined additional material incentives for the respective year. These data once again confirm our thesis that serious reforms are needed in PFIA's control technology. In addition to quality and accurate application of the specified rules of conduct by inspectors, the Agency must ensure full and effective workload of inspectors. According to data from PFIA for 2010, only 65% of the designated effective working time fund of inspectors was allocated to the implementation of financial inspections. Also again, according to PFIA data presented in Figure 1, the average daily expenditure by departments for the 357 financial inspections completed in 2010 ranged from 29 to 67 days.

Table 8. The number of established violations under the PFIA of guilty officials, as well as of persons who work under civil contracts for management and control, for the period from 2008 to 2011

Number of detected violations and enforcement of administrative penalties decrees according to the requirements of art. 32 of the PFIA	For a violation of a normative act regulating budgetary, financial-economic or reporting activities, if no penalty is provided for in the relevant normative act, the fine is from BGN 200 to BGN 1,000.	For not providing financial inspectors with access to the office premises and to the documentation - the fine is from 200 up to BGN 1000	For failure to submit documents, certified copies of documents, information, references, declarations on bank accounts and written reports - the fine is from BGN 200 to BGN 300.	For presenting inaccurate information, references, declarations, documents and certified copies of documents - the fine is from 200 up to BGN 400	For other actions or inaction, apart from the cases under items 2 - 4, which hinder the financial inspectors in the performance of their powers - the fine is from BGN 200 to BGN 1,000.	For failure to comply with the instructions under Art. 18, para. 1, item 1 – the fine is from 200 to 1000 BGN.	For non-compliance with the deadline pointed out in Art. 18, para. 2 – the fine is from BGN 100 to BGN 500.
2011	356	0	1	4	0	5	7
2010	437	1	0	1	1	4	3
2009	482	3	2	2	1	3	4
2008	359	4	0	0	3	2	1

Source: Annual reports on the activity of PFIA for the period from 2008 to 2011

Table 9. Received income from established violations under the PFIA of guilty officials, as well as of persons who work under civil contracts for management and control, for the period from 2008 to 2011

	Fines	Property sanction	Total
2011	1 570 900	823 800	2 394 700
2010	892 500	486 200	1 378 700
2009	751 343	291 107	1 042 450
2008	685 124	341 811	1 026 935

Source: Annual reports on the activity of PFIA for the period from 2008 to 2011

Figure 1. Average daily expenditure by department for the 357 financial inspections completed in 2010

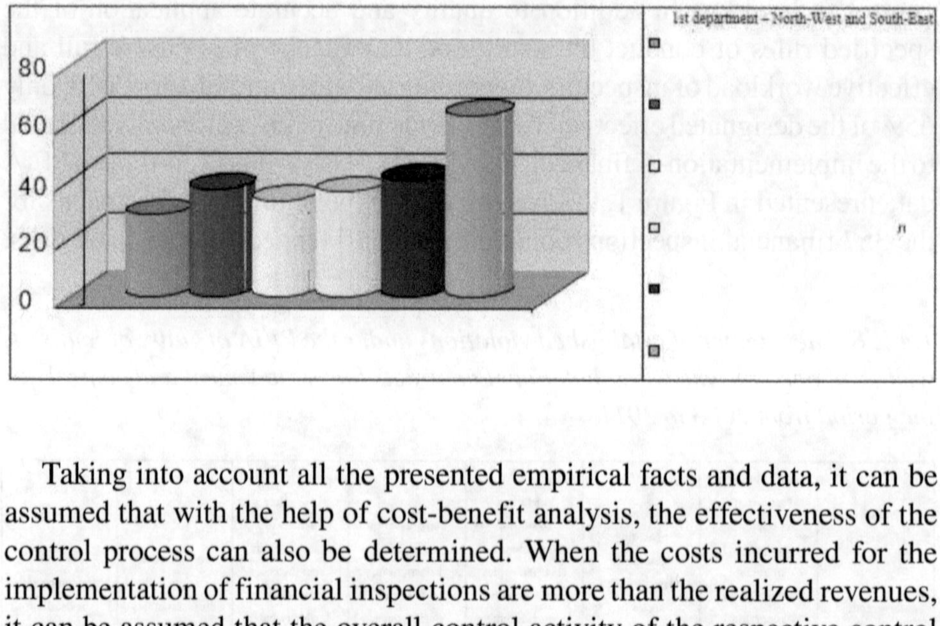

Taking into account all the presented empirical facts and data, it can be assumed that with the help of cost-benefit analysis, the effectiveness of the control process can also be determined. When the costs incurred for the implementation of financial inspections are more than the realized revenues, it can be assumed that the overall control activity of the respective control authority is ineffective. Conversely, if the realized benefits (including revenues) are greater than the costs, then we assume that the control process is effective. Effectiveness can be taken as an estimate of the effect exerted on the controlled object (Drysdale, 2010). But with regard to the control body itself, how effective or ineffective it is, the performance indicator obtained after deducting the costs of its administrative maintenance from the revenues that are realized must be taken into account.

Figure 2. Distribution of "effective fund working time" days used by the financial inspectors in PFIA in 2010

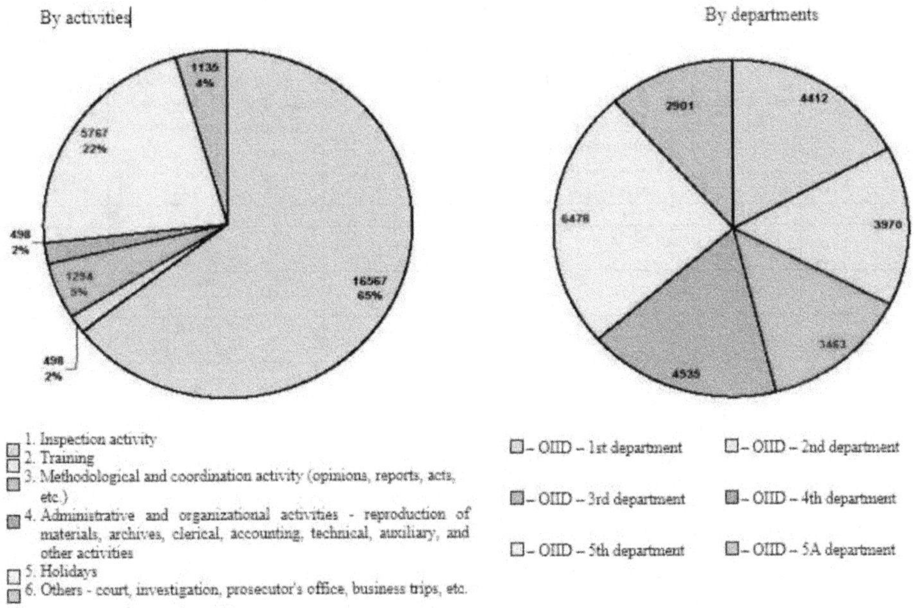

The ratio between the costs realized by the Agency and the benefits achieved is also subject to monitoring by the Audit Office. In audit report No. 0500001410 for an audit of the activities of the State Financial Inspection Agency for the period from 01.01.2008 to 06.30.2010, the information from the acts for establishing administrative violations was taken into account and sample indicators were formed that additionally evaluate part of the results of the Agency's activity (see Table10).

Therefore, in order to determine the usefulness of PFIA's activity, the auditors of the Audit Chamber have formulated the following sample indicators:

1. First sample indicator: the ratio between the number of penal decrees entered into force to the total number of penal decrees, which are acts of the administrative sanctioning body (the director of the Agency). For the relevant period (2008, 2009 and half of 2010) these ratios are: 65%, 73% and 68%.

   These are results of the Agency's activity, from which fines, sanctions and penalties are collected, whether voluntarily or forcibly. For 2008 and 2009, violations of the budgetary, financial and economic disciplines

Table 10. Information on the acts drawn up to establish administrative violations for the period from 2008 to 2010

Year	Number of acts	Acts of an administrative penal authority			Number of penal decrees entered into force	Court acts			Number of voluntarily paid penalty decrees	Compulsory collection of penal decrees by competent authorities (in BGN)
		Number of Penal decrees	Number of RP	Number of letters under Art. 28 of the Law on Administrative Violations and Penalties		Number of decisions on confirmation of penal decrees	Number of decisions on annulment of penal decrees	Number of acts pending in court		
	1	2	3	4	5	6	7	8	9	10
2008	2179	1185	40	945	766	43	65	354	306 938 BGN after 220 penal decrees	25 257 BGN afrer 309 letters
2009	2222	1415	33	829	1033	101	147	184	417 405 BGN after 346 penal decrees	65 329 BGN after 490 letters
2010	1368	394	4	218	269	17	19	106	68 544 BGN after 177 penal decrees	164 letters

were established in the amount of BGN 458,425; from them, revenues in the amount of BGN 815 000 were realized, which is 0.18%. The main conclusion that the auditors draw on the basis of the established data from the analysis is that significant human and financial resources are spent on drawing up acts to establish administrative violations, and small amounts of income are realized from them.

2. Second sample indicator: the ratio between the number of Acts of Penalty Decrees not closed in court to the number appealed in court. For the period they are 77%, 43% and 75%. These ratios indicate a high percentage of penal decrees on which the court does not issue a decision at the time of their formation. Thus, the evaluation of the results becomes unrealistic at the time of its reporting.
3. Third sample indicator: the ratio between the number of letters under Art. 28 of the Law on Administrative Penalties and Violations to the number of Acts for established administrative violations. They are 43%, 37% and 16% and show how many of the acts drawn up to establish administrative violations by the inspectors are determined by the administrative penal authority as unimportant cases and end with notification letters to the offenders. These results of the Agency's activity do not bring real financial means, but they have a disciplinary effect on the offenders, who will be sanctioned if they commit the same offense again. Based on the data presented in this way, the auditors of the Court of Audit found that, regardless of the high percentage of acts drawn up, defined as minor cases of violations, it is clear that a lot of human and financial resources of the Agency are being spent.

Thus, the presented method reveals the effectiveness of the control body, but not the problems regarding the way of applying the control principles. We believe that the application of the ***multiple criteria analysis*** method will provide greater clarity regarding the quality of the control process. If the control process is in the range of 100% to 50% detectability of committed violations and abuses, it can be assumed that the implemented control process is qualitative. If the discoverability of committed violations and abuses is in the interval from 50% to 25%, then it should be assumed that the level of the control process is average. But if the detection of violations and abuses is in the range of 25% to 0%, then it is assumed that the control process is of poor quality (Wilson, 1975). Based on the scale presented in this way, we believe that the method of applying the principles of financial control can be easily determined accordingly. In the high-quality control process, the qualitative application of the principles of financial control will be indisputable. In the control process, the quality of which is determined to be average, accordingly, not a complete, but a partial deviation from the intended rules of conduct will be observed. In the case of low-quality control processes, there is a lack of quality application of the principles of financial control.

The analysis by multiple criteria, according to the EC guidelines on determining the normative impact, includes:

1. Identifying the goal and the options for achieving it
2. Setting up criteria that will be used to compare options (these criteria should be measurable, at least from a qualitative point of view)
3. Highlighting each criterion to reveal its relative importance in relation to the decision to use, for example, preparatory techniques, ethical principles, technical grounds or interactive procedures with the competent authorities
4. Ranking how each option meets the criteria (the ranking should match the base scenario)
5. Ranking the options by combining their respective weight and rating
6. Performing a sensitivity analysis to check the reliability of the rankings

In fact, the analysis by multiple criteria is the so-called SWOT analysis. With its help, the strengths and weaknesses are established, as well as the opportunities and threats in the implementation of a specific regulatory act. Above in the study, the results of the regulatory impact in Hungary, Croatia and Great Britain were presented. We will not dwell again on the established facts and results of regulatory impact in these countries. Here we will only point out again the Western practice that in order to implement the SWOT analysis itself, it is necessary to carry it out by a higher authority. We propose here this analytical method to be carried out by the Ministry of Finance. We believe that it is within the powers of this ministry to analyze the normative acts that affect the regulatory impact of the executive branch.

In recent years, the Ministry of Finance (MOF), based on the Program "Administrative Capacity", 2007-2013, has implemented various SWOT analyses, namely: SWOT analysis of the state of public administration, SWOT analysis of the structure of civil society, and also a SWOT analysis to develop and validate a risk management strategy. Despite the efforts of the Ministry of Finance to establish the SWOT analysis as one of the main methods for establishing accurate facts and results, there is still a lack of organizational principles for the implementation of analysis according to various multiple criteria for determining the regulatory impact of the normative acts of the executive power. We believe that the introduction of this method will contribute to determining the influence and impact of the PFIA and the PFIA regulations for application on the controlled objects. From the point of view of tax control, we believe that this method will also have a positive effect since the exact influence and impact of the most important tax laws will be determined: VAT Law, Corporate Income Tax Law, Personal Income Tax Law and etc. The method will also contribute to a more accurate determination of the weaknesses of already established tax laws and the possibilities for their improvement.

Risk management as a method for determining the regulatory impact, and hence for determining the impact of the rules regulated in the specific legal act, is a basic requirement of the EU for the country. This method assesses the risk of an adverse event occurring and the possible consequences for individuals and society should it occur. Risk analysis is a technique for identifying and evaluating factors that could threaten the success of a regulatory act. This technique also helps to define preventive measures to reduce the likelihood of these factors occurring and to find countermeasures to successfully deal with these obstacles when they occur to avoid the possible negative impact on the implementation, for example, of new legislation.

The study of the risk from the point of view of the application of the normative act itself in the control process aims, on the one hand, to determine the possible factors that have an impact on the correct application and compliance with the legally established norm, and, on the other hand, to define the safety measures as a general rule for making a final control decision (Nedyalkova, 2010). According to a study by the Organization for Economic Co-operation and Development, one of the precautionary measures to reduce the risk of incorrect application of a specific legal act is to apply the precautionary principle. According to this principle, it is necessary to use the available resources very rationally and efficiently, so as to reduce the known and large risks. The application of the principle itself also realizes relevant costs, which must be considered as part of the control impact costs. The rational distribution of resources and the consistency in the development of security policies require identifying what the risks are in the control process itself. The application of the precautionary principle, which from a practical point of view is occasion-specific, is more than once a response to political pressure. Different priorities and compromise coordination of regulatory policies are often violated on its basis. It can be assumed that the precautionary principle in our control practice is still an idea that has yet to be established until it reaches a decision rule. Indeed, despite its application in Western practice, there are still logical reasons for its inherent ambiguity.

The precautionary principle (Vorsorge Prinzip) originated from German control practice and was used in Germany for the first time in 1980. Based on it, a number of important changes in environmental legislation have been justified (Rehbinder, 1991). The German approach is adopted in the legislation of various countries, and the principle is mentioned also in the Treaty establishing the European Community (EC Treaty, 1997).

From a risk management perspective, "the normal state of affairs is neither scientific certainty nor total ignorance. For this reason, a sound decision-making principle is one that uses all available information, weighted by its reliability, in terms of subjective probabilities, rather than prioritizing any particular risk" (OECD, 2012).

Different regulatory methods can be used to manage risks. These include: self-regulation, incentives, technical and economic methods (Baldwin, 2012). According to various specialists, the use of the relevant method is not according to what the risk is, but depending on the initial attitudes of the supervisors, whether they accept that risks can be identified, assessed and predicted, or whether they accept that risks must be negotiated and constructed (Baldwin, 2012).

The risk management of the regulatory impacts by the control authorities, observing the principles of financial control, can be carried out with the help of the so-called an integrative approach to risk management. The integrative approach helps to overcome a number of shortcomings in traditional approaches to risk management, as integrative risk management considers risks through different levels in the control process, covering strategies and tactics for the implementation of the relevant regulatory act. This approach examines how risk management has been extended to give strategic advantage to the principles of financial control while preserving its use as a tactical tool (Marden, 2012).

Taking into account the proposed methods for researching the application of the principles of financial control based on the regulatory impact of the control normative acts: the PFIA, the PFIA regulations for application and the internal regulations of the Agency, the following main conclusions can be drawn:

1. The study of the application of the principles of financial control is a complex process due to the fact that the principles actually represent a qualitative regularity that should be observed by the relevant control authority. The presented approaches are a proposal, which, of course, with a deeper research analysis will form a final and more accurate result.
2. Due to the innovative nature of the proposed research method, we believe that to determine its significance and efficacy, sufficiently large and qualitative empirical studies covering over a ten-year study period are needed. For such research, a good database of control practices in the country is needed, and at the moment there is no such database. This further complicates research work using the method thus proposed.
3. The presented data from the foreign practice of the application of each approach of the method is evidence of the advanced development of the analysis as a means of making final decisions, referring not only to the regulatory impact of a specific regulatory act, but also to the application of the principles of financial control.

REFERENCES

Baldwin, R. (2012). *Risk Regulation, Management and Compliance*. Bristol Inquiry. http://www.bristol-inquiry.org.uk

Drysdale, Al. (2010). *The Financial Controller: The Things the Academics Don't Teach You*. Management Books 2000, Ltd.

Ehrmark, E. N. (2011). Model evaluation of strategic alternatives based on SWOT-analysis. *Rusnauka*. http://www.rusnauka.com/31_PRNT_2010/ Economics/ 74034. doc.htm

Marden, E. (2003). Risk and Regulation: U.S. Regulatory Policy, 44 B.C.L. Rev. 733. http://lawdigitalcommons.bc.edu/bclr/vol44/iss3/2

Nedyalkova, P. (2010). Selection and applicability of financial control rate in the control process. *Trakia Journal of Sciences*, (8), 1–10.

OECD. (2012). *Risk and regulatory policy.* OECD Reviews of Regulatory Reform.

Paredis, F. (2006). *Methodology and Feasibility of Sustainability Impact Assessment.* Academia.

Treaty, E. C. (1997). Treaties of the European Union. *Wikipedia.* https://en.wikipedia. org/wiki/Treaties_of_the_European_Union

Weigel, W. (2009). *The Standard Cost Model A Critical Appraisal.* Center for the Study of Public Law and Economics.

Weihrich, H. (1982). The TOWS Matrix - A Tool for Situational Analysis. *Long Range Planning*, *15*(2), 54–66. doi:10.1016/0024-6301(82)90120-0

Chapter 8
Impact of the Principles of Financial Control on the Quality of the Inspection Activity Carried Out by the Public Financial Inspection Agency

ABSTRACT

Since the issue of the quality of financial control is a wide-ranging and problematic issue, the authors focus only on the quality of the inspection activity carried out by PFIA. The authors believe that the quality of PFIA's inspection activity should be considered as a factor affecting the effectiveness and efficiency of the supervised entity. Also, the quality of the inspection activity should be taken as a category describing the characteristics of PFIA, namely: the procedures of the institution, the attitude of employees towards the controlled object, the access to information, etc. In order to determine what the quality of PFIA's inspection activity is, it needs to be assessed based on the tangible and intangible elements of quality.

DOI: 10.4018/978-1-6684-8883-6.ch008

INTRODUCTION

Determining and accurately evaluating the quality of control actions has always been a topical and highly debatable issue. The problem of giving an accurate assessment of the quality of control actions is related to the incorrect determination of the tangible and intangible components of quality. According to Mayer An, the tangible (material) components of the quality of control actions are the control environment, the technological equipment and provision of the control process, the available control persons who participate in the control process (inspectors, lawyers, directors of departments, etc.), the resource provision for the implementation of the relevant control actions, etc. Intangible (intangible) components refer to: the personal responsibility of the controller, the professionalism and ethics of the controller, the additional administrative-procedural actions that should be taken in order to properly implement the control process, etc. (Hsu, 1968).

From an etymological point of view, the word "quality" was used "for the first time in the Old Bulgarian language as an equivalent of the Greek word ποιότης, which originates from ποῖος, „what". Quality should be defined as a category that describes the characteristics of an object (Wikipedia, 2012).

In one of the most significant philosophical works, *Critique of Pure Reason*, Immanuel Kant discussed quality in terms of categories. For him, "categories are forms of the reasoning ability which, being applied by the imagination to experience, make it possible to know it. The categories are divided into four groups – by quantity, quality, attitude and modality. According to quality, the categories are reality, negation, and limitation" (Kant, 1993).

Other specialists, such as V. Vinokurov and A. Vinokurov, accept that the quality of control can be studied from different angles and from different points of view. However, according to them, the informational-economic aspect is the most comprehensive. According to this aspect, control is considered to be qualitative when "the companies have the skills to successfully conduct business".

V. Vinokurov and A. Vinokurov propose that the quality of control be evaluated as a quantitative measure between the similarity of the results of the regulatory authorities and the control results obtained in the company itself. For ordered structural quantitative features, the degree of similarity is calculated based on correlation (Vinokurov, 2005).

According to R. James, the correct application of control technology, in which attention is paid to the methodology of applying the principles of financial control, will inevitably lead to a qualitative implementation of the control process (James, 1951).

Other specialists accept that control quality is measured as a consequence of factors and events defined in terms of the statistical characteristics underlying certain events. Kenett recognizes that quality assessment will help shift the focus of all those involved in the control activity from mere data and numbers to actual information. (Kenett, 2009).

Based on the opinions thus presented, we believe that they reveal a part of the existing problems in determining the quality of financial control, but, on the other hand, they are too heterogeneous and incomplete. Since the issue of the quality of financial control is a wide-ranging and problematic issue, we focus only on the ***quality of the inspection activity carried out by PFIA***. We believe that the quality of PFIA's inspection activity should be considered as a factor affecting the effectiveness and efficiency of the supervised entity. Also, the quality of the inspection activity should be taken as a category describing the characteristics of PFIA, namely: the procedures of the institution, the attitude of employees towards the controlled object, the access to information, etc. In order to determine what the quality of PFIA's inspection activity is, it needs to be assessed based on the tangible and intangible elements of quality. It is also necessary to establish criteria of indicators, on the basis of which the evaluation will be carried out. These criteria can be:

1. Evaluation of the application of the principles of financial control from the information presented in the findings protocols. In order to display this information, it is necessary to apply the new finding report form proposed in the second chapter of this study. In the currently approved and applied forms for a finding protocol, there is no mention of finding data, which exact principles are applied during the inspection activity, which means that for the time being these criteria cannot be used to assess the inspection activity of PFIA.
2. Development and approval of a policy for improving the quality and qualification of personnel.
3. Approval of general measures to guarantee the quality of the performed inspection activity.
4. Evaluation of the available information, as well as evaluation of the received applications, complaints and reports of violations of the PFIA.

5. Periodic assessment of the qualifications and competence of the inspectors.
6. Entering current data into the quality information system in accordance with the established hierarchy of access to it.
7. Determining whether all actions are properly structured.
8. Determination of the time scope of all individual control activities, i.e. whether the specified time range is realistic.
9. Are the expected results clearly defined and objectively measurable?
10. Assessing whether the set indicators measure the results in an adequate way.
11. Determining and evaluating whether the expected results of each individual inspection activity contribute to the fulfilment of specific goals and objectives.

PFIA has an approved "Methodology for the implementation of control over the quality of the inspection activity carried out by the bodies of the Agency". The methodology regulates the order and manner of carrying out quality control of the inspection activity; determining the criteria for its evaluation; the objects of control; the officials who have the right to carry it out; the procedures for establishing the quality of the inspection activity; the actions, acts and documents performed or drawn up in connection with this activity.

The main goal of the quality control of the inspection activity is to achieve legality and efficiency of the activity with an optimal ratio between benefit and resource for its implementation. Therefore, quality control provides current and subsequent information on the state of the quality of the activity, the causes, conditions and factors affecting it, and serves as a basis for making management decisions and for taking subsequent measures to eliminate irregularities, deficiencies, and violations.

The object of quality control of the inspection activity is the actions performed and the documents and acts drawn up by bodies and officials of the Public Financial Inspection Agency (PFIA) to fulfill the tasks and to achieve the main goal defined in the Law on the Public Financial Inspection (PFIA).

The established methodology defines the main criteria for evaluating the quality control of the inspection activity, namely:

1. At the first level are *the criteria related to the degree of application of the principles of financial control*, regulated in Art. 3 of the PFIA, when carrying out the inspection activity. Their application requires

the legality of actions and documents, impartiality, completeness and accuracy in establishing all facts and circumstances subject to the financial inspections being carried out, official start and confidentiality.

2. At the second level are *the criteria related to the degree of completion of the tasks of the financial inspection*, formulated according to Art. 2 of the PFIA. Subsequent financial inspections of the organizations and persons specified in Art. 4 of the PFIA should be carried out, as well as reports of violations of the normative acts regulating the budget, financial-economic and reporting activities of the same and disclosure of damages caused and indicators of fraud, a mandatory compilation of the statutory acts which bring to administrative criminal and property liability the guilty persons from the inspected objects if there are relevant legal grounds for this.
3. At the third level are *the criteria related to the degree of performance of official duties by the bodies and employees of PFIA*, in order to ensure conformity in the form and content of the actions performed and the documents drawn up by the financial inspectors, with the control procedures and the requirements of the normative acts and the internal acts of PFIA.

The control over the quality of the inspection activity is a permanent activity that covers all stages of the financial inspection - from its assignment to the reporting of the results of the performed inspections and the measures taken to eliminate the violations and realize legal responsibility in the presence of relevant legal prerequisites. Depending on the stage of its implementation, the quality control of the inspection activity is current and subsequent.

In Resolution No. 304 of November 11th, 2011 amending and supplementing the normative acts of the Council of Ministers in the Regulations for the Implementation of the Law on State Financial Inspection, adopted by Resolution No. 197 of the Council of Ministers of 2006 (published in Official Gazette issue 65/2006; amended and supplemented in issue 20/2008 and issue 30/2009), one of the amendments states that the PFIA Specialized Administration refers to: Directorate "Unscheduled inspection activities"; Directorate "Planned inspection activity in the field of public procurement"; Directorate "Analysis and report of inspection activity"; Directorate "Legal assurance of inspection activity". According to the aforementioned decree, the Directorate "Legal assurance of the inspection activity" is responsible for organizing and carrying out the inspections for subsequent control, and the controllers of the European Commission are responsible for the quality of the inspection activity and the activity of providing assistance. All other specialized administrative agencies are obliged to provide assistance in the implementation of quality control of inspection activities.

Due to the complexity of the researched problem, namely establishing the influence of the principles of financial control on the quality of inspections, regulated in Art. 3 of the PFIA, we believe that it is necessary to present all components that influence the determination of the quality of the inspection activity in one matrix. The elements of this matrix are: control technology; the principles of financial control, the stages for applying the principles of financial control and the implemented control actions based on the influence of the previously listed three components. The matrix is presented in Table 1.

The up-to-date approved technology of the control processes implemented by PFIA is aimed at the implementation of the four main policies of the Agency, which are:

1. Carrying out subsequent financial inspections for compliance with the country's legal acts in accordance with the requirements of Art. 4 of the Public Financial Inspection Act
2. Establishing violations of the normative acts governing budgetary, financial-economic or reporting activities, as well as indicators of fraud
3. Implementation of subsequent control over the awarding and execution of public contracts and the implementation of administrative-penal liability
4. Detection of fraud and violations affecting the financial interests of the European Communities

PFIA's internally validated control technology includes:

1. **Initiation of financial inspection.** An instigator for the initiation of a specific financial inspection can be any natural or legal person who possesses sufficiently reliable, documented information about the existence of a specific financial violation leading to the abuse of financial discipline. The initiation in the specific case is done by submitting signals, requests and complaints to PFIA. Other common reasons for initiating a financial inspection are coming by the Agency itself, namely: planned and in cases where a relevant public procurement registered in the public procurement register is of significant public interest arising from its value or public importance of the contractor or the contracting authority. Also, the initiator of the assignment of an inspection activity

Table 1. Matrix representing PFIA's control technology

Technology Principles		Stages for applying the principles of financial control: P1 – Application of the control policy application of the control policy	P2 – compliance with the organizational technology to perform the financial control inspections	P3 – evaluation of the effectiveness of the control process	P4 – a system for individual evaluation of the application of the principles of financial control	Activities
1. Carrying out subsequent financial inspections for compliance with the country's legal acts, according to the requirements of Art. 4 of the Public Financial Inspection Act.	Legality, objectivity, official start and confidentiality	YES	YES	YES	YES	Ensuring the legality of subsequent financial inspections; initiating a financial inspection; assignment of financial inspection; taking action in cases where the relevant organization or the relevant inspected person refuses to grant the financial inspectors access to their office premises; collection of evidence during subsequent financial inspections; control actions when establishing administrative violations and realization of administrative penal liability
2. Establishing violations of the normative acts governing budgetary, financial-economic or accounting activities, as well as indicators of fraud	Legality, objectivity, official start and confidentiality	YES	YES	YES	YES	Ensuring the legality of inspection actions when violations of regulations are established; collection of evidence; taking actions to establish administrative violations and realize administrative penal liability.
3.Implementation of subsequent control over the assignment and execution of public procurements and the implementation of administrative and penal liability	Legality, objectivity, official start and confidentiality	YES	YES	YES	YES	Ensuring the legality of inspection actions when violations of regulations are established; collection of evidence; taking actions to establish administrative violations and realize administrative penal liability.
4. Detection of fraud and violations affecting the financial interests of EU	Legality, objectivity, official start and confidentiality	YES	YES	YES	YES	Ensuring the legality of inspection actions when violations of regulations are established; collection of evidence; taking actions to establish administrative violations and realize administrative penal liability.

may be the prosecution authorities, complying with the requirements of the Law on the Judiciary. Initiators can be the Public Procurement Agency, as well as the Audit Chamber. The Central Coordination Unit for Combating Offenses at the Ministry of the Interior can also be the initiator of a financial inspection by submitting relevant signals for violations affecting the financial interests of the European Communities.

2. **Assigning the financial inspection.** The financial inspection is assigned on the basis of an order of the director of the Agency or to officials authorized by him. The order is prepared by the heads of departments of the Directorate "Organization and performance of inspection activity" in two copies: one for the Agency's records and one for the inspection file. The copy for the archive of the registry is agreed by the directors of the "Organization and execution of the inspection activity" and "Legal and methodological assurance of the inspection activity" directorates. In cases where the financial inspection is assigned to a team, the order shall specify the head of the team. The Director of the Agency may amend and cancel the order on the assignment of the financial inspection, as well as order the suspension and resumption of the financial inspection by separate orders. The head of the audited organization or the relevant audited person shall be notified of the issued order for carrying out a financial inspection, as well as of the subsequent changes through the newly issued order.
3. **Taking action in cases where the audited organization or the relevant audited person refuses to grant financial inspectors access to their business premises to carry out a financial inspection.** The head of the team carrying out the financial inspection (in cases where the inspection is carried out by a team) or the financial inspector suggests to the director of PFIA to request assistance from the authorities of the Ministry of Internal Affairs to ensure access. For this purpose, it is necessary to prepare the corresponding report to the director of the Agency, and also the request itself to the authorities of the Ministry of Internal Affairs is prepared by the aforementioned persons. The request must be in triplicate. One of them is provided to the authorities of the Ministry of Internal Affairs. The request should contain: the subject of the financial inspection; the reason for seeking assistance; the day of providing the assistance and data on the inspected organization or the inspected person, and for legal entities the name, registered office or address of management, EIC (Uniform Identification Code) and the persons representing it are indicated. For persons, the following information must be indicated - full name, social security number, residence and permanent address, and for foreign citizens - full name, personal number of a foreigner and the address at which they are registered in Bulgaria.

4. **Collection of evidence during the financial inspection.** During the implementation of the financial inspection, it is necessary to continuously document the established facts and circumstances established through official and personal checks of all relevant information related to the tasks, mentioned in the order for the assignment of the financial inspection. The financial inspector compiles the evidence required in the PFIA's Regulations for Application - tables, references, finding protocols, opinions, certified copies of the inspected documents, information, declarations, written explanations, conclusions of experts, etc.
5. **Control actions when establishing administrative violations and realization of administrative penal responsibility.** When, during the inspections, evidence of administrative violations committed by officials of the inspected organization or person is collected, the financial inspector is obliged to draw up an Act of Establishment of an Administrative Violation (AEAV). The AEAV is drawn up only in cases of proven violations under the PFIA, Public Procurement Law, Regulations for the Implementation of the Law on Public Procurement, Order on Assigning Small Public Procurement, Resolution of the Council of Ministers No. 55/12.03.2007, or when administrative penal competence is presented in the relevant regulatory act for the PFIA bodies. The act of administrative violation is drawn up in three copies - one for the offender and two for the Agency. Also, the act of establishing an administrative violation must contain the requisites under Art. 42 of the Law on Administrative Offenses and Penalties. With the drawing up of the AEAV, an administrative file is also drawn up. The created administrative file contains a copy of the act, the original evidence to it and the person's objection if any.
6. **Establishing damages under the PFIA and realization of property liability.** In the event of culpably caused damages, the financial inspector is obliged to draw up a statement of account. The findings of the act of accounting are documented with references, tables compiled by the financial inspector, findings protocols, explanations from the obliged persons, data on the movement of goods and material and monetary values, firi tables, certified copies or certified files of documents, conclusions of experts, etc.
7. **Reporting the results of the performed financial inspection.** After the completion of all factual checks in fulfillment of the tasks under the order for the assignment of financial inspections, the collection of evidence, the drawing up of acts for establishing administrative violations and acts of recording, a report on the results of the financial inspection is drawn

up. When copies of documents are submitted as evidence, they must be certified with a stamp "true to the original" by the verified organization or person. Commonly known facts and circumstances reflected in reports, balance sheets, accounting and other documents that are not subject to amendment should not be used as evidence.

The findings in the report must be numbered and arranged according to the tasks defined in the order for assigning the financial inspection. In the findings containing administrative violations, the acts drawn up for establishing administrative violations must be indicated with the number and date, against which responsible persons they were drawn up, as well as the reasons why such acts were not drawn up.

On the basis of everything stated up to this point, it can be assumed that the PFIA technology presented and approved in this way affects in great detail all procedural actions related to the preparation of the relevant control documents. The order, the sequence of the documentary evidence of the carried out inspections from their initiation to their completion are described in great detail, according to the thus presented *Instruction on the form, order, terms and movement of documents and acts drawn up during the performance of a financial inspection by the bodies of the State Financial Agency inspection approved by Order NoFK-09-35/13.03.2008, amended and supplemented by Order No FK-09-41/23.07.2009.* The instruction was provided by the director of the Agency - Temenuzka Petkova, for the implementation of the empirical study of this work.

The Instruction presents the stages of the control technology in PFIA, but does not reveal in depth the methods and means for the implementation of this technology. The control documents, which should be drawn up by the relevant financial inspector or team leader, are described sequentially, so as to realize the documentary justification of the control process. Problems in the technology of the control process, expressed in clearly defined procedural rules of conduct, are reported by various non-governmental organizations in Bulgaria, studying the efficiency and effectiveness of the control processes, especially in relation to the implementation of public procurement. For example, according to the research of the Institute for Legal Analysis and Research (ILAR) "Crisis in the systems for the assignment, execution and control of public procurement in Bulgaria" for the period 2006 - 2011, it was found that "over fifty percent of the procedures carried out according to the order of the Public Procurement Act and the Ordinance on the Assignment of Small Public Procurement in force at the time, according to PFIA data, and over seventy percent of these procedures, according to the data of the Audit Chamber, are flawed due to the lack of the necessary attention or competence in the application of the requirements of the regulatory framework by the principals of public procurements". According to the same study by ILAR, it is established that from the audits carried out by the Audit Chamber, the data are even more disturbing, because "according to them, between 70% and 85% of the public procurements carried out, violations were found, and most often they are related to attempts to manipulate the order itself. Over the past four years, during audits of 5,500 procedures for the assigning of public procurements with a total value of BGN 5 billion carried out by the experts of the Audit Office, administrative violations were found in more than 60% of the cases".

The Audit Chamber also strives to establish the quality and effectiveness of PFIA's control activity by comparing the established control technology and the adopted methodology for subsequent control. In their latest report from 2010, the auditors of the Audit Chamber found that in 2008 the subsidy used to finance the Agency's activities amounted to BGN 3,312,668, and the revenues from fines and sanctions received from its budget according to penal decrees are in the amount of BGN 332,195. In other words, as a result of the effective activity of PFIA, observing the principles of legality, objectivity and official start, a 10% return of the subsidy absorbed by the Agency was achieved.

Again, according to the data of audit report No. 0500001410 of the Audit Chamber for 2009, the absorbed subsidy is in the amount of BGN 3,293,091, and the revenue from fines and sanctions under penal decrees received in its budget is in the amount of BGN 482,734. As a result of the effective activity of the financial inspections, applying the principles of objectivity, legality, official start and confidentiality, a 15% return on the subsidy was achieved, which shows a tendency to increase the number of revenues received in the Agency's budget.

Another important piece of evidence that can be presented regarding the problems that exist in the implementation of control inspection technology by PFIA are the results that the Agency publishes annually the refusals of submitted applications, complaints and signals for the initiation of financial inspections in its activity reports (Table 2)

Table 2. Data on the signals, requests and complaints submitted by interested parties for the initiation of financial inspections for the period from 2008 to 2011

Year	Submitted alerts, requests and complaints for initiation of financial inspections (no.)	Refusal to carry out financial inspections (no.)	Realized financial inspections (no.)	Identified violations from the financial inspections carried out (no.)	Determined caused damages (BGN)
2008	445	165	280	2166	8 798 227
2009	718	296	422	1800	17 728 141
2010	480	112	368	2250	15 000 000
2011	584	150	434	2458	66 000 000

Source: Annual reports on the activities of SPFIA for the period from 2008 to 2011

From the data in Table 2, it is found that for the studied period - from 2008 to 2011, a significant part of the signals, complaints and requests to initiate financial inspections received a refusal. The Agency's annual reports do not state the reasons for the refusal. We believe that the incomplete disclosure of the reasons why the procedure for the implementation of a financial inspection was not opened, casts doubt on the objectivity, impartiality, independence and effectiveness of the supervisory authority's control actions.

On the other hand, proof of the existence of problems regarding the application of the PFIA's control technology presented and approved in this way are also the court decisions in which the penal decrees issued by the control authorities are cancelled. The annulment of the penal decrees is proof that the control processes do not have that administrative control burden, on the basis of which a full and qualitative impact on the controlled object should be sought.

According to data from the Audit Chamber, for the audited period from 01.01.2008 to 06.30.2010, PFIA did not carry out a subsequent control of the administrative penal files, which ended with a court decision to cancel the criminal decree. The report also states that the different practices of the courts have not been analyzed, in regard to preventing new decisions to cancel the legal basis for the implementation of administrative penal liability.

Table 3 presents the Acts of Encashment drawn up by PFIA for the period from 01.01.2008 to 06.30.2010, found during the audit by the Audit Chamber.

Table 3. Acts of encashment, drawn up by PFIA for the period from 01.01.2008 to 06.30.2010

Year	Acts of encashment		Value of voluntarily paid Acts Reimbursed by the date of completion of inspections (in BGN)	Value of Acts of Encashment sent by the object for forced collection by the competent authorities (in BGN)
	Number	Value in BGN		
2	3	4	5	6
2008	55	1 447 038	147 856	6 acts BGN 69 350
2009	39	3 172 933	240 669	11 acts BGN 1 219 368
Until June 2010	15	645 604	114 942	1 act BGN 39 224

For the audited period, Acts of Encashment with a total value of BGN 5,265,575 were drawn up, with which property responsibility is sought from the guilty persons.

Therefore, the analysis of the data shows the following: 1) the total value of the voluntarily paid sums for compensation of damages under the Acts of Encashment and those sent by the objects for forced collection is BGN 217,206 for 2008, and BGN 1,460,037 for 2009, and for the half year of 2010 – BGN 154,166;

2) the value of the sums paid for reimbursement of damages under the Acts of Encashment to the number of damages under compiled acts for the same periods in percentages is respectively 15%, 46% and 24%.

As a result of the effectively performed tasks of financial inspections, the public financial interests of the country are protected in the specified amounts, observing the principles: legality, objectivity, official start and confidentiality.

The impact of financial control principles cannot be directly determined and measured. Their impact can be ascertained:

1. In the implementation of the current and subsequent control over the quality of the inspection actions of PFIA. Based on this control, the degree of achievement of the objectives of the financial inspection, the fulfillment of the main tasks and the compliance of the actions and documents carried out or drawn up during the financial inspections with the requirements for form and content are determined.

2. When determining the effectiveness of the Agency, by comparing the granted and absorbed subsidy and the amount of revenue from fines and sanctions received in favor of the budget. From the information presented by external agencies and analysts regarding the activities of PFIA. For example, according to the 2011 AFCOS report (Directorate "Coordination of Combating Offenses Affecting the Financial Interests of the EU"), in connection with identified weaknesses in the control of public procurement, it is recommended to carry out a permanent risk assessment and adopt an active and a results-oriented approach to prevention and control, as well as to increase the capacity of PFIA. In 2011, during financial inspections, 72 cases of violations and frauds in money spending under EU programs and funds were identified and registered by the PFIA authorities. Of these, 21 cases are under the Operational Program "Regional Development", 26 cases - under the Operational Program "Administrative Capacity", 7 cases - under the PHARE Program, one case - under SAPARD, 9 cases - under the Operational Program "Environment", 3 cases - under the Operational Program "Development of Human Resources", 3 cases - under the Program for the Development of Rural Areas, 1 case - under the Operational Program "Development of the Competitiveness of the Bulgarian Economy" and 1 case - under the Operational Program "Transport". If there is evidence of a crime, the information about the frauds and violations found during the financial inspections is sent to the authorities of the prosecutor's office according to competence on the basis of Art. 19 of the PFIA.

From the data thus presented, it can be assumed that the improvement of PFIA's control actions is necessary. The results found by the Audit Chamber, AFCOS, OLAF, etc. are that the Agency's resources and capacity are not being used effectively. All files prepared by the relevant outsourced workplaces of the Agency (for example, Varna, Shumen, Targovishte, Dobrich, Montana, Vidin, etc.) are sent by post to the city of Sofia for the Directorate "Analysis and Report of Inspection Activity" for the placement of incoming file number and again the entire file is sent to the relevant outsourced workplace to continue further inspection actions. Upon completion of the inspection activities in the outsourced workplaces, the inspectors prepare all the documentation on the completed inspection and send it both to the Directorate "Analysis and Report of the Inspection Activity" and to the Directorate "Legal Assurance of the Inspection Activity" in Sofia. The purpose of this mailing of the information is to competently draw up the relevant closing documents, i.e. the powers of lawyers and inspectors working in the Agency's outsourced workplaces are too limited. Due to this established practice, the Agency's directorates in Sofia accumulate various documentation and information from outsourced jobs, which must be processed correctly. We believe that this distribution of files and documents from the outsourced workplaces to the Agency's directorates in the city of Sofia provides an opportunity to violate one of the main principles of Art. 3 of the PFIA, namely confidentiality.

Due to the established practice in the Agency, due to continuous use of the services of Bulgarian Posts Company, on 27.11.2012, an invitation was published on the PFIA website for assigning a public procurement with the subject "Provision of postal services for the needs of the Agency for State financial inspection' with ID 9009278 in the register of the Public Procurement Agency. In the invitation, a period of 24 months is specified for the execution of the order, starting from the date of signing the contract or until the value limit of BGN 65,000 (sixty-five thousand) without VAT is exhausted.

In order to improve the control activity of PFIA, we make the following recommendations:

1. The entry and serial numbering of the relevant file should not be carried out using the previously approved technology, but an electronic register should be approved, which would be available both to the persons from the Directorates of the Agency in the city of Sofia and to the inspectors and legal advisors of PFIA of outsourced jobs. In this way, the administrative costs of the Agency will be significantly reduced.
2. In order to solve the problems related to the control technology, it is necessary to confirm the stages of the control technology which are adopted in PFIA; to establish the principles that should be observed in each stage of the control technology, and also to establish the control actions that the PFIA inspectors should carry out. A structured proposal is presented in Table 4.

Based on the issues presented so far regarding the influence of the principles of financial control on the quality of inspection activity, the following main conclusions and recommendations can be made:

1. In the PFIA control technology, presented with the help of the Instruction on the form, order, terms and movement of the documents and acts drawn up during a financial inspection by the bodies of the Public Financial Inspection Agency, approved by Order No. FK-09-35/ 13.03 .2008,

Table 4. Presentation of PFIA's control technology and the principles of financial control to be applied by the inspectors

Stages of control technology adopted by PFIA	Principles to be applied	Control actions that PFIA inspectors should carry out
1. Initiation of financial inspection	Objectivity Impartiality Independence Confidentiality Fairness	Verification of received complaints, alerts and requests for initiating a financial inspection. The inspection should not be carried out only on a documentary basis, but if possible (i.e. depending on the nature and specifics of the controlled object), some confirmation of the submitted information should be requested from other control authorities.
2. Assignment of financial inspection	Accuracy in the selection of the team leader or the financial inspector to carry out the financial inspection Confidentiality Legality Objectivity	According to the presented procedural actions at this stage of PFIA's control technology, there is nothing to change. Any other proposal to change the method of assigning financial inspections will be accompanied by more costs for its implementation.
3. Taking action in cases where the audited organization or the relevant audited person refuses to grant financial inspectors access to their premises to carry out a financial inspection	Official start Confidentiality Independence Coordinating the control actions of the PFIA with the actions of the control authorities from which assistance is requested Effectiveness	The recommendation we are making is to change the regulations again, especially the Public Financial Inspection Act. If the controlled person refuses to grant access to his office premises, the legislator should provide the Agency with the possibility to impose administrative penal sanctions and fines in such situations. In this way, on the one hand, the costs that are additionally incurred in order to coordinate the control actions with the other control authorities will be reduced. On the other hand, the imposition of such type of sanctions and fines will have a greater impactful and educational effect on society - to assist the control authorities.
4. Gathering evidence during financial inspections	Official start Independence Objectivity Efficiency Confidentiality Qualification Economy	The necessary evidence must be collected very precisely and accurately so that the most accurate legal findings are presented in the control reports. The reports must correctly and accurately describe the collected evidence, so that subsequently, during the pre-trial proceedings, it is not established that a significant part of relevant facts and events was not taken into account. Also, the findings themselves, before being presented in the control reports, should be presented to PFIA's legal advisors, so that in advance and from a legal point of view, the entire financial control proceedings can be reviewed, and not subsequently during the court proceedings, the findings be overthrown.
5. Control actions when establishing administrative violations and realization of administrative penal liability	Legality Objectivity Efficiency Official start Confidentiality Independence Contemplativeness Truthfulness Equality	The actions of the control body should be suitable for the achievement of the goal (proper goal-means attitude). Among the many suitable means, there should not exist any less onerous means for the attainment of the aim thus set. The control body should fully and thoroughly investigate the factual aspects of the specific case. In the implementation of the control process, there should be a strong connection with substantive legality.
6. Establishing damages under the PFIA and realization of property liability	Legality Objectivity Official start Confidentiality Efficiency Independence Contemplativeness Truthfulness Equality	The control body, on its own initiative and with its own actions, shall ensure the lawful development of the control process. Naturally maintaining the principle of "official start" at the stage of issuing an Act of Encashment is essential for its evidentiary burden when disputing it.
7. Reporting the results of a financial inspection	Objectivity Independence Truthfulness Equality	An accurate and precise presentation of the control situation, correctly presented in the relevant control documents. Support for generally available and comprehensible information should be provided as appropriate.

amended and supplemented by Order No. FK-09-41/23.07.2009, the emphasis is not placed on the way of applying the principles of financial control, but on the requirements for the form, order, terms and movement of the documents and acts drawn up during the financial inspections. We believe that it would be appropriate for the adopted Instruction to comply with the Control Policy proposed in the second chapter of this study. In this way, we believe that the quality and efficiency of the control activity of the financial inspectors will be improved.

2. Table 4 visualizes the mutual relation between the Control Policy and the Instruction on the form, order, terms and movement of the documents and acts drawn up during the financial inspection. At each stage of the approved control technology, Table 4 presents the principles to be observed and applied by the inspectors.
3. The appeal and subsequent cancellation of the penalty orders issued by PFIA are sufficient proof of the existence of problems in the implementation of the control technology. We believe that if a precise methodology for the application of specific rules of conduct is not adopted and approved and its compliance by inspectors is not ensured, such court decisions will continue to be a common practice.

REFERENCES

Hsu, J., & Mayer, An. (1968). *Modern Control Principles and Applications*. McGraw- Hill Book Company.

James, R. (1951). Some aspects of a Governmental Audit. *The Accounting Review*, *26*(3).

Kant, I. (1993). *Towards Eternal Peace*. BAS Publishing.

Kenett, R. (2012). Quality, Risk and the Taleb Quadrants. Available from: http://papersssrn.com/sol3/papers.cfm?abstract_id= 1433490&download=yesq

Vinokurov, V. A., Vinokurov, A. V. (2005). Kachestvo upravlenia kak faktor ukreplenia rынochnыh pozitsiy predpriyatia. *Standartы i kachestvo, 1.*

Chapter 9
Evaluation of the Results of the Implementation of the Financial Control Principles

ABSTRACT

The valuation data considered and presented in this part of the study only refer to the applicability of the principles of financial control in Portugal and Ukraine. The main reason for this is that the state control agencies (respectively the state financial inspection agencies) of a number of countries (such as Romania, Serbia, Italy, France, Great Britain, etc.) have not taken action on the application and impact assessment of the control principles. The lack of sufficient empirical data, even from the countries thus covered in the study (Switzerland, Finland, Greece, Ukraine, Portugal, and Estonia), is proof of the degree of complexity of the issues chosen for research.

INTRODUCTION

The main goal of this part of the study is to prove one of the main hypotheses, namely whether it is possible to give an accurate assessment of the application and impact of the principles of financial control. We believe that in order to give an answer to the question posed in this way, it is necessary:

1. To follow the sequence of stages in the application of the principles of financial control, presented in the second chapter of the work.

DOI: 10.4018/978-1-6684-8883-6.ch009

2. To apply the methodology for researching the principles of financial control by PFIA.

Michael Scriven (Scriven, 2012) assumes that evaluation is a process of determining merit, and evaluation is a product of this process. In 1988, Patton also distinguished assessment from evaluation in the following way: according to him, the practice of evaluation involves the systematic collection of information about the activities, characteristics and results of programs, personnel, and products for use by specific people, to reduce uncertainty, improve performance and decision-making regarding what those programs, personnel, or products do (Patton, 1988).

According to Elizabeth Sommerlad, there are basically three types of problems in the evaluation process in practice. The first problem is ***conceptual***, i.e. how people think about assessment. The following questions relate to this problem: what is the assessment for the interested parties; who cares about the findings; what is the approach or model that will guide the evaluation? The second problem is ***technica***l. The following questions to address relate to this problem: what methods are appropriate; what will be the unit of analysis; what steps will be taken to ensure data quality; what type of data will be collected; how should evaluation be incorporated into the decision-making process? The third problem is the ***operational*** one, which refers to solving questions such as: who will be responsible for the assessment; who will do the assessment; how people responsible for collecting or providing information are involved in planning the assessment; how the assessment will be managed (Sommerlad, 1992).

The opinions thus presented characterize the essence of assessment and evaluation too generally. Taken alone, these statements are true, but also incomplete from the point of view of financial control. We believe that the assessment of the application of the principles of financial control should be considered as a systematized method of gathering information on the impact of the principles of financial control, regulated in Art. 3 of the PFIA. This process should be implemented by expert assessors. Evaluation should be done after each completed inspection. The assessment of the application of the principles of financial control in PFIA should be considered as a process for characterizing and evaluating the various aspects of the application of these principles.

In order to carry out the evaluation process qualitatively, it is necessary for the expert to express his expert opinion unambiguously, competently and accurately and, according to the documents presented to him. Until now, in the control practice of PFIA, there has been no assessment of the application of the principles of financial control due to the circumstances that:

1. There is no established methodology for assessing the degree of application of the principles of financial control, regulated in Art. 3 of the PFIA.
2. There is no approved "Card for expert assessment regarding the implementation of the principles of financial control in the PFIA". The aforementioned document should be drawn up by the expert appraiser, who will present his expert conclusion and ethically evaluate: 1) the manner of conducting the control process; 2) the application of the principle of "legality"; 3) the application of the principle of „objectivity"; 4) the application of the principle of „confidentiality"; 5) the application of the principle of „official start“. The card as a document letterhead should be approved by the Ministry of Finance and approved by the director of PFIA. The card should include criteria of indicators to determine the application of the principles.
3. There is a lack of established practice for researching the application of the principles of financial control, on the basis of which the next problem arises, namely the lack of an information base of indicators, which help to determine their influence and impact on the control process.

We propose that for the development of the methodology of financial control by PFIA, the Ministry of Finance and the director of PFIA should approve the following "Expert evaluation card regarding the application of the principles of financial control in PFIA":

Model 1. of an Expert evaluation card regarding the application of the principles of financial control in PFIA

EXPERT EVALUATION CARD REGARDING THE APPLICATION OF THE PRINCIPLES OF FINANCIAL CONTROL IN PFIA

The present expert assessment was developed by…*(full name of the expert)* under a contril inspection, according to order of the director of PFIA .

EVALUATION CRITERIA

The indicators, which help a concrete assessment of the ethical conduct of the control process to be given, are closely related to the answers to the questions about the need, role and importance of the control policy in the inspection

Table 1. Ethical evaluation regarding the ways of conducting the control process in PFIA

Criteria	Yes	No	Evaluation
Is the control process up-to-date and qualitatively presented in the control documents?			
Have the inspectors complied with the ethical requirements presented in the PFIA Code of Ethics?			
Have significant detections of irregularities been achieved by PFIA inspectors?			
Has a behavior algorithm been developed to ensure the quality implementation of the control process?			
When making a decision, are the potential harms and expected benefits of the specific procedures comprehensively taken into account?			
Are significant violations detected during the implementation of the control process?			
Is there an established general assessment of the reliability of the information presented in the control documents?			

Table 2. Criteria for evaluating the application of the principle of "objectivity" by inspectors

Criteria	Yes	No	Evaluation
Is the degree of independence of the obtained results from the expected and, accordingly, from the desired results correctly determined?			
Is there any bias in performing the control process?			
Has the supervisory body been influenced by outsiders?			
Are the forms of the control study itself correctly applied?: 1. Evidence gathering 2. Examination of the evidence - examination of its content, and also whether the information hidden in it is extracted 3. Is the evidence properly evaluated - the correct definition of its significance and role in the control process			
Are the control methods correctly applied to implement the control process?			
Has a risk management algorithm been developed to include risk identification, monitoring, risk mitigation trends?			
Is a control specialist training program being developed and implemented?			
Is the volume and type of information to be provided to the controlled objects defined?			
Is there a conflict of interest in implementing the control actions?			
Have all the duties of the inspectors on the assigned work been complied with?			
Is the information correctly presented in the finding protocols regarding the state of the controlled object?			

Table 3. Assessment of the application of the principle of "confidentiality" by PFIA inspectors

Criteria	Yes	No	Evaluation
Inspectors do not fabricate, falsify or intentionally misrepresent the information presented			
Data, results, methods and procedures are not publicly disclosed without the knowledge, consent and approval of a higher authority			
All facts and circumstances related to the control activity are collected, analyzed and evaluated truthfully, accurately and impartially, without allowing the influence of own or other interests			
The personal data of the inspected persons are not disclosed			
Are PFIA inspectors offered or promised different services from the inspected sites that would cause erroneous inspection actions?			
Is confidentiality respected in inquiries and reported reports and complaints?			

activity. The defined criteria for evaluating the application of the principles: objectivity, official start and confidentiality, are specified according to the Regulations for organizational technology for carrying out financial control processes. The accurate assessment of the indicators presented in this way will contribute to the effective or ineffective reference by the inspectors to

Table 4. Assessment of the application of the principle of "legality" by PFIA inspectors

Criteria	Yes	No	Evaluation
Are the relevant legal acts known by the persons performing the inspection activity?			
Do the persons carrying out the inspection activity comply with the relevant laws?			
Do the inspectors perform their professional activities in strict compliance with the Constitution of the Republic of Bulgaria?			
Are the established internal work rules followed?			
Are PFIA's interests being violated by the inspectors in compliance with the "legality" norm?			
Has a good organization been created in PFIA so that citizens and affected parties can make reports, complaints and requests for violations of financial discipline and for violations related to public procurement?			
When considering the submitted signals, requests and complaints, do PFIA inspectors cooperate with inspectors from other control institutions legally, observing the agreements concluded between the control organizations?			
Do PFIA inspectors lawfully remove the violations and take the necessary measures to bring the officials responsible for violating the law to legal responsibility?			
Have all the ways and means, which are not legally prohibited, been used to establish the facts and circumstances?			

Table 5. Assessment of the application of the "official start" principle by PFIA inspectors

Criteria	Yes	No	Evaluation
Do the facts and circumstances verified by the inspectors objectively and accurately reflect the established results of the performed inspection activity, the established violations and damages, the reasons for their occurrence and the guilty persons?			
Is there an initiative on the part of the financial inspectors to establish all the facts and circumstances related to the inspected financial and economic activity of the inspected organizations and persons?			
Were the procedural actions followed during the official inspections regarding the reliability of the information established during the inspection activity?			
Are the successive stages in the control process followed, namely the initiation to start the inspection, its conduct and its subsequent completion?			
Did the inspectors properly collect all the necessary evidence, even when there was no request from the interested parties?			
When appealing the acts, according to the Law on Administrative Violations and Penalties, was all the evidence provided taken into account?			

Expert's conclusion
First and last name of the expert, signature
Date:

the regulated methods in the Regulations on organizational technology for carrying out financial inspections.

In the Republic of Finland, inspectors apply similar control cards. The purpose of these cards is to give a reasoned opinion by the inspectors regarding the condition of the controlled object, and also with their help, the experts declare the application of the approved control technology. In Finland, the Ministry of Finance has the following departments: Economic Department, Budget Department, Financial Markets Department, Tax Administration Department, Local Self-Government and Regional Administration Department, Administrative Management and Development, International Relations Secretariat, and Media and Communications Unit Department. The main duties of the financial inspectors of the Republic of Finland are to lead, coordinate and develop internal control and risk management. Their main task is to be responsible at governmental level for control activities and reported control results related to the prevention of abuse and control of EU funds. The strategic objective of the financial control of the Republic of Finland is to promote fairness between generations by preserving good administrative management and accountability of government finances and operations.

The Ministry of Finance in Finland is responsible for all guidance and development of public procurement procedures. Finnish legislation on competitive tendering is based on Directives 2004/18/EC and 2004/17/EC of the European Community on public procurement procedures as well as the World Trade Organization's public procurement agreements. The purpose of these provisions is to enable an open competition for equal and non-discriminatory treatment of tenderers and a reasonable use of public resources. For 2011, public procurement in Finland amounted to EUR 22.5 billion, which is equal to about 15% of the Gross Domestic Product.

Control over the implementation of public procurement has always been one of the fundamental problems that OLAF points out not only for Bulgaria, but also for a number of developed countries. For example, OLAF reports significant problems in the implementation of control over financial discipline and the effective implementation of control over public procurement in the Republic of Estonia. According to data from the OLAF report for 2010, "only one citizen submitted information on the basis of which the European Office launched an investigation last year." According to the same OLAF report, the problems of the Republic of Estonia are due to: firstly, the incorrect distribution of responsibilities between the control authorities, and secondly, the incorrect application of the principles of financial control and the lack of subsequent evaluation of their impact in the control process.

In a comparative analysis between the established control bodies of Bulgaria and those of Estonia, it is established that in the studied North-Eastern European country there is no established Agency under the Ministry of Finance, as is the case in Bulgaria, which is entrusted with the control of financial discipline and the subsequent control to establish fraud and violations affecting the financial interests of the European Communities. In Estonia, there is an established Public Procurement Agency, which has similar rights and obligations as the Public Procurement Agency in Bulgaria. Another significant difference between the established control bodies of Bulgaria and Estonia is that, in addition to the control activities carried out by the Public Procurement Agency, in Estonia there is an established State Audit Office whose purpose is to carry out audits in ministries and state departments, as well as to implement internal audits in ministries and local authorities, and it is also assigned to exercise control over the implementation of public procurement rules. Therefore, it can be assumed that OLAF's criticisms of Estonia's established control system and the need to improve it, including distinguishing the responsibilities and duties of control bodies, are justified.

In Ukraine, the State Financial Inspection (SFI) is a specialized body of the executive power. Its activity is directed by the Cabinet and coordinated by the Ministers of Ukraine through the Minister of Finance. The main task of the SFI of Ukraine is the implementation of state policy in the field of state financial control. The purpose of the SFI of Ukraine is the preservation and use of public funds and other non-transferable assets; accuracy in identifying the need for budget funds and the obligations of the budget enterprise; the effective use of funds and state property; the reliability of the accounting and financial reporting of ministries and other executive bodies, public funds, public mandatory insurance and insurance funds, budgetary institutions and economic entities from the public sector, as well as the economy of companies, entities and organizations that receive (in the period that is checked) funds from the budgets at all levels, public funds and mandatory insurance funds or public use (used during the period being checked) of public or municipal property; compliance with the law at all stages of the budget process in the state and local budgets.

The State Financial Inspection of Ukraine also aims to control the observance of the required compliance with public procurement legislation. It analyzes the state of compliance with financial discipline and informs the executive authorities, local authorities or the public about the results of this analysis. It develops and presents proposals regarding the elimination and prevention of causes and conditions that have led to violations and deficiencies of commitment within public authorities. The implementation of state financial control by the SFI of Ukraine is carried out through checks in the form of planned and unplanned inspections on some complex issues.

For the implementation of financial inspections by the SFI of Ukraine, the established concepts and requirements of the EU are observed. The state financial control of Ukraine must ensure the correct (lawful, economical, effective, efficient and transparent) management of public finances, which is considered as a set of three components: internal control, internal audit and their harmonization (CONCEPT, 2017).

The results of the performed financial inspections of the SFI of Ukraine show a continuing and negative practice of illegal and improper use of state resources and budget funds. In the first half of 2012, the State Financial Inspection of Ukraine found violations of financial and economic discipline in more than 4,700 public sector enterprises. The total amount of violations is over 2.3 billion euros. Measures were taken to improve financial discipline, and for the first half of 2012, the SFI received 1,600 reports of violations in the spending of budget funds. After reviewing the submitted complaints and reports, 815 penal cases were opened, and in 712 of them, a penal decree was appealed against persons performing the internal audit of the audited budget organization.

The problems regarding the implementation of the principles of financial control and the subsequent assessment of their impact and influence are fundamental for the SFI of Ukraine. The principles on which financial inspections in Ukraine are based are: legality, objectivity, prevention, openness, accountability and separation of powers. The SFI of Ukraine lacks a developed and approved methodology for evaluating the application of the principles of financial control, which OLAF reports in its report as a weakness in the control practice of Ukraine. According to its 2003 report, OLAF recommends various preventive measures as prevention of financial and economic fraud, one of which is the strict reference to the principles: transparency, objectivity, timeliness and correct conduct of control investigations.

The Organization for Economic Co-operation and Development (OECD) in its report states that the failure to evaluate the application of the principles of financial control is a basic prerequisite for the incorrect and inaccurate determination of the efficiency of financial control. According to the OECD, "the criteria by which it can be determined whether a principle has been applied should be chosen in a way that does not presuppose a judgment of the value of the means as such, but rather of the effectiveness and efficiency of the current arrangements in relation to of achieving outcome goals. The chosen methodology for assessing the implementation of the principles should recognize that the relative costs and benefits of alternative means of implementation may vary over time. On the other hand, the OECD notes that the focus of the principles together with their scope means that the individual principles are themselves "unobservable reviewers" and that what is assessed is a combination of the legal framework and other implementation measures. Therefore, assessing whether the principles of financial control apply in a jurisdiction is necessarily a matter of "informed judgment based on various sources of information". The fact that the proposed methodology of the Organization for Economic Development and Cooperation is focused on jurisdictions rather than on specific inspections leads to some specific challenges in its implementation.

Another financial control practice that can be taken into account is the Greek one. In Greece (as well as in Bulgaria) there is no established policy on assessing the application and impact of the principles of financial control by the General Financial Inspectorate of the Ministry of Finance (Γενική Διεύθυνση Οικονομικής Επιθεώρησης). But what the Greek government did in 2011, after taking into account numerous criticisms from Germany and the EU for poorly implemented financial inspections, was to establish a Commission for the General Financial Inspection. The main task of the

Commission is testing both old inspection cases and operational (current) inspections. The commission has 7 members - one chairman, who is also the head, and six members. On the basis of Law No. 4002/2011, the head of each financial inspection is obliged to prepare the complete documentation relating to the financial inspection both on paper and in electronic form. The paper media after completion of the inspection are handed over to the "Archive" department. Regarding the created files, they should be submitted to the Secretary of the General Financial Inspectorate, and be numbered according to the number of the relevant file. The secretary of the General Financial Inspectorate in Greece has the responsibility and commitment to send the files to the head of the Commission for assessing the quality of the inspection activity. Since its establishment, from March 2011 to the end of 2012, the Commission has checked 2450 current financial inspections. Of these, the Commission has defined 932 as very good, 734 as good and 784 as bad, for which repeated inspections have been assigned.

In Portugal, the General Financial Inspectorate (InspeçãoGeral de Finanças – IGF) is the oldest control body of the Portuguese state. It is equivalent to the supervisory authority General de la Administracion in Spain. The IGF was established in 1930 and since then its purpose and role has been amended several times to adapt to changes in the entities it controls. The main financial inspection is within the Ministry of Finance of Portugal. As financial controller, the IGF exercises control over budgetary and financial discipline fairly, in accordance with the principles of "legality, regularity and sound financial management" (Blanco, 2006).

The IGF works closely with the General Directorate of the Budget at the Ministry of Finance in Portugal. The powers of the IGF are aimed at carrying out strategic control of financial management, including control of legality and financial audit. The General Financial Inspectorate of Portugal covers all public sector entities. At the end of each financial inspection, a document entitled "Analysis and reporting of irregularities identified by the IGF" is prepared. The document provides guidance not only to prevent misconduct in the management of public finances, but also to avoid some degree of subjectivity and inaccuracies that may arise in control actions. This document also contains a "check list" of assumptions to be checked during the inspection. The purpose of the "checklists" is to assist inspectors in developing possible scenarios that would occur during control actions. In this way, inspectors have prior guidelines and expectations from the applied control procedures. This document was approved in September 2011 amid strong public criticism and questioning of the effectiveness of IGF inspections.

In its 2011 report, the Portuguese General Financial Inspectorate reports the relative weight of the application of financial control principles based on the assessment of the final inspection results (Figure 1).

Figure 1. Scale for reporting effectiveness, efficiency and the quality of implementation of the principles of financial control by the General Financial Inspectorate in Portugal

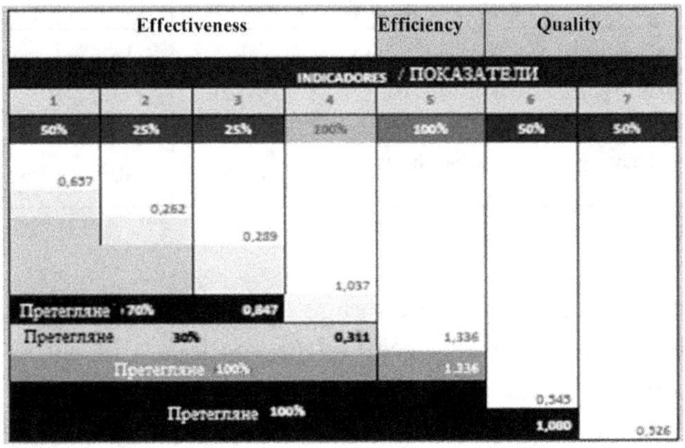

The relative weight of the influence of each principle on the final financial control results can be presented in more detail using the estimates presented in Table 6.

Table 6. Presentation of the relative influence of the principles of financial control on the effectiveness, efficiency and quality of the control results realized by the General Financial Inspectorate in Portugal

Effectiveness	Efficiency	Quality
55%	25%	20%
0,636	0,334	0,214

The data from Fig. 1 and Table 6 were obtained as a result of 118.44% summary results of realized financial inspections by the IGF. The general opinion of the General Financial Inspectorate (IGF) in Portugal is that the performed self-assessment on the application of the principles of financial control is relatively good, as three main operational objectives have been achieved. The indicators for the evaluations presented in this way are: the

Table 7. Indicators for determining the assessment of the application of the principles of financial control by the General Financial Inspectorate in Portugal

Indicators	2008	2009	2010	2011
Ind. No. 1. Scope of financial control	No data	5%	11,76%	8,87%
Ind. No. 2. Coverage of management services in the management of human resources in the IGF	No data	22,70%	13,49%	9,42%
Ind. No. 3. Index - result (60% financial value + 20% creation of financial-control knowledge + 20% consistent decisions)	1195,24 (points)	1275,80 (points)	1902,80 (points)	1037 (points)
Ind. No. 4. Number of controlled objects/Number of inspectors	1,58	1,48	1,82	1,67
Ind. No. 5. Total collected points from the inspections/ Number of controlled objects	6,93 (points)	7,45 (points)	7,59 (points)	7,58 (points)
Ind. No. 6. Number of training and qualification hours provided	No data	No data	No data	8883 hours

scope of financial control; the coverage of managed services in personnel management; the total points received (earned) by the supervisor during the implementation of the financial inspection; the number of training and qualification hours, etc. These indicators are presented in Table 7.

The comparative information according to the investigated indicators (control body authorized to carry out financial inspections; applied principles of financial control; application of a card for evaluating the application of the principles of financial control and other methods for researching the application of the principles of financial control) between inspection activities of the surveyed countries is presented using Table 8.

The information presented in Table 8 regarding the control practice of applying an evaluation method for determining the influence of the principles of financial control is for Bulgaria, Greece, Portugal, Ukraine, Estonia and Finland. We believe that the inclusion of other countries in the scope of the study, apart from those indicated, requires characterizing the established practice for carrying out financial inspections in the relevant country under study, as well as presenting the goals and tasks of the control body, which is authorized to carry out inspection actions. The control technology for carrying out financial inspections in Greece, Portugal, Ukraine, Estonia and Finland is specific. This is due to the peculiarities of the state policy, as well as the presence of some dissimilar problems in the implementation of financial inspections. Regardless of the differences, the positive directions of development of the control actions of the State Financial Inspection of Ukraine and the Financial Inspection of the Ministry of Finance of Finland are a prerequisite for being designated as a model for improving the control

Table 8. Comparison of established inspection activities of Bulgaria, Ukraine, Estonia, Portugal, Greece and Finland

Country	Control authority authorized to carry out financial inspections	Applied principles of financial control	Application of the Card for assessing the application of the principles of financial control	Other methods for researching the application of the principles of financial control
Bulgaria	Public Financial Inspection Agency (PFIA)	Legality Objectivity Official start Confidentiality	No	There is no methodology for researching the application of the principles of financial control
Ukraine	The State Financial Inspection of Ukraine	Legality Objectivity Preventiveness Openness Accountability Separation of powers	No	There is no methodology for researching the application of the principles of financial control
Estonia	There is no specialized control body that only carries out financial inspections. The control activity is carried out by the Public Procurement Agency (PPA) and also by the State Audit Office	Legality Objectivity Official start Confidentiality	No	There is no methodology for researching the application of the principles of financial control
Portugal	General Financial Inspection (InspeçãoGeral de Finanças – IGF)	Legality Economy Legitimacy Independence Impartiality	No	An evaluation of the final inspection results is carried out based on the summarization and analysis of the information presented in the control documents
Greece	General Financial Inspection at the Ministry of Finance (Γενική Διεύθυνση Οικονομικής Επιθεώρησης)	Legality Objectivity Official start Confidentiality	No	There is no methodology for researching the application of the principles of financial control
Finland	Financial Inspection at the Ministry of Finance	Legality Objectivity Official start Confidentiality Economy Legitimacy	Yes	With the help of the expert assessment cards on the application of the principles of financial control, their influence and impact are examined

technology of the State Financial Inspection Agency in Bulgaria. The adoption of the methodology for assessing the influence and impact of the principles of financial control through the introduction of the "Expert Assessment Card on the Application of the Principles of Financial Control", as in Finland, and, on the other hand, the analysis and reporting of irregularities found in the financial inspection, as in the example of Ukraine, we believe will improve the control practice of PFIA in Bulgaria.

In other developed countries, such as Switzerland, Great Britain, the USA, etc., the Ministry of Finance does not have a separate structure exercising control over financial discipline. This control in the aforementioned countries is assigned and carried out by the Audit Office. The established structure of state power determines the place of the Audit Office as a control element of the control system of the respective country. For example, in Switzerland, the Ministry of Finance has the following control institutions: General Secretariat – SG; Federal IT Steering Unit – FITSU; State Secretariat for International Financial Matters – SIF; Federal Finance Administration – FFA; Federal Office of Personnel – FOPER; Federal Office of Information Technology, Systems and Telecommunication – FOITT and Federal Office for Buildings and Logistics – FBL. The following institutions are related to the activities of the Ministry of Finance in Switzerland: the Swiss Federal Audit Office – SFAO; the Swiss Financial Market Supervisory Authority – FINMA and the Federal Pension Fund – PUBLICA.

Switzerland, which is a federal state that acquired its federal government after being a confederation, consists of twenty-six cantons. The specific legislation in the various cantons also determines the differences in the implementation of control in the public sector. Although the individual cantons have many points of contact, their special status and powers can vary greatly. The historical development of the individual cantons is also a prerequisite for the disparate definition of the essence of control in the public sector, and hence the disparate implementation of the control technology. Thus, for example, in the German-speaking parts of Switzerland, the term „Finanzkontrolle" („financial control") is used; in the French-speaking part of the country they use the terms „Inspection des finances du canton" („inspection of cantonal finances"), „Inspection Cantonal des Finances" („cantonal finance inspection"), Inspection des finances de l'Etat („state inspection of finances "), Contrôle cantonal des finances („Cantonal Financial Control Office ") or Contrôle des finances de l'Etat („state financial control"). Despite these names, they all refer to the audit activity of the Audit Office. In some individual cantons, the Audit Chamber adheres to the approved cantonal Constitution. In other cantons it is established by law or decree of parliament. Administratively, in the 1980s, there were separate audit services to the executive power. With the adoption of the Audit Office Act in the canton of Bern after 2000, the Audit Office is an independent executive body. This practice was also adopted in the canton of Zurich in 2001.

In the canton of Zurich, the Audit Office, in carrying out its control actions, observes the principles: regularity, legality, efficiency, suitability and economy. The audit activity of the Swiss Audit Office can be the subject of research in other studies. Comparing the established control practice for the public sector in Switzerland and the control practice in Finland, a number of differences are identified. Apart from the fact that in Switzerland there is no control body under the executive power, which is authorized to carry out financial inspections, as is the practice in Finland and in Bulgaria, but also the peculiarity of the control practice in Switzerland is distinguished by some peculiarities:

1. The established organizational methods and measures applied within public administration are similar to those applied in private business in order to protect state property, ensure the accuracy and reliability of accounting reporting.
2. Internal control in public sector organizations has been strengthened. The adopted internal control mechanism (IKS) in Switzerland ensures: proper and efficient administration; compliance with the basic policy of administrative law; protection of public assets; detection and reduction of errors and irregularities and timely reporting accompanied by reliable financial information.
3. There is no established methodology for studying the application and impact of the principles of financial control. The reports of the Audit Chamber of Switzerland indicate the principles of financial control applied during the audit in the relevant canton, as is the control practice of the Audit Chamber and PFIA in Bulgaria. The lack of assessment of the impact of the applied principles, following the example of Finland, we consider to be a gap in the control technologies of both Switzerland and Bulgaria.
4. Of all the main principles, the Swiss Audit Office checks whether the audited object has complied with the principle of "legality" in the implementation of the budget. For this purpose, it is checked whether all business operations carried out by the audited budgetary organization are legal, and also whether they are properly documented.

The presentation of other control practices, other than the one established in Bulgaria, we consider not imperative, since the following conclusions and recommendations can be made based on the information thus presented for Switzerland, Finland, Greece, Ukraine, Portugal and Estonia:

1. The valuation data considered and presented in this part of the study only refer to the applicability of the principles of financial control in Portugal and Ukraine. The main reason for this is that the state control agencies (respectively the state financial inspection agencies) of a number of countries (such as Romania, Serbia, Italy, France, Great Britain, etc.) have not taken action on the application and impact assessment of the control principles. The lack of sufficient empirical data, even from the countries thus covered in the study (Switzerland, Finland, Greece, Ukraine, Portugal and Estonia), is proof of the degree of complexity of the issues chosen for research.
2. The Organization for Economic Cooperation and Development (OECD), whose main purpose is to stimulate economic progress and trade, with the help of its research, has reached important conclusions for financial control practice, one of which is that it is necessary to adopt and regulate uniform criteria on the basis of which to effectively assess the application and impact of the principles of financial control in the control processes.
3. Evaluating the application and impact of financial control principles should be considered as one end of financial inspection technology. This process can be implemented both by the control institution itself and by another authorized body at the Ministry of Finance. The established results should be made publicly available so that any interested person has free access to them.

REFERENCES

Blanco, Sl. (2006). Auditoria do sector público no contexto da nova gestão pública. Revista de Estudos Politécnicos/Polytechnical. *Studies and Reviews (General Fisheries Commission for the Mediterranean)*, *3*(5/6), 201–225.

CONCEPT. (2017). CONCEPT of Development of Public Internal Financial Control till 2017. *DKRS*. http://www.dkrs.gov.ua/kru/en/publish/article/50363

Patton, M. Q. (1988). Six honest serving men. *Studies in Educational Evaluation*, *14*(3), 301–330. doi:10.1016/0191-491X(88)90026-0

Scriven, M. (2012). The Nature of Evaluation. RISMES. http://www.rismes.it/pdf/ Scriven_domain_evaluation.pdf

Chapter 10
Comparative Analysis of the Results of the Implementation of the Principles of Financial Control in Bulgaria

ABSTRACT

Based on everything stated so far regarding the presented empirical results of the foreign practice of applying the principles of financial control, the following main conclusions can be drawn: 1. The presented control foreign practice regarding the application of the principles of financial control is proof of the relevance of the studied problem. 2. The data presented by the foreign specialists reveal that the main problems regarding the incorrect application of the principles of financial control are due to irregularities in the implementation of the control technology. 3. Western specialists maintain the thesis that it is necessary to adopt additional general control principles, and with their help, it is expected to improve the quality of control work. The proposed new general control principles exist in the UK as unwritten rules. The purpose of their normative regulation, according to specialists, is to transform them into written rules that have legal weight in case of their inaccurate application.

DOI: 10.4018/978-1-6684-8883-6.ch010

INTRODUCTION

The purpose of this part of the study is to apply one of the methods of empirical research, namely the comparative analysis. It is aimed at comparing the application of the principles of financial control in the implementation of financial inspections in Bulgaria with the practices in the USA, Great Britain, Australia, Germany and Russia. The scope of the basic principles of financial control includes a number of rules that cannot be analyzed in detail in the studied countries. For this reason, the object of investigation are the principles of *objectivity, legality* and *confidentiality*, which, according to data from OLAF (European Anti-Fraud Office), are often violated.

The studies of foreign specialists, which are presented in this part of the development, are not aimed at analysis and research of the application of the relevant principle for a specific financial control situation and for a specific financial control authority. Their studies are aimed at the general impact and application of a specific control principle for the overall state-authority control practice. For example, according to research by Jay Weiser, the principle of "confidentiality" is not respected in the implementation of the following legal acts in the USA (Weiser, 2010):

- The Children's Online Privacy Protection Act of 1998
- The Cable Communications Policy Act of 1984
- The Drivers Personal Data Protection Act of 1994
- The Law on Electronic Communications
- The Fair Credit Reporting Act of 1970
- The Financial Secrecy Act of 1978
- The Confidentiality Act of 1974
- The Access to Stored Telegraphic and Electronic Communications and Transaction Reports Act
- The Personal Data Protection Act 1988

The damage caused by non-compliance with the confidentiality principle by the control authorities is about $100 to $1000 per day. The most significant violations found by Jay Weiser are by the cable operators, who, by virtue of an agreement with the specific control institutions, are obliged to provide the information recorded with them for the respective subscription. The study also includes abuses by online operators who research information about persons under 18 using the Internet. Government agencies that check and access the information of motor vehicle owners and drivers also appear to misapply the principle of "confidentiality". A number of violations of financial institutions are noted, which unlawfully exempt a number of government expenses from their monitoring (Weiser, 2010).

According to another study, TL Beauchamp also reported significant violations of the principle of "confidentiality" in the UK, which are presented in Table 1 (Beauchamp, 2011).

From the data in Table 1, it is established that the principle of "confidentiality" in Great Britain is violated by the relevant control bodies relatively moderately - from 5% to 25%. The values are relatively moderate and, according to TL Beauchamp, the violation of the principle of confidentiality is due to the premise of unethical behavior of the treating doctor towards his patient, and also of unethical behavior of the control authorities towards the controlled object. Usually, the violation of confidentiality is most strongly revealed and established in the transfer of established facts and available information to third parties, which is inadmissible without the confirmed permission of the relevant authorities in court proceedings.

Table 1. Reported violations in the application of the confidentiality principle for the period from 2007 to 2011

Types of activities	2007	2008	2009	2010	2011
The relationship "doctor - patient"	16%	21%	17%	19%	22%
The activity of the tax authorities	24%	20%	27%	19%	21%
The activity of the customs authorities	14%	17%	11%	15%	14%
The activity of the financial inspectors	8%	14%	17%	19%	11%
The activity of the judicial authorities	9%	10%	7%	5%	12%
The activity law enforcement (police)	15%	16%	18%	17%	15%

According to research by Sue E. Estroff, the principle of "confidentiality" is actually the ethical principle of "privacy". Its correct compliance by persons involved in a control situation is a complex process. The complexity arises, on the one hand, from the fact that the controller "enters the personal space of the inspected object", and on the other hand, due to the fact that a third interested party may intervene in this process, whose intentions are other than to establish the received information during the control process, but also to use it against one of the parties. The general presumption in the literature is that the requirement to maintain confidentiality is related to the moral requirement to respect examinee autonomy. But in the control process, the meaning of autonomy applies in the protection of freedom of choice, but not in the protection of personal information.

Violation of the "confidentiality" principle is also established in cases where the controller acted to achieve personal benefit or interest in a specific control situation. Using his official position, as well as the available resources available to the control organization, the controller can make a final control decision that is aimed at follow-up actions that bring personal benefits.

The problem with the application of the "confidentiality" principle is found in the application of the "transparency" principle. The public release of information from the control process must comply with the Personal Data Act. In the disclosed information, the "integrity of the individual and his private life should be guaranteed by ensuring the protection of physical persons in case of unlawful processing of the personal data related to them in the process of the free movement of data". The disclosed information must be presented in a systematized form, summarized and correct. It should purposefully reflect the irregularities found during the control process, and should also present the measures taken to eliminate the irregularities found. According to research by L.P. Francis violation of the "confidentiality" principle, due to "excessive observance of the "transparency" principle, is observed very often and in almost all the studied countries (Table 2) (Francis, 2011).

According to the research presented by Francis in Table 2, it is found that the principle of "confidentiality" is violated in all the countries studied. The violation is from 20% to 50% of the control processes carried out in the studied countries, which is in average values. The values of violations of the principle are highest in Brazil. For the period studied, from 2007 to 2011, violations ranged from 42% to 49%. These values show that the principle is not violated in all control situations. The purpose of the surveyed countries is to change this trend, and if there are violations, they should be from 1% to 20%. Violations of the principle in more than 50% of the cases in control practice mean that the constitutional rights of the inspected are violated.

According to research by the Australian Institute of Criminology, non-compliance with the control principles "objectivity" and "legality" is due to the influence and impact of the corruption factor (McCusker, 2006). According

Table 2. A study by L. P. Francis on the breach of principle confidentiality

	2007	2008	2009	2010
Argentina	28%	29%	26%	24%
Australia	32%	26%	28%	27%
Brasil	48%	49%	43%	42%
Greece	42%	40%	39%	35%
Germany	29%	26%	24%	23%
Estonia	49%	45%	43%	42%
Italy	35%	33%	31%	29%
France	41%	48%	39%	31%
The USA	25%	27%	26%	27%
The UK	27%	28%	25%	23%

Source: Francis, L.P. Environmental Ethics, 2011.

Table 3. Factors influencing control practice

Factors	%	Rank
1. The norms and values of politicians and civil servants	88,4	1
2. The lack of quality control, supervision and audit	87,2	2
3. The relationship between business and politics	86,6	3
4. Government/state values and norms	84,6	4
5. Public sector culture (values/norms)	83,3	5
6. Lack of quality management commitment	82,2	6
7. Bad organization and bad management	80,7	7
8. Increasing the power of organized crime	79,3	8
9. Established norms and values in private and public life	78,0	9
10. The growing importance of lobbying	76,5	10
11. The broken relationship between politics and administration	67,0	11
12. Social inequality	66,7	12
13. Low wages in the public sector	56,9	13
14. Economic problems (inflation/recession)	62,2	14

Source: McCusker, R. Review of anti-corruption strategies. – *Technical and Background Paper*, 2006, No. 23, p. 4.

to experts, the presence of corruption in control practice is due to the low incomes of the controlling authorities. Table 3 presents the main factors that influence the presence of corruption in control practice.

On the other hand, it is argued that corruption is actually largely self-perpetuating, resulting from the actions and reactions of certain elements within a given society. Key elements include payments for political party lobbying and the lack of quality control in the employment of control specialists (McCusker, 2006). The question of the qualified quality of control specialists has been repeatedly raised before various non-governmental organizations and media. This can be considered as one of the painful problems of control practice, because control bodies, in addition to having access to specific accounting information, but based on it, must apply relevant knowledge and qualified experience to make the precise and accurate decision.

Therefore, in order to determine the final result of the applied principles of "legality" and "objectivity" in control practice, the impact of corruption levels in a number of sectors and industries should be taken into account.

The presented study was done based on a survey of 55,000 people. The survey covers issues related to the prevalence and impact of corruption, including an assessment of corruption levels. According to the specialists who carried out the study, the principles of "objectivity" and "legality" are manifested most strongly in the limitation and prevention of corruption by the control bodies. In interventionism (a type of control approach), the control bodies tactically wait for the moment when the corrupt actions take place, "to appear and then intervene, applying the principles of 'objectivity' and 'legality' in order to catch the violation itself" (Bull & Newell, 2003). This approach incentivizes retribution and deters corrupt practices, but it also has corresponding disadvantages: the damage has already been done and may not be undone; the majority of crimes may go unreported; the demand for certain

Figure 1. World corruption barometer
(McCusker, 2006)

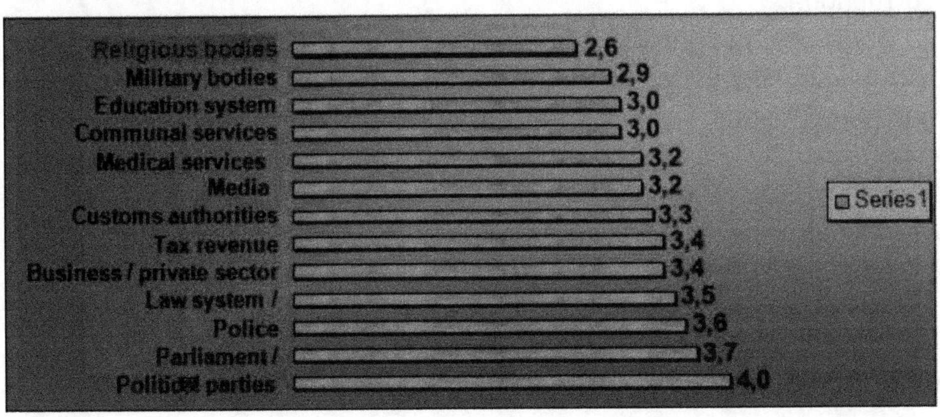

resources will inevitably be infinite given the degree of oversight. For this reason, it is necessary to ensure that the deterrent effect is actually working.

In the managerial approach, whose representatives are James Lincoln, Pierre Dupont, Alfred Sloan, etc., the supervisor must study the practice so as to develop specific recommendations that have immediate practical application. Essentially, in this approach, those in control advocate reducing or eliminating corrupt opportunities so that those who benefit from them cease to be able to do so. There are limitations in this approach due to the fact that the control persons are not obliged to work with the pre-determined principles of management, namely: to be agents who want to be included in the specific corruption scheme in order to uncover it (McCusker, 2006). Along with the principles of management, the controlling person should also observe the main principles of financial control: *objectivity, independence, legality* and *official start*.

In Germany, public procurement financial inspections are carried out by the Federal Procurement Agency (FPA). It is the second largest federal agency after the Federal Office for Defense Technology and Procurement. FPA has taken a number of measures to promote integrity among its staff, including the provision of advice by staff on the prevention of corruption, the organization of seminars and training, dealing with corruption and the rotation of its staff. Since 2001, in order to better apply the principles of financial control in control corruption environments, the Federal Public Procurement Agency in Germany has obliged its inspectors to participate in corruption prevention seminars. The seminars are organized by a prosecutor. They explain possible risky corruption situations and possible strategies for providing bribes. Another part of the training is directed at how to behave when these corrupt situations arise. The seminars emphasize the central role of inspectors, whose ethical behavior is an essential part of preventing corruption.

Another way to prevent corruption is adopted in German control practice, and it is the rotation of personnel after a period of five to eight years. The purpose of rotation is to avoid control practice becoming routine. However, FPA reports that the low level of specialization does not allow a large proportion of employees to change their organizational unit, due to the lack of sufficient knowledge of the new organizational unit.

We focus our attention on the German control system, as it is very different from those of other countries. Each sector of the government, as well as each government organization, is responsible for developing its own management and control mechanisms. Given the hierarchical structure of the German public administration, the decision-making body is built between different levels of administration. The higher authority is usually able to instruct the lower authority to put in place specific control systems. For this reason, in German control practice, the division of control principles into basic and derivative is most strongly manifested (OECD, 2015). The main principles of financial control in German control practice are: institutional independence; judicial independence; efficiency; compliance with specific legal norms; independence in the choice of administrations, which must be controlled in objectivity (SIGMA, 2012).

From the research that was done by SIGMA, it was established that in the German audit practice, the application of the principle of independence is distinguished according to the purpose of the audit. It can be assumed that German control practice most accurately distinguishes independence.

As a federation, Germany consists of 16 states, each with individual legislation aligned with federal laws. From the point of view of budgetary control, each province has a separate Audit Office, which is subordinate to the Federal Audit Office in Germany. The application of the principles of financial control by the audit chambers in the individual provinces is confirmed by means of the internal audit regulations and also by complying with the international auditing standards. When performing the audit on budget funds, the goal of the auditors is to achieve efficiency and economy of the audit process. The requirement for efficiency refers to the obligation to achieve the maximum possible results with the available resources. The requirement for efficiency in the context of financial management should be seen as optimization of spent budget funds. Also, efficiency should be aimed at establishing the best possible relationship between set goals and objectives. According to German specialists, in order to give an accurate assessment of the effectiveness of the audit process, it is necessary, in addition to the audit principles, to observe the principles of business administration during the control process. The research presented in this way does not indicate what the established principles of business administration are in Germany, and a more comprehensive study cannot be done by applying the method of comparative analysis.

Institutional independence is explicitly stated in Art. 130 and Art. 282 of the Treaty on the Functioning of the European Union. The independence of the control institutions is guaranteed through the method of constitution, the mandate of the governing body and the renewal of the composition. The independence of the various control institutions, despite the aforementioned factors for its guarantee, manifests itself in a different direction. Thus, for example, for the Audit Chamber, independence is expressed in its freedom to plan its audit activity and to carry it out in accordance with the law and internationally recognized auditing standards. From the point of view of the Bulgarian control practice, and in particular of PFIA, the Directorate "Planned inspection activity in the field of public procurement" realizes the institutional independence of the Agency by organizing, directing and carrying out the planned inspection activity of the Agency. It determines the frequency of carrying out financial inspections and the specific contractors based on the analysis of information on the activity of awarding and execution of public procurement, on the assessment of risk factors and prepares an annual plan. It performs subsequent financial inspections, establishes violations of the legal acts governing the awarding and execution of public procurement, as well as budgetary, financial-economic or reporting activities, and brings the guilty parties to administrative criminal liability if there are relevant legal grounds. It reveals damage caused to the property of organizations and individuals and brings the guilty parties to property liability if there are relevant legal grounds. And it establishes indicators of committed fraud within the meaning of the State Financial Inspection Act.

In the control practice of the Russian Federation, it is also accepted that control is not an end in itself, but rather an integral part of the country's regulatory system. Its purpose is to reveal deviations from accepted standards and violations of the principles of legality, efficiency and economy in the use of state funds. The control activity should "catch these problems at the earliest possible stage in order to take corrective measures so as to ensure compensation for losses and to take measures to ensure that similar violations do not occur in the future".

From the point of view of the hierarchical structure of the executive power in Russia, it differs significantly from the hierarchical structure of the executive power in Bulgaria. This can be taken as a basic premise for the different control goals and tasks that are set for each of the control bodies that make up the executive power of the Russian Federation. For example, the Ministry of Finance consists of the following 17 departments: Department of Administration and Control; Department of Budgetary Policy and Methodology; Department of Tax and Customs Tariff Policy; Department of Government Debt and Government Financial Assets; Department of Financial Policy; Department of Intergovernmental Relations; Department of State Financial Control Regulation, Audit and Accounting; Legal Department; Administrative Department; Department of Long-Term Financial Planning; Department for Development and Implementation of the Federal Budget;

Department of International Financial Relations; Department of Fiscal Policy in the Field of Innovation, Industry, Energy, Communications and Public-Private Partnerships of the Ministry of Finance of the Russian Federation and Department "Information Technologies in the Management of State and Municipal Finances and Information Management in the Budget Process".

The control actions in the so-named institution of the executive power are within the powers of the Department for the Regulation of State Financial Control, Audit and Accounting and the Administrative Department. The first department carries out state control (supervision) over self-regulating audit organizations. The second department carries out the organizational-methodical management and control of the activity of the federal offices and organizations, part of the organizational structure of the Ministry of Finance. What the two departments have in common is that when exercising their control powers, they apply the principles of *legality, objectivity, economy, efficiency and expediency of the funds spent.*

Both in our control practice and in the control practice of Russia, a number of problems in the application of the principles of financial control are also observed. For example, according to a 2010 study by the Association of Accounting and Control Authorities in the Russian Federation, the following weaknesses are identified:

1. For the most part, the compiled control acts are based on various types of norms regarding the implementation of monitoring for the effective use of public funds. There are no legal norms regarding the effectiveness of control, regulating the activities of the authorities.
2. There are significant differences between the legislation in determining how to monitor the object's performance. There are "18 different possibilities for controlling the same object in different ways, each with different areas of control over the efficient use of public funds, as well as their different combinations" There are "18 different possibilities for controlling the same object in different ways, each with different areas of control over the efficient use of public funds, as well as their different combinations".
3. Only three of the regions in the Russian Federation implement quality control over the effective use of public funds. This, according to specialists, is due to the fact that in these areas the control is entrusted to be carried out by: the Audit Chamber of the Kaliningrad region; The Audit Chamber of the Republic of Altai; The Audit Chamber of Nizhny Novgorod Region.

4. In 14 acts, or in 18% of the total researched control acts, problems were noticed in the determination of effectiveness, but their implementation (i.e. whether public funds were used correctly and efficiently) was not noticed by other control bodies related to these specific control functions. Such results are noticeable in the control acts and reports of control institutions from Moscow, Lipetsk, Leningrad, Smolensk, etc.
5. A characteristic feature of a large part of the acts of the control bodies is that they do not indicate the list of specific areas continuing their control over financial discipline.
6. Despite the fact that, in their activity reports, the control institutions report the fact that they have determined the most correct control tools and have correctly formulated the tasks set for them, only 38% of the control inspectors themselves report that these tools were correctly and accurately applied during their inspection actions.
7. In a number of acts of the control bodies, the determination of the pre-set control objectives contains imprecise and incorrect formulations, which mix the actual legal content of the problem with the method of implementation and with the defined functions.

From the information thus presented, it should be assumed that the main problems in the implementation of financial control in the Russian Federation are due to shortcomings in the established control technology. Deficiencies in control technology are the result of gaps regarding the sequence of stages through which the control process should pass, the incorrect determination of the content of the control problem and the methods for its resolution. All this is a prerequisite for the incorrect and inaccurate application of the principles of financial control in the control practice of the Russian Federation.

As in other countries and in the UK, the Ministry of Finance and the Government are responsible for the development and promulgation of management and control systems in public administration. The established management and control systems are in accordance with the requirements of INTOSAI (SIGMA, 2012). Regarding the principles of financial control, it is assumed that a strict regulatory environment is maintained with their help and good control results are achieved as well.

The application of the principles of financial control was studied from various aspects for the period from 2018 to 2021 by P. Nedyalkova, i.e. (Nedyalkova 2018; Nedyalkova, P., Andreeva, A., Yolova, G. 2021; Tsoncheva, G. 2018), both from the point of view of internal audit and from the point of view of internal control. The main problem is that when applying the corresponding principles, the control persons are not aware of the scope, power, intensity of influence of the rule itself, and also due to the lack of the relevant professional competence and, above all, the lack of control will, they do not apply the relevant control in a timely manner principle. They rely more on chance, on the current state of the object and on the fact that after them no further control actions will be implemented in which the weaknesses of the control production will be revealed.

According to leading specialists from the London School of Business and Finance, the trend in the development of financial control is to increase the number of basic principles with the help of which the evidentiary approach is implemented, as well as to establish the basic inherent control risk in the control situation. This is an ongoing process that will require a significant change in the behavior of both firms and the Financial Services Authority (the FSA). There are, of course, limitations in the speed of application of the new basic (basic) principles, as well as the possibility of different precedents in control practice. For this reason, it is necessary for all research centers in the field of control practice to assist interested parties and regulatory authorities - both at local and intermediate level - to "make most of the basic principles regulatory real".

According to UK experts, the purpose of the basic principles of financial control is not to impose control dictates or overly restrictive measures, but to lay the groundwork and define responsibilities, "deciding how best to reconcile business objectives and processes relating to regulatory outcomes'. The purpose of the new basic control rules is to accommodate changes in market conditions, as well as changes in the political-economic conjuncture. It has been found that in more dynamically changing economic conditions, established principles are more durable and very difficult to change, unlike those that are stagnant.

The new general (basic) control rules that are proposed are:

- *Presence of a regulatory culture.* The controller should focus on identifying broader control problems affecting the audited object. The existing problem situations and questions that will be checked should be flexibly defined and oriented towards the presentation of a final result. The controller must properly manage and analyze the incoming information. This requires, accordingly, certain control experience, knowledge of the regulatory framework, restraint in the presentation of certain facts at a higher level and further use of the established facts and evidence.

- *Setting reasonable deadlines*. In order to be able to correctly apply the principles regulated in each legal act, both by the controller and by the controlled one, the relevant legal conditions for the implementation of a given regulatory requirement must be regulated in the relevant reasonable terms. Normative acts do not regulate this principle, but it is applied by the state authorities very moderately. The change of a given normative act, which regulates, for example, a new model for taxation, is promulgated earlier than the date of entry into force of the legal requirements themselves. The purpose of this time interval is to allow all interested parties to familiarize themselves with the new amendments.
- *Regulation of self-trust*. In order to make the most correct decisions, it is necessary for the controller's behavior to be reasonable, to question everything and to be able to correctly ascertain the control situation based on the available information. If the information is provided by another control authority, not to accept it as 100% accurate and true, but to question it and cooperate with other control sources in order to confirm or reject it.

Based on everything stated so far regarding the presented empirical results of the foreign practice of applying the principles of financial control, the following main conclusions can be drawn:

1. The presented control foreign practice regarding the application of the principles of financial control is a proof of the relevance of the studied problem.
2. The data presented by the foreign specialists reveal that the main problems regarding the incorrect application of the principles of financial control are due to irregularities in the implementation of the control technology.
3. Western specialists maintain the thesis that it is necessary to adopt additional general control principles, and with their help, it is expected to improve the quality of control work. The proposed new general control principles exist in the UK as unwritten rules. The purpose of their normative regulation, according to specialists, is to transform them into written rules that have legal weight in case of their inaccurate application.

REFERENCES

Beauchamp, T. L., & Childress, J. F. (2011). *Ethics principles* (5th ed.). Oxford University Press.

Francis, L. P. (2011). Environmental Ethics. *Annual Review of Environment and Resources*, (39), 150.

McCusker, R. (2006). Review of Anti-Corruption Strategies. *Technical and Background Paper*, (23), 4.

Nedyalkova, P. (2018). Features, characteristics and methodology of internal control over nanotech manufacturing and nano-production in food industry. *Ikonomicheski Izsledvania, 27*(3), 157–189 ID: 57204010473

Nedyalkova, P., Andreeva, A., & Yolova, G. (2021, June). Digitalization and the new legal and economic challenges to employers in implementing internal control. *Ikonomicheski IzsledvaniaVolume*, *30*(5), 158–175.

OECD. (2015). *Management Control in Modern Government Administration, Some Comparative Practices*. OECD.

Tsoncheva, G. (2018). Researching the quality of accounting information and building a high-quality accounting information system. Free University.

Weiser, I. (2010). *Measure of Damages for Violation of Property Rules: Breach of Confidentiality*. Zicklin School of Business.

Conclusion

The study revealed a significant part of the still unexplained - both theoretical and practical-applied issues of the application of the principles of financial control. We believe that the existing practical irregularities and inaccuracies regarding the mechanisms and methods of application of the established control rules are the result of the accumulated over the years unexplained scientific research questions in the theoretical and practical field of financial control. Entering the core of the theory of financial control hides its risks, and the more we go into the depths of this matter, the more we find that with the scientific research approach presented in this work, not all existing theoretical and practical problems in financial control can be covered and investigated.

Through the interdisciplinary research approach, it has been proven that the principles of financial control determine its methodological foundations. Practice overtakes the theoretical clarification of a significant part of the processes and phenomena that are a prerequisite for changing the methodology of financial control. Once established, the principles of financial control, as written rules, regulated in a relevant legal act, are not subject to substantive change. Their regulation means that they have practically proven their purpose, first, as unwritten rules. The control methodology is subject to change, but this change is the result of the influence of a number of factors that affect the control process. In such situations, according to J. Hsu, the direction (stages) of the control methodology can be changed, but not the established principles (Hsu, 1968). In the presence of risky situations and prerequisites that seek to provoke the controller, and thus also to undermine the control actions, other control rules can be imposed in addition to those established, but these principles must not contradict and invalidate the effect of the normatively regulated ones.

In this study, the established methodology for determining the normative impact of a given normative act has been proven. It can also be applied as a methodology for researching the application of the principles regulated in the relevant normative act. Compliance with the regulatory requirements by the supervisors in the implementation of their control actions is carried out with the help of the control norms regulating certain provisions. Each norm of control has a certain structure, especially in regard to laws, decrees, regulations, acts, etc. The regulated rules are one of the constituent elements in this structure, and following them, the regulatory texts of the normative act will be achieved.

The proposed systematic stages for applying the principles of financial control, namely: **the approval of a control policy, the approval of organizational technology for the implementation of a control process, and the development and implementation of an individual assessment system for evaluating the application of the principles of financial control**, are a prerequisite for the establishment of a methodology for the study of these principles. The individual assessment can be formulated using the findings protocol, in which each inspector must individually and impartially assess the rules he follows in the control process. The assessment criteria are presented in the Expert Assessment Card on the application of the principles of financial control. The card should be prepared individually by the PFIA inspector, and the assessment data from it should be presented in the findings protocol. All information regarding compliance with the sequence of stages, and the indicators, on the basis of which the relevant assessment of the influence of the control principles is formulated, should also be revealed in the final reports of the inspection activity. The lack of this type of information, as is currently the case in PFIA's control practice, is a prerequisite for drawing a number of contradictory conclusions about the performed control process.

Correlation analysis as a statistical-mathematical method is applied as a method to prove the influence and impact of control environments on the controlled object. With the help of the graphic construction of the active, passive and corruption control environment, it was proved that theoretically the environments so specified can be distinguished from each other, but in practice, they are of a mixed type such as active-passive, active-corruptive and passive-corruptive. The complex nature and specificity of the control environment are a prerequisite for problems on the part of inspectors to qualitatively and effectively apply the principles of financial control. The more clearly defined the control environment, the easier the principles of financial control are applicable.

Considering all the presented research theses, evidence and information sources, on the basis of which the empirical study of the development was carried out, the following more important conclusions can be drawn:

1. The control principles are the main building block, on the basis of which not only the entire control process, but also the control technology, takes place. It can be assumed that they are the design or idea for its implementation and progress.
2. The control principles themselves are interconnected and form a single control system. Despite the existing variety of control principles, the characteristic is that no principle contradicts another. They complement each other and reveal the specifics of the controlled object.
3. There is no historical information and data on when exactly the principles of control appeared, but what is known is that they are the result of practical traditions existing since ancient times for the implementation of control in various forms and modes of manifestation.
4. The main problems that are a prerequisite for the incorrect and inaccurate application of the principles of financial control by financial inspectors are: a) the lack of an internally regulated methodology for a specific control institution for the application of the principles of financial control; b) the absence of a methodology approved for the control practice for researching the application of the principles of financial control; c) the violation of the sequence of control stages of the control process; d) the incorrect implementation of the control technology.
5. The development and implementation of a methodology for researching the application of the principles of financial control in Bulgaria should be within the competence of the Ministry of Finance. The obtained results should be provided and officially published by the National Statistical Institute, so that all interested persons have access to this information. In this way, we believe that control practice will be significantly improved because comparability of the obtained results will be realized for the same set control goals and tasks by the relevant control authorities. The development of such a methodology will contribute to the clarification and modern solution of a number of control problems, such as: the timely change of the control technology; the application of new rules of conduct in relation to the change in the country's political and economic situation; the introduction of stricter restrictive control measures, etc.
6. During the empirical study of the applicability of the principles of financial control, a number of practical problems were identified. This is due to the fact that the mechanisms for applying the principles of financial control are not sufficiently legally regulated, especially in regard to the specific (derivative) principles. This also proved our thesis that significant reform is needed in the control technology of PFIA

regarding the principles of control since our country still does not have established traditions regarding the mechanisms and their application, as is the case in other countries belonging to the Anglo-Saxon control system.

7. The incorrect and inaccurate application of the principles of financial control by any control institution, including PFIA, is not due to inaccurate regulation of their nature in the normative acts but is a result of the lack of an internally approved methodology regarding the manner of their application. Therefore, the main recommendation we make to the control authorities is the development of such a methodology.
8. The proposed sample methodology regarding the application of the principles of financial control must be tailored to the specifics, goals and tasks of the control organization.

The limited volume of work and the problematic application of the principles of financial control are the main prerequisite for claiming that the research questions presented in this way are not exhausted. The completeness of the development refers only to the achievement of the previously set goals and objectives. An object of subsequent research could be the analysis of the dependence between the functions and principles of financial control. Similarities and differences can be explored between the principles on which control strategies are constructed and the principles that are implemented during the control process itself. The different points of view and opinions on the issues presented in each part of this study can also be the subject of independent research and analysis.

We believe that the topic set in this study is a major key, which helps much larger and more important issues for society to be investigated, such as, for example, the study of the mechanisms and applicability of the principles and norms of financial control applied by the European Commission as the main control body of the member states of the European Union. In addition, the principles and norms of control can be the object of study from the point of view of internal control for a particular company. Also, the subject of research can be the principles of financial control of other control institutions, not only the principles of PFIA. All presented alternative options for research once again prove the impossibility of covering and researching all current issues related to the principles of financial control in a single study.

The problems and questions presented in this work are a small part of the unexplained and unexplored problems in the field of control theory. It is likely that the proposed research approaches are not the only ones to investigate the questions presented. The methods proposed here to investigate problematic and practical issues, such as the method of applicability of principles to control theory, can be considered daring and too innovative. The presented study is a small attempt to outline the theoretical-applicable problems of the principles of financial control, as well as to present a research approach for their resolution.

Glossary

Control Environment: The environment status and development determine the development of the control system and the development and change of the object and subject of control. It can be assumed that the relevant environment determines the mechanisms of impact, interaction, and monitoring. A distinction needs to be drawn between the environment of a control system exercising state control and a control system which is an element of the financial management and control system (FMCS) to carry out an internal audit in an organization or an entity. The environment in which control systems of state control develop represents the political, social, cultural, and economic situation within the relevant territorial unit. However, this is a very "simplified idea of the scope and structure of the environment in which the relevant control system develops since the relevant environment comprises problems such as distribution of responsibilities and division of powers, solving religious problems, determining the degree of government influence (state power influence, respectively) on people and the economy.

The control environment includes the following elements:

integrity and ethical values;

management's philosophy and operating style;

organizational structure;

assignment of authority and responsibility;

human resource policies and practices;

competence of personnel.

Control Systems are Strongly Dependent on the Established Form of Government: The financial monitoring of the budget implementation and the control over the spending of budget funds in the control systems concerned are carried out by different control institutions.

Established Impact System: The last element, i.e., the impact system is defined based on the above major components of the control system. The impact system is aimed at removing deficiencies and violations, recovering the damage caused to the state property or the property owner, offering appropriate measures to eliminate the causes and factors which constitute a prerequisite for the occurrence of violations to influence the subjects who committed the violation. In different state control systems, different methods for seeking responsibility and imposing penalties on guilty persons are included in the scope of the defined measures to eliminate violations. In Bulgaria, for example, the measures to eliminate violations and to seeking responsibility include the liability to pay compensation, disciplinary liability, administrative criminal liability and criminal liability.

Established Models and Methods of Regulation, Control, and Supervision: Established models of regulation, control and supervision incorporate the methods of their implementation. The primary purpose of state control systems is to achieve the functions of regulation, control, and supervision. The functions of regulation, control and supervision are carried out at certain stages of the state government process at which a certain state decision is formed, made or implemented. The regulatory function of the control system is seen in two aspects. One of them is maintenance of the control system within the defined parameters of state government decisions to achieve specific state aims and tasks. The second aspect is that through the regulatory function of the control system adjustments can be made to initially taken state decisions according to the changes in the environment. The regulatory function is achieved by various means and methods; it mostly depends on the regulation object and the place of the regulatory body in the state apparatus.

The Financial System: This is considered in two aspects - economic and institutional. Considered through the economic aspect, the financial system is a set of financial relations, on the basis of which the corresponding funds are formed and the public production is redistributed. The financial system consists of two structural units - fiscal and relations, which are financial relations expressing the income and expenses of public legal affairs and non-fiscal relations, considering the income and expenses of individuals and legal entities.

Public Relations: They are the major component of control systems; they present the relationships, interactions and relations between people. Relations arise as a result of the interaction of at least two parties, two persons or organizations, i.e. relations between social objects. Consequently, public relations arise between two or more persons who have a certain social (public) status and perform a certain social (public) role. The control system content is determined by the direct connection and interaction between the subject and object of control, as well as by their manifestation in the various forms of government.

State Apparatus: Something that should be considered a system of state authorities and institutions through which state power is exercised. Two basic methods are used to exercise state power: coercion and persuasion. Persuasion creates preconditions for effective government but it is not always enough to achieve certain goals. For this reason, state power often applies the methods of coercion. Therefore, in practice, both methods are applied in combination.

Compilation of References

Alekseev, S. S. (1981). *The General Theory of Law: In 2 vols* (Vol. 2). Legal Literature.

Alexandrovich, B. (2008). *Political Science*. Business and Educational Literature.

Bairova, M. (1982). *Dictionary of foreign words in the Bulgarian language*. BAS Publishing.

Bakardzhieva, M. (2006). *Quantitative methods in management, Svishtov*. Tsenov Academic Publishing House.

Baldwin, R. (2012). *Risk Regulation, Management and Compliance*. Bristol Inquiry. http://www.bristol-inquiry.org.uk

Beauchamp, T. L., & Childress, J. F. (2011). *Ethics principles* (5th ed.). Oxford University Press.

Blanco, Sl. (2006). Auditoria do sector público no contexto da nova gestão pública. Revista de Estudos Politécnicos/Polytechnical. *Studies and Reviews (General Fisheries Commission for the Mediterranean)*, *3*(5/6), 201–225.

Bogdanov, Hr. (2006). Otnosno efektivnostta na kontrola. V: Mezhdunarodna nauchno-prakticheska konferentsia „Evrointegratsionnite protsesi i predizvikatelstvata pred stopanskata otchetnost, analiza i odita“. Svishtov: AI „Tsenov“.

Braverman, H. (1974). *Labour and monopoly capital: The degradation of work in the twentieth century*. Monthly Review Press.

Burtsev, V. V. 2001. Basic principles of state financial control organizations in modern conditions. Financial management, N° 2.

Chipev, P. (2002). In Search of Mechanisms for Better Corporate Control, Sofia: COALITION 2000

Clive, B. 2006. Managing As If Faith Mattered: Christian Social Principles in the Modern Organization. Review of Business, Spring, 27, No. 2.

CONCEPT. (2017). CONCEPT of Development of Public Internal Financial Control till 2017. *DKRS*. http://www.dkrs.gov.ua/kru/en/publish/article/50363

Consolidated version, (2012). Consolidated version of the treaty establishing the European Community. Available from: http//www.eur-lex.europa.eu [seen on 10.07.2012]

Corcuff, Ph. (1973). *Les nouvelles sociologies*. Nathan.

Cornyu, Zh. (2004), Legal Dictionary, Sofia: "Sophi-R" PH

Crockett, A. (1996). The Theory and Practice of Financial Stability. *De Economist*, *144*(4), 57. doi:10.1007/BF01371939

Dinev, M. (1986). *Kontrol i regulirane na ikonomicheskite sistemi*. Profizdat.

Dinev, M. (1999). Kontrol v sotsialnoto upravlenie. Sofia: Trakia-M

Dinev, M. (2008). *Obshta teoria na schetovodstvoto*. Trakia-M.

Dochev, D. (1997). Izsledvane na operatsiite. Varna: Universitetsko izdatelstvo na IU

Dochev, D. (1997). Izsledvane na operatsiite. Varna: Universitetsko izdatelstvo na IU

Donev, I. (1984). *Istoria na matematikata. V. Tarnovo: UI „Sv. sv*. Kiril i Metodiy.

Donev, K. (2002). Darzhaven finansov kontrol – teoria i praktika. God. na IU Varna, 74.

Donev, K. (2002). Darzhaven finansov kontrol – teoria i praktika. God. na IU Varna, 74.

Drysdale, Al. (2010). *The Financial Controller: The Things the Academics Don't Teach You*. Management Books 2000, Ltd.

Dworkin, R. (1978). *Taking Rights Seriously*. Duckworth.

Ehrmark, E. N. (2011). Model evaluation of strategic alternatives based on SWOT-analysis. *Rusnauka*. http://www.rusnauka.com/31_PRNT_2010/Economics/ 74034. doc.htm

Engels, F. 1963, Writings. T. 37

Fayol, H. (1937). The administrative theory in the state. In: L. Gulick & L. Urwick (Eds.). Papers on the science of administration. New York: Institute of Public Administration. Golikov, A. P. (2003). Эkonomiko-matematicheskoe modelirovanie mirohozyaystvennыh protsessov. Harykov: Harkovskiy natsionalynыy universitet im. V. N. Karazina.

Francis, L. P. (2011). Environmental Ethics. *Annual Review of Environment and Resources*, (39), 150.

Georgiev, G. 2002. Modeling Markov Chains in Ms Excel. Scientific works of the University of Ruse, 47.

Georgieva, P. I., & ... (1987). Mathematical-Statistical Methods in Technological Research. *Agricultural Science*, *XXV*(1).

Grozdev, B. (2005). The tax officials would refuse a bribe for an 800 BGN salary. SEGA, N°19

Hadjolyan, M. (2012). The Bulgarian Judiciary in the System of Separation of Powers. http://ejournal.vfu.bg

Hart, H. L. A. (1961). *The Concept of Law*.

Heizer, J., & Render, B. (2011). *Principles of Operations Management* (8th ed.).

Hirsh, S. (1990). *Introduction to Type in Organizations*. Consulting Psychologists Press, Inc.

Hsu, J., & Mayer, An. (1968). *Modern Control Principles and Applications*. McGraw- Hill Book Company.

Ifandiev, G. (2013). It's time to take back the church. http://www.forumat-bg.com

Italy – Constitution. (2012). Available from: http://www.servat.unibe.ch/icl/it00000_. html [seen on 10.04.2012]

James, R. (1951). Some aspects of a Governmental Audit. *The Accounting Review*, *26*(3).

Kaczmarek, P., Kent, S. T., Rus, G. A., Stockbridge, R. H., & Wade, B. A. (2007). Numerical solution of a long-term average control problem for singular stochastic processes. *Mathematical Methods of Operations Research*, *66*(3), 456. doi:10.100700186-007-0166-9

Kant, I. (1993). *Towards Eternal Peace*. BAS Publishing.

Kazakov, N. (2013). Principles of regulation of internal financial control and forms of its implementation in the system of economic security of Russia. http://oad.rags.ru

Kelsen, H. (1962). *Theorie pure du droit*.

Kenett, R. (2012). Quality, Risk and the Taleb Quadrants. Available from: http://papersssrn.com/sol3/papers.cfm?abstract_id= 1433490&download=yesq

Kushner, H. J., & Dupuis, P. (2001). *Numerical Methods for Stochastic Control Problems in Continuous Time* (2nd ed.). Springer. doi:10.1007/978-1-4613-0007-6

Lazarov, K. (2009). *Administrative law*. Fenea.

Lima Declaration. (1977). Lima Declaration of Control Guidelines. http://www.intosai4kni.org/wiki/ [seen on 14.07.2009]

Lynch, Ch. (2012). *The Budget Control Act of 2011: Elements and Options (Economic Issues, Problems and Perspectives)*. Nova Science Pub Inc.

Marden, E. (2003). Risk and Regulation: U.S. Regulatory Policy, 44 B.C.L. Rev. 733. http://lawdigitalcommons.bc.edu/bclr/vol44/iss3/2

Marinova, S. (2009). Towards the concept of legal principle. Economic alternatives, N° 5.

Marx, K. (1988). *Capital: A Critique of Political Economy*. Partizdat.

McCusker, R. (2006). Review of Anti-Corruption Strategies. *Technical and Background Paper*, (23), 4.

Milev, A. (1970). *Dictionary of Foreign Words in the Bulgarian Language*. Science and Art.

Mladenov, M. (2009). Conflict Management. Alternative dispute resolution methods in the tax process. www.eprints.nbu.bg/408/ [seen on 24.05.2009]

Moffett, J. (2011). Control Principles and Role Hierarchies. Available from: http://www. moffett. me.uk

Moffett, J. (2011). *Control Principles and Role Hierarchies*. Moffett. http://www. moffett.me.uk

Monks, R. (2001). *Corporate Governance* (2nd ed.).

Nedyalkova, P. (2010). Selection and applicability of financial control rate in the control process. *Trakia Journal of Sciences*, (8), 1–10.

Nedyalkova, P. (2018). Features, characteristics and methodology of internal control over nanotech manufacturing and nano-production in food industry. *Ikonomicheski Izsledvania, 27*(3), 157–189 ID: 57204010473

Nedyalkova, P. (2020). Empirical Study of the VAIA Metric (Value Added of Internal Audit) and Determination of the Internal Audit Quality for Shumen Municipality for the Period 2011–2016. In *Quality of Internal Auditing in the Public Sector. Contributions to Management Science*. Springer., doi:10.1007/978-3-030-29329-1_11

Nedyalkova, P. (2020). Presentation of the Dependence Between the Chosen Internal Audit Approach and the Methods for Assessing the Quality of the Internal Audit in the Public Sector. In *Quality of Internal Auditing in the Public Sector. Contributions to Management Science*. Springer., doi:10.1007/978-3-030-29329-1_8

Nedyalkova, P. (2020). Specifics of the Assessment as a Process of Internal Audit Activity. In *Quality of Internal Auditing in the Public Sector. Contributions to Management Science*. Springer., doi:10.1007/978-3-030-29329-1_4

Nedyalkova, P., Andreeva, A., & Yolova, G. (2021, June). Digitalization and the new legal and economic challenges to employers in implementing internal control. *Ikonomicheski IzsledvaniaVolume*, *30*(5), 158–175.

Nedyalkova, P. 2020. Quality of internal auditing in the public sector perspectives from the bulgarian and international context. pp. 1-151 ID: 57204010473

Nikolov, N. (2011). On the nature of the performance audit and its directions in the public sector. International jubilee scientific conference "Economy and management in the 21st century - solutions for stability and growth", Svishtov

OECD. (2012). *Risk and regulatory policy*. OECD Reviews of Regulatory Reform.

OECD. (2015). *Management Control in Modern Government Administration, Some Comparative Practices*. OECD.

Paredis, F. (2006). *Methodology and Feasibility of Sustainability Impact Assessment.* Academia.

Pashev, K. (2013). Corruption in taxation. *Challenges to tax policy and administration.* CSD. https://www.csd.bg/fileSrc.php?id=1412

Patton, M. Q. (1988). Six honest serving men. *Studies in Educational Evaluation*, *14*(3), 301–330. doi:10.1016/0191-491X(88)90026-0

Preffer, J. (1978). *The external control of organizations: A Resource Dependence Perspective.* Harper & Row Publishers.

Report of the EC, (2008). Report of the European Commission on the management of EU funds in Bulgaria, July 2008.

Schaad, A. (2011). A Framework for Organisational Control Principles. Available from: http://www.alloy.mit.edu

Schinasi, G. (2006). *Safeguarding Financial Stability: Theory and Practice.* International Monetary Fund.

Scriven, M. (2012). The Nature of Evaluation. RISMES. http://www.rismes.it/pdf/ Scriven_domain_evaluation.pdf

Slavchev, Z. (2010). *Tax-insurance procedural law.* Sofi-R.

Slavchev, Z. (2010b). *Appeal of revision act.* Nova Zvezda.

Spasov, K. (2003). *Social Management.* Apis.

Stengers, I. (1994). (ed.). L'effet Whitehead. Paris: Vrin.

Tarantino, A. (2011). *Financial Internal Controls Best Practices.* WILE Global Finance.

Tashev, R. (2000). Contemporary legal positivism. Modern law, N° 5.

The 6 Basic Principles of the Constitution. Available from: http://voices.yahoo.com/ the-6-basic-principles-constitution -1608845.html [seen on 8.04.2012]

Treaty, E. C. (1997). Treaties of the European Union. *Wikipedia.* https://en.wikipedia. org/wiki/Treaties_of_the_European_Union

Tsoncheva, G. (2018). Researching the quality of accounting information and building a high-quality accounting information system. Free University.

Velichkova, M. (1977). *Edinni printsipi, metodika i kriterii za kontrol.*

Vinokurov, V. A., Vinokurov, A. V. (2005). Kachestvo upravlenia kak faktor ukreplenia rынochnыh pozitsiy predpriyatia. *Standartы i kachestvo, 1.*

Weigel, W. (2009). *The Standard Cost Model A Critical Appraisal.* Center for the Study of Public Law and Economics.

Weihrich, H. (1982). The TOWS Matrix - A Tool for Situational Analysis. *Long Range Planning*, *15*(2), 54–66. doi:10.1016/0024-6301(82)90120-0

Weiser, I. (2010). *Measure of Damages for Violation of Property Rules: Breach of Confidentiality*. Zicklin School of Business.

Zingales, L. (1997). Corporative Governance. Working Paper 6309. National Bureau of Economic Research.

Zlatarev, E. (2007). *The State Financial Inspection and Property Liability*. Ciela.

Apostolov, Iv. (1946). Evolyutsia na kontinentalnata talkuvatelna teoria. GSU YuF, N° 41

About the Author

Plamena Nedyalkova is the chief assistant at the Department of Accounting, Economic University of Varna, Bulgaria and a certified internal auditor at the Ministry of Finance. Also a member of the Institute of Internal Auditors in Bulgaria, she has gathered extensive professional experience as an accountant, chief accountant, and assistant auditor. Since 2014, she has been a certified internal auditor in the public sector at the Ministry of Finance in Bulgaria. Over the years, she has been a guest lecturer at numerous foreign universities. Works with various non-governmental organizations to support society.

Index

S

T

V

www.ingramcontent.com/pod-product-compliance
Lightning Source LLC
LaVergne TN
LVHW061534290926
849162LV00004B/787